The Life
and Death of
Pretty Boy Floyd

Pretty

The Life & Death of Boy Floyd

JEFFERY S. KING

The Kent State University

Press · Kent, Ohio, &

London, England

© 1998 by The Kent State University Press,
Kent, Ohio 44242
ALL RIGHTS RESERVED
Library of Congress Catalog Card Number 97-36166
ISBN 0-87338-582-9
Manufactured in the United States of America

05 04 03 02 01 00 99 98   5 4 3 2 1

Library of Congress Cataloging-in-Publication Data
King, Jeffery S., 1940–
    The life and death of Pretty Boy Floyd / Jeffery S. King
        p.   cm.
    Includes bibliographical references and index.
    ISBN 0-87338-582-9 (cloth : alk paper) ∞
    1. Floyd, Pretty Boy, 1904–1934.   2. Criminals—United
States—Biography.   I. Title.
HV6248.F563K56   1998
364.1'092—dc21
[B]   97-36166

British Library Cataloging-in-Publication data are
available.

Contents

 **Acknowledgments**

Many people from such institutions as the FBI, Library of Congress, Postal Inspection Service, Oklahoma Historical Society, East Liverpool (Ohio) Public Library, Oklahombres (an Association for the Preservation of Lawmen and Outlaw History of the Indian Territory), and the National Association for Outlaw and Lawmen History have helped me greatly.

I am particularly grateful to Mary Ann Johnson, Dee Cordry, Rick Mattix, Jeff Maycroft, Michael Webb, William Helmes, Rick Cartledge, Neil Scott, Marley Brant, Brad Smith, and Postal Inspector B. R. Posey. John T. Hubbell was a wonderful editor and had a native Oklahoman's interest in Pretty Boy's saga.

The Life
and Death of
Pretty Boy Floyd

 # Introduction

Charles Arthur "Pretty Boy" Floyd was one
of the key figures in the development of
the modern FBI. By 1935 "G-men" were national heroes who had
wiped out major public enemies such as Floyd, and the time was ripe
to set up the powerful Federal Bureau of Investigation. Before that
the FBI was simply a minor federal agency named the Bureau of Investigation or the Division of Investigation. The Kansas City Massacre
of June 1933 had convinced the public that the outlaws were a national menace; yet at that time there were only 266 agents with limited authority.[1]

Two years after Floyd's death FBI Director J. Edgar Hoover told an
audience of high school boys that Floyd was "a skulking, dirty, ill-
clothed hobo and, as such, he was hunted down to his end, as a hoodlum, an ego-inflated rat."[2]

For Depression-era America, gangsters were a form of cheap enter-
tainment. Some citizens sympathized with them because of a resent-
ment of banks. After the tragic ends of the outlaws, they could believe "crime does not pay" and feel superior. In the early 1930s people
thought there was a "new" crime menace—the freelance criminals
or small gangs who specialized in bank robberies or sometimes in

kidnappings. They were extremely mobile, using fast cars instead of horses and machine guns instead of six-guns. But they were very much in the tradition of the frontier outlaws. They arose from the Depression and flourished in the Midwest crime corridor.

But such criminals as Ma Barker, John Dillinger, Machine Gun Kelly, Bonnie and Clyde, Pretty Boy Floyd, Baby Face Nelson, and Alvin Karpis were not a national menace; they actually represented the end of the old West. As late as June 1, 1932, a cowboy on horseback robbed a bank at Hatch, New Mexico, and got two thousand dollars.[3]

In truth, comparatively little was stolen. Clyde Barrow's biggest robbery netted only fifteen hundred dollars. The Dillinger gang's take was only about a quarter of a million dollars. Floyd was reported to have robbed from twenty-five thousand to half a million dollars, but probably netted less than a hundred thousand dollars. This was small change to organized crime.

Barrow, arguably the worst outlaw of the Depression period, killed thirteen men. Floyd himself killed some eleven men. But Depression-era outlaws concentrated on robbing banks. Ironically, these outlaws contributed to the rise of the FBI.[4]

In 1907, the new constitution of Oklahoma, Floyd's home state, provided for no statewide law enforcement organization. There were only elected county sheriffs. By the 1930s, however, increasing urbanization led to more crime. To make matters worse, good state roads and cars that could go as fast as a hundred miles an hour led to increased mobility for criminals. Farmers were poor then, and young people were desperate. There was the famous criminal hideout, the Cookson Hills in eastern Oklahoma. Nearby were "open cities" for criminals—Joplin, Missouri, and Hot Springs, Arkansas—where there were corrupt politicians and friendly police.[5]

Little aid came from the Cookson Hills residents. Honest farmers were too smart to talk. Of course, moonshiners and others who had been harboring fugitives would not talk. In September 1932 alone, three officers and three criminals were killed in the Hills.[6]

The law was understaffed. Most rural counties had at most four law enforcement employees: a sheriff, an undersheriff, a deputy, and a jailer. Moreover, one-third of the time they were officers of the court, often spending no more than six hours a day actually enforcing the law.

Too little money, sparse population, and the Depression were worries. The advantage was with the criminals: radios were rare, sheriffs were limited to their county boundaries, and many officers were poorly trained.

The Oklahoma State Bureau of Criminal Identification and Investigation was not created until 1925. At first there were only seven agents, and the number was about the same by the early 1930s.[7] The need for a state police was obvious even in 1929, but there was resistance. That year a Tulsa police captain said, "Present day law enforcement reminds me of a 'sherf' of the late nineties mounted on a pinto and trying to run down bandits in airplanes. It just can't be done. The old-time theory that a big hat and a gun is all a man needs to be an officer of law has been exploded." The *Tulsa Daily World* of May 29, 1931, wanted a "Highway Patrol" like the new Missouri State Police, which it thought would be a good defense against bank robbers. As a substitute, unpaid vigilantes organized in several towns.[8]

But bank robbery in Oklahoma was still a dangerous job. Between mid-year 1929 and the end of 1930 51 banks were robbed by 208 bandits. Many of these were repeaters, of course. Eleven were killed and 118 arrested. Five were sentenced to life. The rest received a grand total of 540 years in jail.

In 1931 and 1932 about 120 Oklahoma banks were robbed. However, in 1933, with increased security, only twenty-nine banks were robbed.[9]

Oklahoma crooks such as Ford Bradshaw, Aussie Elliott, Wilbur Underhill, Jim Benge, Tom Carlisle, Troy Love, and Ed Newt Clanton were tough. One sheriff said they would "charge hell with a bucket of water." So sometimes lawmen felt they had to shoot to kill. But these outlaws never made it big. Only Pretty Boy Floyd is well-known today.[10]

Floyd was a guerrilla who could live off the territory he knew so well, with the support of a friendly population. According to some accounts he got his "Pretty Boy" sobriquet because his neighbors thought he was vain. In the words of one author he was "a unique figure in U.S. crime annals, this broad-shouldered, apple-cheeked bumpkin with the cattle reflexes and the stainless steel nerves. An unsettling mixture of Little Abner, Cole Younger and Emiliano Zapata. An outlaw as outmoded as Black Bart in some ways, yet strangely contemporary in others."[11]

The gangster was neither highly intelligent nor polished. But his cool demeanor and a certain shrewd cunning helped him over rough spots.[12]

Although Floyd had many good friends, he was reserved; and he could be dangerous when angry. He was a very religious person and attended church even during intense manhunts. He had a loving relationship with his son and visited his father's grave each Memorial Day despite risk of capture. Floyd was known for his honesty and generosity, even to outsiders. One relative later said he "never suffered no one's charity."[13]

But some thought little of the bragging Floyd. "Floyd is just a crossroads chicken thief," said C. A. Burns, chief of the Oklahoma Bureau of Criminal Investigation. Harvey Bailey, a notorious criminal of the 1920s and 1930s, said Floyd and Clyde Barrow "are just small fry. They got [sic] out and hijack a couple of filling stations, hold up a country bank or two and think they are tough. Just a couple of small fry, that's all." But others thought Floyd was "the most dangerous gunman in the southwest" or even "the most dangerous man alive." He came to be called "the most daring, relentless, picturesque bandit and murderer of our nation and our time."[14]

The public was outraged because of Floyd's participation in the brutal Kansas City Massacre and wanted the "extermination of this mad dog." Many years later, on October 5, 1967, columnist Earl Wilson said "that I was as poor as anybody in the 1930s when Pretty Boy was killed. I saw him stretched out on a slab in East Liverpool [Ohio]. He was never a folk hero to me."[15]

Often the press wrote about Floyd and some thought him to be a Robin Hood. "He could go anywhere and find people who would hide him out. . . . He wasn't brutal like Bonnie and Clyde. One thing that's never told is that he never harmed anybody during a robbery," his son Jack later said. Floyd could make a public appearance without getting into trouble. He went to Earlsboro, a central Oklahoma oil field town, and left a large contribution at a church there, but no one told of the visit. Floyd would drop in at a county dance and dance with the prettiest girls. He did this often and paid the fiddler well.[16]

He wrote to the acting governor of Oklahoma, "I have robbed no one but moneyed men." Bankers were believed to be the enemy of widows and orphans. According to legend, Floyd tore up first mortgages if they were not recorded.[17]

He was deadly with guns. One newspaper reported, "The steel-vested desperado is noted for the breakneck speed at which he drives and the machine guns which are always with him." A joke was that newsboys yelled, "Four officers escape from Pretty Boy." He was good with all kinds of guns, but his favorite was the machine gun. Kansas City Chief of Detectives B. H. Thurman said Floyd was "one of the quickest men on the draw and the surest pistol shot I have ever known." He was one of the first outlaws to add a machine gun to his arsenal.[18]

His exploits excited the rural public. They said, "Give 'em hell, Chock" when he robbed the bank in his hometown, Sallisaw, Oklahoma. In the early 1930s the bank robbery insurance rate in Oklahoma doubled.[19]

Children were named for him. Legend was that he kept a rural school in fuel one winter. His wife, Ruby, said that he fed several hundred poor families.[20]

Some bandits claimed to be Pretty Boy, but they were usually unsuccessful. One bank robber was not believed because he was too old and "poorly dressed."[21] Another criminal, who tried to demand the keys to a new car from two Tulsa sisters in their early twenties, was instead subdued by them while their nine-year-old brother ran for help. The young women knew he was not the infamous outlaw because he was rude and very rough, whereas newspapers had reported the actual Pretty Boy was "very polite to women."[22]

One Tulsa reporter wrote, "Some officers and not a few average citizens consider [Floyd] 'a pretty good fellow who would go right if he had a chance,' claiming that he never shot anyone who wasn't trying to kill him." The reporter even praised those who gave him shelter and protection, as the people in the Cookson Hills had done.[23]

This book will investigate several questions concerning Floyd:

First, was he really a worthless "public rat"?

Second, was he one of the killers in the Kansas City Massacre?

Third, where did he hide out after the Massacre?

Fourth, what role did the FBI's well-publicized "scientific method" have in the Floyd investigation?

Fifth, did he have any contact with other notorious outlaws of the period, such as Dillinger and the Barker-Karpis gang?

Sixth, was Floyd executed by the FBI?

PART 1

The Robin Hood of the Cookson Hills

A Cornbread Living

Over twenty thousand people from at least twenty states, some from half a continent away, went to the funeral of Charles "Pretty Boy" Floyd, "Public Enemy No. 1," at Akins, Oklahoma, on October 28, 1934. Floyd, wanted for numerous crimes, including the murder of five men during the notorious Kansas City Massacre on June 17, 1933, had been killed six days before on a farm near East Liverpool, Ohio, by FBI agents and local police. The *Muskogee Daily Phoenix* called the funeral the largest in Oklahoma's history, a "Saturnalia."[1]

The day before the funeral, relatives and close friends had kept the death watch over Floyd's body at his mother's house in Sallisaw, the small county seat of Sequoyah County, while thousands passed beside the casket heaped with flowers contributed by his mourners. Mrs. Walter Floyd, "a gnarled woman, with a lean, strong jaw," had succeeded in barring photographers and reporters, whom she blamed for her son's bad reputation, from the private rites at her home. His friends claimed, "Charles was a good boy who got a dirty deal."[2]

At daybreak the day of the funeral, Sallisaw was host to the largest gathering it had ever seen, even to "perhaps the most motley crowd in

9

history. Booted hills men with 'ten gallon hats,' city dwellers, Indians and 'toughs' alike descended upon the city." Farm women dressed in calico aprons carried babies in their arms. Lawmen from every county in Oklahoma came for a chance to see the man they had never been able to catch. The city fathers were concerned that flags draping Sallisaw for a convention would be taken as a memorial for Floyd.[3]

Most had come by car, but there were some wagons and buggies and some riders on horseback. A few had come on foot from as far away as thirty miles. School buses brought children.

Local stores were crowded with buyers of picnic items such as lunch meat, buns, cheese, cookies, and fruit, at premium prices. Grocery stores and restaurants were out of food before dark.

A steady stream of people left the small town that hot day and headed toward the Akins cemetery, nine miles away. Dust was thick as the cars went out, and at midafternoon, headlights were necessary. Fences were torn down to make room for the six thousand parked cars that overflowed onto the pastures near the cemetery. Hundreds of others were parked along the road to Akins and in Akins itself.[4]

The funeral procession left the Floyd home shortly after noon and made its way to a small arbor in the center of the Akins cemetery. Three cars heaped with flowers preceded the hearse, as did several cars bearing members of Floyd's family. The arrival of the body in its simple casket was delayed by the traffic. Before the doors of the hearse could be opened, more than half an hour was spent persuading the crowd to fall back.

Floyd's four sisters and two brothers, accompanied by his ex-wife, Ruby, and their nine-year-old son, Jackie, had to fight their way to cane-bottomed chairs sheltered in the small arbor away from the eyes of the crowd. Already there were his mother, sitting stone-faced and unweeping, his aged grandfather, and his grandmother, a wrinkled old woman wearing a new sunbonnet. Ruby wept in the arms of Mrs. George Birdwell, the wife of Pretty Boy's slain lieutenant.[5]

At 2:30 in the afternoon the Reverend W. E. Rockett of the Sallisaw Baptist Church, of which Floyd's mother and a sister were members, conducted final services, with the Reverend Owen White of the Akins Baptist Church assisting. The funeral rites were simple, followed by several songs by the Akins choir and a sermon on the folly of crime by Rockett, who ended it with Christ's last words on the cross: "It is finished." Most could not hear the funeral oration, and there were calls from the crowd for loudspeakers.

Then the casket was opened for public display as an example that "crime does not pay." Only the upper part of Floyd's body—dressed in a dark serge suit, white shirt, and tie—was visible, with no sign of bullet wounds. "My boy never hurt anybody!" his mother screamed, and then she was quiet.[6]

With a single line on each side of the shingle-roofed shelter, directors of the Moore funeral home of Sallisaw and special officers appointed by the Floyd family guided the procession. Sheriff Bill Byrd of Sequoyah County stood at the head of the bier but was unable to preserve order. Men were reminded to uncover their heads and the greatest respect was demanded. Individuals were told not to be boisterous, to laugh, or to make "improper" remarks.

The Floyd family's desire to bar the press and photographers had only limited success. Many writers and cameras were present. A woman carrying a folding camera in a purselike case had been ordered to leave before the body arrived. Another camera was smashed after being taken from a man under the pavilion.

It was a circus with the mob eating peanuts, drinking corn liquor, spreading picnic lunches, carrying pistols, upsetting gravestones, trampling graves, and ripping down fences as they tried to hear the sermon and catch a glimpse of the notorious outlaw. Funeral wreaths were reduced to fragments by souvenir hunters.

Some forty people fainted from lack of air in the melee outside the pavilion, and three woman near the little shingle arbor were nearly trampled.[7]

Less than half the people had seen the body when Floyd's mother ordered the coffin closed. "I drove 1400 miles to see the body and got within three feet of it," one man said. Some then left, but most waited for the actual burial, which was delayed until almost dark. Floyd was buried to the left of his father; the grave of his brother Chester Lee, who had died in infancy in 1925, lay on his father's right. It was dark before many left. The traffic crawled the nine miles to Sallisaw and was heavy for fifty miles in all directions.[8]

. . .

Charles (or Charley, according to his friends and relatives) Arthur Floyd was born on a Bartow County, Georgia, farm on February 3, 1904. He was the fourth of the eight children of Walter Lee Floyd and Mamie Helene Echols, who had married on December 19, 1897.

Except for Charles, the Floyd children—Carl Bradley, Rossie Ruth, Ruby Mae, Emma Lucille, E. W., and Mary Delta—were law-abiding. The family was proud of Carl Bradley's service in World War I.[9]

Walter Floyd was born in Bartow County on November 2, 1878, and lived there for many years. He was a fireman on the W. & A. Railroad. After a railroad accident he worked in bauxite mines and then turned to farming. He was "remembered as a friendly man, always ready to help anyone in need," and as a hardworking, industrious farmer.[10] He was reported to be a strict father. Mamie Echols, born on March 13, 1881, was a religious woman and a stern parent.[11]

In 1911 the family moved to Hanson, in Sequoyah County, Oklahoma (populated by clannish ex-Georgians), where they rented land to produce cotton (one year they had a yield of one bale of cotton per acre), corn, and other crops. Only a few years before, the county, which had a population of barely twenty-five thousand, had been part of the Cherokee Nation. Walter, who also did summer road work for the county, made enough to buy a few luxuries, such as his first automobile, a Ford touring car.

The Floyds became active members of the Hanson Baptist Church, where Walter was baptized.[12] They lived on the southern edge of the Cookson Hills, four hundred square miles with only a few poor roads and underbrush so thick that a man could walk within thirty feet of someone without seeing him or being seen. Since the Civil War the Hills had furnished hideouts for such notorious outlaws as Belle Starr, the Dalton Gang, Bill Doolin, Cherokee Bill, Mont Cookson, and the Kimes Brothers. "They were believed to be headed for the Cookson Hills" was a familiar saying. Everyone there was suspicious of the law and of strangers, and lawmen got little aid. Even honest farmers were afraid to talk.[13]

In 1921 Henry Starr, "Last of the Real Badmen," who was well-known in Sequoyah County, was killed while robbing a bank in Arkansas.[14] Three years later the famous lawman Bill Tilghman was killed in Cromwell, Oklahoma, by a drunken Prohibition agent.[15]

Young Charles Floyd heard many tales of these outlaws. He was espe-cially interested in the exploits of a Wichita, Kansas, badman named Eddie Adams, who once escaped while being taken to prison by train. He asked to use the bathroom, where he broke a window and jumped out. Adams was killed in 1921 at Wichita.[16]

For many Cookson Hills residents, who made only a meager living, "runnin' likker" was a source of income. A few dollars was big money. It was hard to raise anything, so they didn't farm much. A typical hill-side farm had a mule or a horse, a cow, a corn patch, and a poor, ram-shackle shanty. Schools were open only a few months a year, and chil-dren were lucky to get one pair of shoes a year.[17]

After a few years in Hanson, the Floyds moved to a farm near Akins, also in Sequoyah County, where they raised most of their own food, such as sweet potatoes, Irish potatoes, apples, peaches, and vegetables for canning. There were chickens and cows, and hogs were raised for slaughter. The family was proud of their several excellent foxhounds. They cured their own meat, produced lard, made corn meal, and raised sorghum for molasses. Soap was made from meat scraps and Eagle lye.

Walter made enough money to buy a truck and earned extra money by hauling freight between Sallisaw and Akins. Finally he opened a general store in Akins.[18]

For a score of years the Floyds were one of the most reputable fami-lies in Sequoyah County. They were hardworking and able to live in modest comfort, better than many of their neighbors. But their daugh-ter Mary later said they "worked in the sand hills for a cornbread liv-ing." A religious family, they held nightly Bible readings in the kitchen before bed.[19]

Charles, who loved his mother, revered his father, and was protec-tive of his brothers and sisters, did all the chores expected of him but hated the bone-wearing work on the farm.

According to Mary, Charley was fun to be with and usually made her laugh. But sometimes, when he went too far and talked about re-volting things at the dinner table, he would laugh until the others got sick to their stomachs.[20]

The lively and cheerful Charley left Akins School after graduating from the sixth grade. Although he did not care to study, he did learn to read and write somewhat and to do simple arithmetic.[21]

His mother later said, "Charles has not done one-thousandth of the crimes he has been accused of. As a little boy he would tell the truth regardless of the consequences. He was loyal to his family and friends," and he was always "courteous and truthful." His wife, Ruby, said of him: "When we were kids, Charles was the school hero. He wasn't studious, he was too busy laughing." He was "just an ordinary school boy," according to a friend and former schoolmate, Fred Green, who later became county attorney of Sequoyah County. "I don't think he ever did anything that amounted to much until he went to St. Louis and got tough." Even Sheriff George Cheek of Sequoyah County admitted he had been "a good boy."[22]

As a youngster he was suspected of a few petty thefts, and it is known that he stole some cookies from the Sallisaw grocery store of J. H. Harkrider, who later said in an interview:

> I guess the first thing Pretty Boy Floyd ever stole was from my grocery store. I had some little cakes in boxes and they kept disappearing. I marked some boxes and watched to see where they went. He was just a kid at that time, and came in the store and stood around and left. I counted the boxes and one was missing. I got an officer and we went around to the ally [sic] and he was there eating some cookies. I asked him where he got the cookies and he admitted getting them out of my store, after I showed him the mark. We tried to scare him up and show him he couldn't steal, and let him go.[23]

When Charles was fourteen, he was a harvest hand in the Kansas and Oklahoma fields. "That's when he met the wrong kind of men. They changed his ways of thinking and doing," his sister, Ruth Wofford, said later. His mother agreed: "He changed when he came back from the harvest."[24]

Before that time he seldom fought, and was involved only in the usual schoolboy scrapes. But now the muscular Floyd liked to fight and was good with his fists, with a "punch like the kick of a mule." His favorite hangout was a Sallisaw pool hall, a place popular with rough oil field workers, and he never left a challenge unanswered.[25] Usually he won his fights, but once a gang of farm toughs attacked him, beat him up badly, and tried to gouge out one of his eyes. Fortunately, an immediate operation saved his eyesight.[26]

He continued to be suspected of minor thefts, but was never convicted of any. On the evening of May 16, 1922, there was a burglary at the Akins post office; $3.50 in dimes, nickels, and pennies was stolen (newspapers would later mistakenly report that it was $350 in pennies). The next morning bloodhounds were used in an unsuccessful attempt to hunt down the robbers. Floyd and a twenty-year-old friend, J. Harold Franks, were arrested for the crime on June 4, 1923, in Sallisaw by a deputy U.S. marshal and were indicted by a grand jury on June 7. Franks pleaded guilty, told authorities Floyd was his partner in the burglary, and served a year in jail.

Floyd insisted on his innocence, and two friends of the Floyd family put up a thousand dollars in bail, so he did not have to spend any time in jail before being acquitted at his trial on March 18, 1924. Franks was a government witness. Floyd may have been acquitted because two key witnesses were missing. Postal Inspector F. L. Clampitt could not be found, and store owner and postmaster Margin Thomas was not at the trial for some unknown reason.[27] Walter Floyd said Charley was sound asleep in his bed at the time of the burglary.[28]

Floyd liked girls. An attractive and friendly young man with a clever glibness and a nice smile, he spent a lot of time grooming his hair and buying and taking care of the best clothes he could afford. Some say he was called "Pretty Boy" in his youth by some of his neighbors, who were impressed by his careful pompadour that was "slick as axle grease."[29]

He was 5 feet, 8¼ inches tall; weighed 155 pounds (he later gained weight); had dark hair, gray eyes, and a medium complexion; and was chunky, with strong shoulders. Floyd had a tattoo of a nurse in a rose on his left forearm and four gold caps on his upper front teeth.[30]

Although he worked hard on the farm during the day, Floyd partied at night as far away as Fort Smith, Arkansas. One uncle later said approvingly that he "never thought of nothin' but girls and engines." His nickname, Chock, came from his love for Choctaw beer, a home brew from the days of the Indian Territory.[31]

Floyd enjoyed dancing and attended the local pie suppers. A superb athlete, he played several sports, especially baseball and basketball. The hill people considered him to be the "best basketball player ever seen in these parts." A favorite activity was to wander the Cookson Hills, hunting squirrels and rabbits, camping, trapping, and hiking. On rare occasions he would go on hunting and fishing trips with his father. Once in a while Charles would shoot craps in the woods with some older boys.[32]

His arrest for the Akins post office robbery apparently sobered him, and he decided to look for a job. He found one at the Allen Redford farm south of Muskogee, where he was well-liked. Later he was a roustabout in the oil fields, but he hated the grease and mud.[33]

There was a story that around 1920 Floyd worked for a short time with the John Callahan gang in Wichita, Kansas, but there are no contemporary accounts, even in the Wichita newspapers, and no police record. He was even reported to have run booze from Joplin to Wichita. Supposedly police knew him as a Callahan "handy man." Wichita Captain W. O. Lyle once said, "We considered him a no-good kid, but hardly worth bothering about." A veteran Wichita newspaperman, Bliss Isely, insisted the story was true.[34]

There is also a dubious report about his relationship with a major outlaw of this period, Harvey Bailey, but Bailey denied that he had ever known Floyd.[35] Supposedly, during a visit to Kansas City in 1923, Floyd had met Bailey and invited him to visit him in the Cookson Hills, and Bailey accepted the invitation in 1924. At that time there was a serious drought and the Cherokees were particularly bad off. Floyd and Bailey decided to do something for them. According to James Evetts Haley:

> . . . Upon seeing their condition he and Pretty Boy, deeply moved in sympathy, drove into Sallisaw and after dark borrowed a pickup parked on the street, kicked in the back door of a well-stocked grocery store, and loaded it and his own Hupmobile car to the limit.
>
> They took off into the Cookson Hills, stopping at the humble cabins along the passable trails to share their bounty with the poor settlers in a sort of pre-Roosevelt poverty program—commendable for its greater economy, fairness and lack of politics, except, unfortunately, such free-handed larceny had not yet been legalized by federal law.
>
> No matter! It ingratiated them with the ignorant Indians even as its lush federal counterpart endeared Washington politicians to the educated public in the years to follow. Thereafter

Harvey, along with Pretty Boy, found welcome refuge in those Hills—and there were times when it was needed.[36]

It was rumored, too, that Bailey and Floyd teamed up in 1930 in the Cookson Hills and robbed a bank near Tulsa, in addition to other forays.[37]

On June 28, 1924, Floyd married Ruby Leonard Hargraves, a tall, feisty part-Cherokee sixteen-year-old farm girl from Bixby with dark eyes, auburn hair, and a pretty face. They moved into a two-room wooden cabin near Akins and tried to make a living at farming. Their only son, Charles Dempsey ("Jackie"), was born on December 29, 1924. His middle name came from the boxer Jack Dempsey.

In the summer of 1925 Floyd traded a neighbor five gallons of moonshine whiskey for a pistol. He told him, "Here, you take this, I'm tired of tryin' to make a livin' with this stuff. Now I'm gonna give this here [the gun] a try." Soon after, he went with the harvest crews traveling the Midwestern states but returned home in a short time. He left again a little later, and Ruby did not hear from her husband for several weeks. She became suspicious when he sent her money.[38]

While working on the harvest, Floyd met Fred "the Sheik" Hilderbrand, a handsome, five-foot-ten-inch nineteen-year-old St. Louis hoodlum who liked to call himself a "two-gun" robber. Hilderbrand had robbed the Kitlark Electric Manufacturing Company in St. Louis of $1,822 on July 25, 1925. In the process he had "frightened to death" fifteen employees by displaying his two guns and clubbing the president of the company on the head with a revolver. He then commandeered a passing car and told the driver "to go ahead fast." Although he exchanged shots with a police officer, he escaped. When he climbed out of the car, he thanked the couple and offered them twenty dollars for their help![39]

Floyd, using the alias of Floyd Schmitt, decided to leave the hard work of the harvest fields and join Hilderbrand in a crime wave in the St. Louis area. August was a busy month for them. Together, they robbed five Kroger stores, for a total of $565, as well as several filling stations.[40]

The two youthful bandits, armed with revolvers, held up a Kroger store on August 22 at 5 P.M. One of them ordered the grocery department clerk, Virgil Burton, the store butcher, and several customers to raise their hands while the other rifled thirty dollars from the grocery department register and twenty-five dollars from the meat counter register. They fled in Burton's roadster, which was parked in front of the store, after forcing him to give them the keys.[41]

Hilderbrand by himself robbed one Kroger store of $130. After his arrest he would say, "I hated to take the money at this place. The old man was so gentle." Late in August they decided to hide out in Sallisaw for a few days.[42]

Early in September 1925, Floyd and Hilderbrand left Sallisaw and rode the brake rods of a freight back to St. Louis, where they camped out on the Meramec River.

Two girls accused the two men of molesting them in a river clubhouse. Warrants charging assault were sought against them, but apparently nothing came of it.

A wiry twenty-six-year-old, five-and-a-half-foot-tall man named Joe Hlavatry, who ran a grocery store at Meramec Highlands near the river, came across the two men. They told Hlavatry that they were looking for a place to stay, and he let them rent rooms above his store.[43]

Hilderbrand applied for a job at Kroger Food Stores headquarters and was rejected. While he was there, a payroll was brought in from an armored truck and taken to the second-floor cashier's office. This gave him an idea for a robbery, and he returned the following Wednesday to case the second floor.

Floyd and Hlavatry agreed to join Hilderbrand in the robbery. On the morning of Friday, September 11, Floyd and Hilderbrand left the store in Hlavatry's Ford. They drove aimlessly through the St. Louis streets, looking for a car to steal. At 11 A.M. they saw a black chauffeur seated in a Cadillac, reading a newspaper. They stopped their car, pulled their guns, and forced the chauffeur to get out of the Cadillac. They drove the big car back to the store, picked up Hlavatry, then drove to Kroger headquarters. The Ford was parked nearby. Hilderbrand carried a sawed-off shotgun, and the other two had revolvers.

The payroll money got to Kroger headquarters at 1 P.M., right on schedule. Ten minutes later the gang arrived and went to the second floor. At the cashier's office they leveled their guns at the cashier, her female assistant, a male clerk busy counting the money, the construction superintendent, and the timekeeper. "Don't scream—or we'll have to kill somebody. All we want is the payroll money," yelled Hilderbrand, who threw $11,784 in payroll money and an additional $200 into a sack; the three bandits then fled. The victims noticed an iodine-painted wound on Hilderbrand's left hand.

It was a quick, professional robbery. Outside the cashier's office the hundred employees on the second floor were unaware of what was happening. The cashier immediately told General Manager Phelan, who raced downstairs in time to see the robbers flee in the stolen Cadillac.

One of the company's drivers, Louis Vazis, also saw the robbers head south at high speed, with Floyd driving. He trailed them until Hlavatry jumped from the Cadillac, took the wheel of the Ford, and sped away. Vazis meanwhile had picked up a policeman, and they managed to overtake the Ford. The Cadillac came up behind them and Hilderbrand opened fire. The fire was returned, but the robbers escaped after a lengthy chase throughout the southwestern part of the city.[44]

After the narrow escape, the trio went to Hlavatry's store and divided the loot. Later that day the abandoned Cadillac was found in Webster Groves. Newspaper reporters loved it when the paymaster told them, "The fellow who carried the gun was a mere boy—a pretty boy with apple cheeks." They labeled Floyd "Pretty Boy." Police at first confused him with a petty criminal called Pretty Boy Smith. (This is most likely how Floyd got his nickname.) St. Louis Detective Sergeant John Carroll was also reported to have used the name "Pretty Boy." The robbery was called "one of the most sensational of recent payroll robberies in the city."[45]

In two expensive brand-new Studebakers they had just purchased, Floyd and Hilderbrand fled to Sallisaw on Sunday, September 13, 1925. Their lavish spending made the local police suspicious, and they were picked up. At first Floyd was not a suspect and was only held for questioning. He was called "Floyd Smith" or "Floyd Schmitt" and a "well-known police character."[46]

Two thousand dollars and money wrappers bearing the stamp of the Tower Grove Bank of St. Louis were found in their possession; Floyd and Hilderbrand failed to explain this, but still denied responsibility for the holdup. Three St. Louis lawmen picked up Floyd and Hilderbrand; the cars were seized and nearly all the money was recovered.[47]

Ruby had not heard from Charles for several weeks when he was arrested at Sallisaw. She later said, "I couldn't believe it. Charles had never been in trouble. He was so kind and likable."[48]

Three days later, Floyd, called "Pretty Boy" Smith, and Hilderbrand were detained in the Fort Smith jail and formally charged with the robbery. Hilderbrand, well-known to the police, had been identified by five Kroger employees from a rogues' gallery the day before. St. Louis policemen also recognized him from the Kitlark robbery. Moreover, he had the telltale discoloration on his left hand. Hilderbrand confessed to the crimes and proudly told of the robbery of the Kitlark Electric Manufacturing Company.[49]

The police continued to look for a third suspect. Hilderbrand told of Hlavatry's participation, which led to a large squad of police arresting him at his store. He confessed after the lawmen found a straw valise, covered with a burlap sack and leaves, containing $2,311.[50]

In turn Hlavatry and Hilderbrand accused Floyd of the Kroger headquarters robbery and of the five Kroger store robberies, as well as the filling station holdups. At first Floyd denied the charges, but finally he admitted his guilt. After pleading guilty in November 1925, he was sentenced to five years in the Missouri State Penitentiary which he entered on December 18, 1925. Hlavatry was also given a five-year sentence, and Hilderbrand got eight years.[51]

Just seven blocks east of the state capitol in scenic Jefferson City, Missouri, on the Missouri River bluffs, stood the Missouri State Penitentiary, one of the oldest and largest prisons in the United States and the first west of the Mississippi River, as well as the only prison in the state. When it had opened in 1836, it could hold forty prisoners on four acres. Less than two years later it was overcrowded, and two men had to be placed in cells originally built for one. By the time Floyd got there, it covered forty-seven acres—called "the bloodiest forty-seven acres in America"—and held about three thousand inmates.

John S. Crawford, the warden at the time Floyd was there, 1925 to 1929, and his staff were strong believers in tough discipline. The ball

and chain, whipping, cold baths, and the sweatbox were routine punishments. Floyd left thirty-nine months later, a hardened and dangerous man.

Seven years before Floyd entered prison, the State Prison Board, in-
fluenced by Progressive ideas, took over the supervision of the institution. Among its numerous reforms were that prisoners were given a
small wage; inmates earned time off under the 5/12 rule (five months
off for every year of the sentence, for good behavior); the terrible punishment of being placed in the "rings"—being suspended by the wrists
for a long time—was abandoned; the office of warden was removed
from political appointment; and a few rehabilitative programs were
added.

But other improvements for inmates were minor. There was no
emphasis on education. Guards, who were political hirelings, got low
pay, had a high turnover rate, and received little training.

Two woman prisoners, Kate Richards O'Hare and Emma Goldman,
convicted for antiwar activities, had come to "Jeff City" in 1919. They
proved to be effective critics of the system who cried "slave labor" and
denounced unsanitary conditions. The two told their story to newspapers, magazines, state legislators, and Congress.

But the inmates continued to have twelve-hour workdays, and
such punishments as flogging remained common. As before, all inmates had to walk in lockstep to and from meals and work. There
were still too few guards and few rehabilitation programs, and the food
and medical care were inferior. Inmate violence, drug trade, and open
gang warfare were widespread.

The penitentiary also remained a human warehouse. Blacks, who
suffered the worst overcrowding, were confined to one building—"A"
Hall—where seven or eight men were crowded into cells meant for
three. Women were housed in a separate building.

The inmate count was increasing at an alarming rate. In 1925,
when Floyd entered, there were about three thousand prisoners. When
he left in 1929, there were about four thousand, approximately 80 per-
cent over official capacity.

From the 1880s to the 1930s the prison was as much an industrial
enterprise as it was a prison. Labor for profit was the major part of the
penal system. The superintendent of industries made more than the
warden. Although anything produced was sold to farmers at reduced

prices, the state made big profits from it, in part because little of the money was spent to feed and clothe prisoners.

There were factories for shoes, for work clothing, and for binding twine. Also produced were gloves, soap, and furniture. The tag plant made state license tags and highway signs.

In 1923, the warden's biennial report stated, "A healthy and proper rivalry obtains among the different factories as to which can best serve the state." The prison was making about five million dollars a year in profit when Floyd arrived there on December 18, 1925.[52]

Upon admittance Floyd was bathed, fingerprinted, and photographed; he was also given clothing and a physical examination. He was then placed in the reception center for about thirty days; there he was tested, interviewed, and given a series of orientation lectures. Floyd facetiously gave his occupation as "waiter."[53]

First Floyd was on kitchen duty, and then he worked in the machine shop as a plumber's helper. The staff thought he was intelligent and a good worker. He kept to himself, was quiet, and had no desire to be a troublemaker. Assistant Deputy Warden Charles Hargus later said:

I doubt if Floyd was a wanton killer. He would shoot and shoot to kill when cornered, but he didn't impress me as the type who would slay a man for the pleasure of killing. That doesn't mean that he was a model prisoner. He would steal things, like most of the convicts, but he didn't go out of his way to hunt trouble.[54]

On December 18, 1927, Floyd was discovered with narcotics in his possession. His punishment was to lose sixty days of good time. The next year, on May 15, he lost another sixty days and earned a few days of solitary confinement for striking a guard. At one morning call the guard swore at him for being slow in getting up, and Floyd, "who was always hot tempered," punched the guard and knocked him down.[55]

Harry Hayes, in charge of the cold storage plant at the prison, later told the press he once boxed Pretty Boy's ears for stealing potatoes:

Floyd used to come after ice and he would take advantage of the opportunity to steal potatoes, which the convicts used in making whisky.

The potato room was not visible from my office, and while I

was sure Floyd was stealing potatoes every time he came after ice, I couldn't catch him at it. I tried to be out in the hall when he came, but he was smart and came at a different time every day.

Finally I saw him pick up a bag of potatoes, carry them out and throw them in the wheelbarrow with a block of ice.

Floyd saw me coming after him, dropped the wheelbarrow and started running. He was rounded up in the yard. He acted insolent and I cuffed his ears a few times.[56]

Floyd remained married until shortly before he got out of prison on March 7, 1929. On January 4, Ruby, through her attorneys, had filed a divorce action in the Tulsa court. The charge was neglect, and she told the court he was serving time at the Missouri prison. Floyd signed a waiver to the action with a scrawled "Chas. Floyd." He did not contest the suit, and the divorce was granted on January 7, with Ruby getting custody of their son.[57]

Floyd had a few friends in prison, among them a cellmate, Alfred "Red" Lovett, and James Bradley, who was serving a thirty-year sentence for highway robbery.[58] Like Floyd, Lovett was quiet and no troublemaker. Born in 1890 in California, he had seven years of education and had been employed as a baker. Until May 1924, when he was sentenced to seven years for a robbery in Jackson County, Missouri, he had avoided prison. On September 9, 1924, he had entered the Missouri State Penitentiary.[59]

Lovett (who had been released a year before Floyd, on June 6, 1928) had suggested that Floyd go to Kansas City when he was freed. It had many advantages for an ex-convict, including a powerful underworld.[60]

2

They Just Wouldn't Let Me Alone After I Got Out

In 1929 Kansas City, Missouri, was a center of the meatpacking industry. It was also a major headquarters for the underworld. Thomas J. Pendergast, its political leader, ran a powerful Democratic machine founded by his brother James. Thomas was also a wealthy businessman who mixed his business with politics. The T. J. Pendergast Liquor Company had to close when Prohibition came, but Tom still owned the Red-D Ready-Mixed Concrete Company. He was one of the first contractors to mix concrete in a plant and then transport it to a job site in revolving-drum trucks. His numerous other operations included the Pen Jack Oil Company.

One of the most important people in Pendergast's operations was John Lazia, head of the North Side Democratic Club, who ran a lucrative bootlegging operation. Lazia had grown up in Kansas City's Little Italy, where he learned how to succeed in organized crime and how to buy off the corrupt local police.

Even in the days of the Old West, Kansas City was known as a safe city for outlaws, such as members of the James and Younger gangs, who were willing to pay the police for protection and who agreed not to cause any trouble while in town. Lazia insisted that he be told what criminals were in the area, what their plans were, and how long they intended to stay. Any crooks from out of town who did not pay him off would be arrested or forced to leave the city. Any money found on them would be appropriated.

For criminals on the run, Lazia provided hideouts. Judge Cas Welsh, one of Lazia's lieutenants, was the justice of peace who provided other services. Most of the regular police would help criminals willing to pay.

There were also fences who accepted stolen goods, "bankers" who handled hot money, and tailors who were willing to make clothes with concealed pistol pockets, as well as criminals who would help in planning robberies.

The houses of prostitution, speakeasies, and nightclubs were near Twelfth and Main and were a center of nightlife for the out-of-town criminals.

Gambling was wide open. Harry Brewer, a blind man who ran the unpretentious Harry's Cigar Store, used it as a cover for a large gambling and betting establishment in the back of the store, known as "Blind Harry's." Only a block away, Johnny Kling and Benny Allen ran the pool hall in the Dixon Hotel, also a front for a large gambling operation. Nearby the Sexton Hotel offered gambling for high stakes. All these operations were around Twelfth and Baltimore, a block from the center of the downtown shopping area. Leroy "Gold Tooth" Maxey, Benny Portman, Johnnie Johnston, and Solly Weissman were among the colorful gamblers.

Even the innocent amusements in the city, including some of the best golf courses in the country, were enjoyed by the visiting hoodlums.[1]

Floyd never had gone along with the members of the crime syndicates, and there is no evidence he did so at this time. He went directly from prison to move in with "Red" Lovett in Kansas City. Police harassed him from the very beginning. Later he would write to a newspaper columnist, J. R. Scott, "I'm not as bad as they say i am, they just wouldn't let me alone after i got out."[2] Floyd was arrested on March 9,

1929, just two days out of prison, and held for investigation. He would be arrested by the local police a total of six times during 1929.[3]

Detectives Thomas J. Higgins, Burt Haycock, and George Hayes saw Lovett enter his rooming house, accompanied by Floyd, a man unknown to them. After following them into the house, they took Floyd and Lovett in for questioning, having caught Floyd laying a revolver on a shelf. Perhaps the police just wanted to tell Floyd the ground rules: that so long as he did not cause them any trouble and paid them off, they would leave him alone.

Soon Floyd was arrested again, this time for vagrancy and suspicion of highway robbery, but they could not pin anything on the docile suspect, so he was released the next day.[4]

Kansas City Captain of Detectives Higgins would say later, "I found this youthful ex-convict living among thieves and I tried to turn him aside from the ways of crime."[5]

After a few days staying with Lovett, Floyd moved to Sadie Ash's place on Holmes Street, where "Mother Ash," as she was called—a strong-jawed ex-Sunday school teacher who had brought her eight children from a country town to Kansas City—ran a cooling-off place for criminals.

Mrs. Ash's two sons, William and Wallace, minor members of the North End mob, were dope dealers and pimps who did odd jobs for the mob. They were also police informers and drug addicts. Wallace had become a drug addict when he was injured in the army and hospitalized. He was the only brother ever convicted of anything, and that was for two drug offenses.

William and Wallace had married the Baird sisters, twenty-one-year-old attractive, blond Juanita Beulah and twenty-two-year-old happy and dark Rose, but William and Rose had gotten a divorce.[6]

Unfortunately for Wallace, it was love at first sight for Juanita and Floyd; they began living together on March 14, 1929. Soon after, Wallace and Juanita divorced.[7]

Frequently visiting the brothels around Thirteenth and Cherry, Floyd became well-known among the night people. Supposedly a madam (perhaps Ann Chambers) told him during one of his visits, "I want you for myself, Pretty Boy." Already he hated his nickname.[8]

Homesick, he visited his relatives in Oklahoma after a few weeks in Kansas City; they told him Ruby and Jackie had moved away, and she had become involved with another man. He worked briefly as a roustabout in the oil fields, though he hated that type of work. Nevertheless, he was greatly upset when he was fired because of his prison record.[9]

Immediately after leaving the oil fields, Floyd returned to Kansas City and got a job dealing dice at a Fifteenth Street pool hall for very little money.[10]

Floyd associates at the time included Lovett; two bandit brothers who were bootleggers, Dan and John Sheehan; Billie Howard, a bootlegger and gambler; Eddie Dickey, an alumnus of Jeff City; Nathan King, also from Jeff City and known to Juanita as "Bob"; and two Italians without criminal records. Often his companions would get boisterously drunk, but Floyd was more circumspect.[11]

After Floyd was arrested once more on May 6, 1929, and released the following day, he decided he had had enough and claimed he wanted to look for work elsewhere. He and Juanita went to Pueblo, Colorado, and settled in a rooming house. Meanwhile, the Pueblo police received a false report that an escaped convict wanted by Kansas City police was hiding in the same rooming house. Four policemen raided the place and arrested the couple, two women, and a man, and took them to the municipal court on May 9. Floyd was not wanted, but all five were sentenced on vagrancy charges to fines of fifty dollars or sixty days in jail. None of them could pay the fine, so they were put in jail. But they served only a week, then were released on condition they leave the city at once.[12]

When Floyd and Juanita returned to Kansas City, he tried to hide under the alias of "Joe Scott," but it did no good. In the next four months he was arrested three more times for "investigation" and held briefly. On September 17, 1929, he was arrested and questioned about a major robbery of the Sears-Roebuck plant in Kansas City, but was not held.[13]

Floyd received tragic news about his adored father on November 14, 1929. Walter Floyd had been killed by Jim Mills, a neighbor, after they had quarreled over the ownership of a pile of wood at a general store run by the Mills family in Akins. According to Mills, Walter threatened him with a knife and then stormed out of the store. Believing him to be getting a gun, Mills grabbed a sawed-off shotgun and shot Floyd, who fled into his grocery store and died shortly afterward, in front of his wife.

of a "resort proprietor" in the neighborhood. As soon as her friend arrived, she expected to join her escort in the car across the street. "Get off the street," the officer ordered, and she promptly crossed to the waiting sedan.

Mrs. Gannon was well-known to the police. She was celebrating her birthday and was drunk when she came out of a house of prostitution the police had planned to raid that night. She also got into the car.

Making a reckless turn as he swung back down the boulevard, Bradley crashed into a vehicle approaching from the opposite direction. Patrolman Manes and Sergeant Kovach rushed to the spot. Kovach grabbed King, who was sitting next to the driver, and took him to the parked police car.

At first there was no sign of trouble, but suddenly Bradley fired at Manes, hitting him in the stomach. Manes staggered a few paces and reached for his gun. As he fell, two officers started shooting. Bradley, wounded in both arms, jumped from the small sedan and ran. He escaped amid a fusillade of bullets.

Kovach helped Manes to the police car and the other officers, who were preoccupied with their chase of the gunman, did not attempt to hold the two women, both of whom fled. King, however, was not able to get away.

The police car broke down and a civilian passing by took Manes to al hospital, where he was operated on shortly after three in the morning, but was given little chance to live.

Every available officer was pressed into service to throw a net around the entire district where the shooting occurred. Police vigorously questioned the three officers involved on the scene and King, who would not tell who his companions were.

Later the two women were traced through a taxicab driver and arrested together with six men and two other women alleged to be members of a bootlegging gang. From this and three quarts of liquor in the car abandoned by Bradley and company, police believed King's gang was a liquor ring in the process of delivering liquor. All suspects were questioned.[26]

The Gannon residence was searched by officers, who found a number on a wall; it proved to be for the headquarters of the gang, on the far side of town. Although Mrs. Gannon denied about the house and tried to hide the bright red clay on her

Floyd, Juanita, and Rose went to Sallisaw for about a month, for his father's funeral and Mills's trial. When Mills was acquitted on the grounds of self-defense, Floyd was outraged. Mills soon vanished, never to be seen again. Local rumor had it that "Chock done what he had to"—had killed Mills and hidden his body.[14]

Floyd returned briefly to Kansas City in early December. The local underworld had asked him to help eliminate the threat of "crack detective" Burt Haycock, who was a police hero. Only the week before, he had arrested three Italians thought to be involved in the big Sears-Roebuck robbery, for which there was a ten-thousand-dollar reward. He also had recently arrested a bandit who carried a tear gas bomb in what looked like a fountain pen. More than a year before, he had been shot in both arms by a bandit gang led by the notorious Gus Nichols.

On the morning of December 2, 1929, Haycock, on his way to police headquarters from home, was driving past South Sixty-first Street when a small closed car with no glass in its back window pulled alongside. It was a busy street, and a streetcar was taking on passengers. Haycock recognized Floyd and escaped injury when he dropped down just as two gunmen opened fire on him with shotguns.

There was no pause in the traffic. He pulled on the emergency brake as two more shots struck his car's front. Twenty bullets hit the radiator, the hood, and the cowl. The vacuum tank had been punctured, but the windshield was unbroken. All the shots had been fired too low to hit Haycock. After a while he looked through the windshield and saw that the would-be assassins had fled. The authorities informed the public they were looking for unknown gunmen, but failed to mention that Haycock had recognized Floyd.[15]

E. P. Boyle, chief of detectives, called the attempted assassination a challenge to the police and told his officers

> to oil up their shotguns. Bring in the crooks. Visit their hide-outs and round them up. Somewhere you may find the right men or you may get a tip that will lead to them. These crooks are becoming so bold they are sure to tip their hands. If the attempted assassination of Burt Haycock is a result of his efforts in the Sears-Roebuck case, it may not stop there. Attempts may be made on the lives of other detectives. Get out and get busy.[16]

The *Kansas City Star* editorialized under the head "Making War on the Police" that "The attempt to assassinate Detective Haycock . . . denotes a bolder and more calculated criminal policy, a purpose to get conspicuously active officers out of the way and to intimidate others."[17]

After the shooting Floyd returned to Sequoyah County. In the middle of December he went back to Kansas City with the Baird sisters and spent the Christmas season there. But an uneasy Floyd fled the city once more, leaving the sisters behind. He joined the Bradley gang, which consisted of James Bradley (alias Bert Walker), whom Floyd had known in prison, Nathan King, Nellie Maxwell—all experienced middle-aged criminals—and others. The gang set up their headquarters in Akron, Ohio.[18]

Bradley had first been arrested in 1919, when he was picked up in Parsons, Kansas, with a first-class kit of burglar tools and two .45 caliber revolvers. In 1920 he was arrested for murder in connection with a Buckner, Missouri, bank robbery, and sentenced to life imprisonment. But the next year he was retried and was cleared. Later he was convicted of highway robbery and sentenced to thirty years. However, on October 2, 1929, Bradley escaped from prison farm no. 3. Charles Hargus, the assistant deputy warden at Jeff City, believed Floyd had set up the escape.[19]

Nathan King was an Oklahoma City outlaw, a.k.a. Jack Arnold, who had committed many holdups. Nellie Maxwell, a well-known Kansas City shoplifter called "the notorious Nellie Maxwell, wanted from coast to coast as a shoplifter extraordinary," served as their housekeeper.[20]

The gang rented a house on the sparsely populated outskirts of Akron from William Gannon, who thought Floyd was "a regular fellow." He later said:

> I guess he was bad all the time, but he was able to conceal it, at least to some of us for a while. It has been a great regret that my wife and I ever knew him. We have had so much notoriety about him—we hoped there would not be any more.[21]

Early in 1930 the gang robbed several places near Toledo. Their biggest robbery, about two thoudand dollars, was that of the Farmers & Merchants Bank of Sylvania, Ohio, on February 5. But they missed

twenty thousand in cash, negotiable Liberty Bonds, a they were outwitted by their victims.

The five robbers entered the bank and announce covered the lobby while King rifled the five cash dr Eleven employees and patrons, including the traf Toledo & Western Railway Company, who had bee company's large payroll, were herded together. O several valuable rings from her fingers and hid th

Just before the robbery a couple had asked cashier of the bank, to get their papers from the bers burst in, Iffland immediately set the tim gang's chances of getting more money. King l with his revolver butt; other bandits brutally until he passed out, but he could not open t time lock.

Meanwhile, at a filling station across from vice president of the bank and owner of the s bery was going on when he saw the victims He telephoned the operator, who arranged f alarm to be sounded. The robbers were t when the siren went off, and they fled.

Getting a shotgun, Howard stepped in robbers when they ran to their car, but n a nearby vehicle was ripped up. A consta crooks in the village fire truck, but los all-night search turned up nothing.[22] D gang robbed three more places in the changed.

At 1:30 on Saturday morning, Mar in a small closed sedan on a downt women.[24] Floyd was not with them local jail, trying to bail out a man theirs.[25]

Three officers, who had just raid the car standing at the curb. Also i Harland F. Manes. One of them st by and asked what she was doing

She told him she was waiting

shoes, Chief of Detectives Edward J. McDonnell noticed it matched the red clay the police found when they checked out the gang's headquarters.

Late that day, March 8, Chief McDonnell and eight of the best pistol shots in the Detective Bureau, all of whom wore bulletproof vests, conducted one of the most spectacular raids ever in Akron on the Walker-Mitchell mob headquarters. Two detectives were detailed to guard the back. The front door was locked, but McDonnell kicked it in and was met by Nellie Maxwell. "Where are they?" demanded McDonnell, as Maxwell was grabbed and silenced. She pointed to the second floor.

The detectives rushed up the stairs. One room was locked, but they broke through the door and found Bradley, who had not gotten medical attention because he was afraid of being arrested. He was in bed with a bloody blanket around him, and a young girl was bathing his wounds. They were unarmed and offered no resistance.[27]

Covering Bradley, McDonnell told one of his men to point his gun under the bed, where there had been a commotion. "If he doesn't come out when I count two, blow his damn head off," yelled McDonnell. One of the detectives, a close friend of Manes, did not wait for the count. He ignored the gun and, grabbing a leg, dragged Floyd out. "I never shot anybody," Floyd insisted. The detective gave him "one of the most severe cuffings in Akron police annals."[28]

Everything was set for flight. Bags were packed. A machine gun, with a clip of 150 bullets, was wrapped in a blanket in the room where the gangsters were found. Rifles, revolvers, and shotguns were distributed throughout the house in case of a police raid. Three sets of license plates were found for Ohio, Indiana, and Michigan. There was also a lot of very expensive luggage, nitroglycerin, and rubber gloves. Parked outside was a stolen car with glass removed from the back window to make room for a machine gun muzzle.

"Mitchell [i.e., Floyd] is believed to be a ring-leader in the Egan's Rats gang of St. Louis, of which Fred Burke was the accredited chief, and to whom is attributed the wholesale massacre of seven men on St. Valentine's Day 1928, in Chicago, Ill.," wrote the *Akron Beacon Journal*. Bradley and his gang also were identified as notorious Chicago–New York gunmen.

Charged with first-degree murder, Bradley was taken to the same hospital where Manes was a patient. Manes, who identified Bradley as the man who had shot him, died the next morning. Frankie Mitchell, alias Frank Schmitz (Floyd); Nellie Maxwell, alias Nellie Denny or Nellie Coleman; and Nathan King were held on the most serious charge allowed, as material witnesses who had assisted or harbored a fugitive, until the trial was over.

All day Sunday the gang was interrogated at the police station and heavily guarded because of rumors of a plot to free them. Each was thought to be guilty of murders elsewhere, as well as of the Sylvania, Ohio, bank robbery. One of the license tags found at the gang's Akron headquarters was the same as the one used in the Sylvania job. Checking with New York, Chicago, Kansas City, and St. Louis authorities, officers tried to identify the prisoners and to see if any were wanted elsewhere.

On Monday the three male prisoners were put in the jail and Maxwell was sent to the women's detention home, with bond set at ten thousand dollars each.

Bradley confessed to being at the scene of the crime, but said, "I was drunk and don't know what happened." He would see the funeral procession for Manes from his cell window the following Wednesday.

Two Toledo detectives interviewed the prisoners on March 10, believing they might have been involved in two recent murders, but they were later cleared of the suspicion. They were still suspects in three other Toledo crimes.[29]

When Pretty Boy got to the jail, he showed great duplicity and charm. He was twenty-six but could pass for nineteen, which he claimed he was. That way, he could portray himself as a young, immature, and naive person who came under the domination of much older and experienced men. With a fake name (Frank Mitchell) he could hide his criminal and prison background, and pretend this was his first experience in crime. Floyd was arraigned in police court March 10 and pleaded not guilty to bank robbery.[30]

The following day Bradley and King were identified by three of the victims as the Sylvania bank robbers. Bradley, supposedly a "big gunman of Chicago," was identified because of a twitch in his neck. They failed to identify Floyd.[31]

On March 12, police learned who the members of the gang actually were.[32] Bradley was indicted for first-degree murder on March 15, and his trial began the following month. On May 21, he was found guilty and sentenced to death. Floyd and King remained in jail.[33]

On May 20, 1930, Floyd and King, still at the Akron jail, were arrested by police officers from Toledo for the Sylvania robbery, and were taken to the Toledo jail.[34]

Two days later, Floyd, who was still referred to as Frank Mitchell, and King were identified as the Sylvania bank robbers by two bank employees and two customers.[35]

Juanita, who learned of Floyd's confinement in Toledo from the newspapers and in letters from him, took the train to see him and stayed for a month. Later she made another visit to see him.[36]

Maintaining a stoical calm all day, Bradley, supposedly "an Akron gambler" who "stole" the show by stony humor, went to his death on November 10, 1930. "It looks like we're in for rather a shocking evening," Bradley said as he sat down in the chair, from which another condemned murderer's lifeless body had just been lifted. He had told Detective McDonnell in jail, "You haven't heard the last of that Mitchell boy yet." Just before he was electrocuted, he said with a sneer, "If you think I'm tough, wait until you run up against this man Floyd."[37]

On November 24, 1930, Floyd and King were sentenced to twelve to fifteen years for the Sylvania bank job, to be served at the Ohio State Penitentiary at Columbus.[38]

Only a few months before, on April 21, a terrible fire had killed 320 inmates at that prison out of a population of 4,300. (It was supposed to hold only 1,500.)[39]

An hour before their sentencing, the "dapper" Floyd made an escape attempt from the Lucas County jail. Floyd and King had been permitted to visit the jail barbershop while there were only three deputies on duty. Bill Jacobs and Joe Packo were talking in the jailer's office. Chet Allyn was with the prisoners, taking them back to their cells.

When Floyd slipped out a side door, using a line of prisoners as cover, Allyn missed him at once and raised the alarm. Packo chased him across the courthouse lawn. Floyd tried to escape down the middle of Michigan Street with its heavy traffic, but within five minutes

Packo closed in on him in front of the Elks' Club, next to the Y.M.C.A. Just at this point a jail officer and a police detective were leaving the club and overpowered Floyd as he eluded Packo.[40]

Joe Packo and Joe Danielak were assigned to deliver Floyd, King, and a third prisoner to the penitentiary on December 10, 1930. Floyd swore to King he would die before he would ever go back to the pen. During his stay in jail he talked little. A jail pal, Billy "the Killer" Miller, who himself had escaped from the jail on September 2, had given him the idea of having a handcuff key smuggled in to him and hiding it under his tongue.[41] Probably he also thought of the train escape of the badman Eddie Adams, who asked to use the train toilet, then broke a window and jumped out.[42]

Floyd appeared resigned to his fate when he boarded the train with the deputies and impressed them with his "foppish" appearance. He had dressed in his best clothing, apparently with the intention of making a good appearance before the warden.[43]

According to Packo:

We got on the train about five o'clock that night after searching the prisoners and cleaning them up for the trip. It was pitch dark within a few minutes after the train left Toledo.

Floyd wanted to go to the lavatory all the time but we wouldn't let him. It was too dangerous and we were afraid he would try to get away. When the train stopped at Kenton to pick up passengers, he asked us again, and we finally told him he could go after the train started.

When the train got going again, we agreed it was all right to let him go. I was handcuffed to a prisoner named Ralph Ball, and Floyd was handcuffed to another prisoner, Nathan King. Danielak went to the end of the car and the door to the lavatory, where he could catch them if they tried to break out. He left the lavatory door open.

They hadn't been inside more than 10 seconds before we heard a window crash. I pulled the cord that stopped the train, and then hauled my prisoner with me to that end of the car. . . . Danielak rushed in and found King standing alone with the handcuffs dangling at his side. The window was smashed. Floyd was gone.

Danielak didn't wait for the train to stop before he jumped out. He couldn't find Floyd. It was too dark to see.[44]

Floyd had jumped only ten miles before the prison stop. Police suspected he may have hitched a ride with someone passing through Kenton. Packo and Danielak notified the Kenton police chief and then continued on to the prison with King and Ball.

For four years Floyd would not be caught.[45]

3

Billy "the Killer" Miller

After his sensational escape from the train, Floyd made his way to Kansas City, where he met Juanita, Rose, and William Miller.[1]

Floyd's record at this time was as a punk who had been arrested many times. During the last five years he had been in prison or jail most of the time and had committed only two major robberies. But he could boast of his sensational escape.[2]

In contrast the slim, dapper Miller, called "Billy the Baby-Face Killer," from Ironton, Ohio, a bigamist with two wives, was known to police throughout the Midwest as the "torpedo" of various Ohio gangs who had already killed five men and as an escape artist. Less than three years before, he had escaped from the Ohio State Penitentiary. After being arrested twenty-eight times, Miller now boasted he would not be taken alive.[3]

Miller, born at Ironton in 1906, lived quietly on the family farm after his father's early death. When his mother remarried as he neared manhood, he left to be on his own. The *Toledo News-Bee* reported his brother Grover said Miller had "a dislike for farm work and the desire to be on the loose," which was the "cause" of his criminal career.

Grover continued:

> Billy never did like the farm. He liked good clothes and a good time. When his mother remarried he went to the West Virginia coal fields and worked for a while, then tried switching in the Ironton yards of the Chesapeake & Ohio railroad, but hard work didn't appeal to him very much. . . . He often told me the guys he bumped into in the coal fields as a kid didn't do him any good.

When Grover had seen his brother for the last time two years before, Billy had advised him, "You ought to get off the 'make' kid while you've got a chance."

Billy's criminal record began on September 18, 1925, when he shot and killed his brother Joseph over a woman in Beaver County, Pennsylvania. He was tried and acquitted. During the next three years Miller was arrested several times, but never convicted. In 1928 he and Grover were arrested in Ironton for robbing a man in an alley. Grover claimed that "they set us up . . . it was a bum rap." For the first time in their lives they had to go to jail. Billy was sent to the Ohio State Penitentiary, but soon escaped.

Miller became a "torpedo" for various Ohio gangs and committed several robberies. After he was captured in August 1930 at Lakeside, Michigan, he boasted that he was the triggerman in the shooting of Detroit Police Inspector William Garvin six months before, then later denied it. At the Lucas County, Ohio, jail, where Miller was sent to be tried for two robberies in Toledo, he met Floyd and they became good friends.

On September 2, 1930, Miller escaped from Lucas County deputy sheriffs while being sent back to the county jail from the courthouse, where he had pleaded not guilty. Handcuffed to a long line of prisoners, he suddenly dodged out of the line, the handcuff dangling from his wrist, ran across the lawn of the Safety Building, then through a parking lot, and escaped in a waiting taxicab.

Miller immediately went to work. The day after his escape, he robbed a bank near Kansas City. The police believed the real aim was to kidnap the president of the bank, who was away at that time. He also robbed an Oklahoma City bank.[4]

. . .

The Floyd-Miller gang stayed in Kansas City until early 1931, when Floyd, Miller, and Juanita moved to a house on the outskirts of Shawnee, Oklahoma, for several weeks.[5] Miller and Floyd robbed the Earlsboro, Oklahoma, bank of three thousand dollars on March 9. They went into the bank shortly after noon, herded three employees and five customers into a vault, and locked them in after forcing Assistant Cashier Charlie Littleton to open it. A third robber, George Birdwell, drove past the bank and picked the gangsters up in a small green coupe. But Littleton was able to escape after a few minutes and spread the alarm. After the robbery the gang went back to Kansas City and joined Rose.[6] The Ash brothers, outraged that Floyd and Miller had stolen their girls, set up Floyd for a police raid on March 23, 1931. That night Floyd went to a Linwood Boulevard speakeasy, where he rented a private room. Three Kansas City detectives burst into the room and found Floyd at the closet. "Can't a fellow even put his hat away?" he asked the detectives, his hands gripping the edge of the closet shelf. The police patted him down, and one of them said, "Okay, turn around." Floyd did just that, and blasted away with the two .45 automatics he grabbed from the shelf as he turned. Stunned, the slightly wounded policemen let Floyd get away. Floyd suspected that the two Ash brothers had informed on him. Moreover, he was furious that the Ash brothers had taunted him with cries of "Pretty Boy," with the connotation of "sissy."[7]

Two nights later Wallace Ash received a telephone call from a woman asking him and William to come and see their ex-wives. "You'd better be careful," Wallace jokingly told a woman friend at his mother's home. She answered, "How about yourself?"

The two brothers left the Ash home shortly before ten in the evening to go downtown, stopping briefly to talk to Detective Burt Haycock. At about eleven they were last seen alive by one of their sisters; Wallace was driving past the Ash home at a fast rate, with Floyd and Miller following in another car.

The Ashes were overtaken and forced off the road about a mile south of Kansas City, Kansas, about fifteen minutes before midnight. Forced from their car at gunpoint, the Ash brothers were ordered to turn their backs to the gunmen at the edge of a ditch.

Will was down with one shot, but it took four to flatten Wallace.

Both were then shot in the head, Will twice and Wallace once. The murderers took about five hundred dollars from Wallace and about two hundred dollars from William, and left the bodies in the ditch. After setting the Ashes' car on fire, Floyd and Miller sped away.

At a house fifty yards away, a farmer named J. A. Grider was awakened by the gunfire. Peering out a window, he saw a car burst into flames and heard two more shots about ten seconds apart. But he heard no outcry or car being driven away. Two other farmers within a quarter-mile also heard the shooting. After Grider dressed hurriedly, he ran to the burning vehicle, saw the two bodies in the ditch, and then drove to a police station to report what happened.

The car was still burning furiously when officers arrived at the scene. They found no clues and little on the bodies, except for a small amount of morphine and a hypodermic needle on Wallace.[8]

Relatives of the slain men denied they were stool pigeons. They believed Floyd had been responsible for the murders because he had a grudge against the Ashes, and he had been seen in Kansas City during the previous two weeks.

Kansas City, Kansas, police were looking for the brothers for the murder of a police chauffeur in 1929. Mrs. Ash wondered why her sons had not been arrested, since the police knew where to find them.

Another alleged stool pigeon, Claude Abbott, an associate of the Ashes, went into hiding after he was warned he, too, was "on the spot" for "tipping off" to police the joints raided two days before. Officers were unable to find him.[9]

Police investigators believed Floyd and Miller were the killers of the Ash brothers, and some members of the underworld sought revenge. But Floyd, Miller, Rose, and Juanita had fled the city. They traveled through Kentucky and Ohio, armed with pistols, staying at tourist camps and hotels.[10]

On April 6, 1931, the bandits robbed the smallest bank in Grant County, Kentucky, the Mount Zion Deposit Bank at Elliston, near Williamstown, about 10:30 in the morning. They picked up about $2,000, including $250 in gold. Rose had cased the place when the bank had opened that morning. One robber stayed in the car in front of the bank, while the other went in and threatened Cashier W. C. Smith, the only person in the building, with a pistol, tied him up with ropes, and placed a gag over his mouth. The gangsters then escaped to the Dixie Highway. A few minutes later, Smith got out of his bindings and called the sheriff's office.

Four miles further on, the robbers were spotted picking up two women and then heading north. They stopped at a farm owned by a James Burroughs, whom Miller had known (but who was unaware of Miller's criminal past), and pretended to be looking at farms to buy in the area. While a posse searched fruitlessly, the quartet ate a leisurely meal at his farm and paid generously.[11]

That night they traveled to Bowling Green, Ohio, near Toledo, and rented rooms at a good hotel. Miller's younger brother, Grover, was being held at the nearby Lucas County jail on a burglary charge. Almost immediately their lavish spending brought them to the attention of the police, who suspected them of being shoplifters or counterfeiters. The members of the gang bought expensive clothing, ate in the best restaurants, and liked to flash their money, especially large bills.

On April 10 the two gangsters stole a jeweler's car from a Toledo parking lot early in the morning and headed for the nearby town of Whitehouse, where they jauntily entered a bank shortly before noon and drew their revolvers. The only person inside was the bank clerk, the other two employees being at lunch. One of the robbers held his gun on the clerk while the other took about eighteen hundred dollars from the counter.

When the clerk stepped on a buzzer that sounded in a nearby store, the gangsters forced him to go with them across the street and act in a friendly manner. People in the store assumed that it was a false alarm. As Floyd and Miller drove off, the clerk took the license number and called the police. As the getaway car turned a corner, a butcher ran into the street, fired one shot from a revolver, and missed. Roads leading into Toledo were guarded, but the gangsters escaped.[12]

On April 15 the couples got drunk on corn whiskey given them by a bellhop during an all-night party. The next morning they were still drunk. The men felt generous, and decided to allow the girls to go on a shopping spree at Uhlman's Clothing Store while they got haircuts at a barbershop next to the store.

Chief of Police Galliher had asked merchants to report seeing any of the suspects. At noon a stenographer at Uhlman's called the chief at his home and told him the two women were in the store. Galliher took Patrolman Ralph Castner with him; they staked out the corners opposite the store and waited. Soon they saw the two men saunter out of the barbershop and enter Uhlman's. A few minutes later the quartet left the store and were followed down Main Street by the police car. As the two couples turned the corner, the car stopped at the curb. The two officers jumped out, and the chief drew his revolver. Quickly stepping a few paces forward, Galliher demanded the four put up their hands.

"Billy the Killer" and Floyd turned sharply, pulled out their guns, and opened fire.

Pedestrians screamed as they ran for cover.

Miller managed to squeeze off one shot before he fell dead, a bullet from Galliher having ripped open his neck.

As Miller's gun fell to the ground and Juanita reached for it, Galliher shot her in the back of the head. She sprawled on the ground, seriously wounded. Rose bent over her.

Floyd fired his gun until it was empty, piercing Castner's intestines in seven places. The patrolman collapsed in a sitting position, firing as he did so.

Floyd started to run, with Galliher close behind him.

When Rose also ran, the chief chased her instead, caught her, and handcuffed her. City Councilman Elmer Bowers ran out of the house on the corner and took charge of Rose.

Galliher resumed chasing Floyd, who was running between houses to his car, parked in front of Uhlman's. He fired his last two shots at Floyd, but missed.

Meanwhile, Rose had gotten away from Bowers, but Galliher grabbed her and handed her over to Bowers once more.

By this time Floyd had reached his car and had driven off. No one saw which direction he had taken.

The Reverend C. B. Halberg, pastor of the Gospel Tabernacle, ran across the street and bent over Castner. The officer's father, Zibe Castner, who worked in a nearby lumberyard, heard the shooting, ran to the street, and helped the pastor carry his son to the curb. Soon ambulances took him and Juanita to a hospital three blocks away.

Doctors operated immediately on Castner, but without much hope. He had been a football star and team captain at Bowling Green

High School and Bowling Green State Normal School; he had been on the police force for only a year and a half. Juanita, unconscious for several days, was not expected to live.

Shortly after Castner and Juanita arrived at the hospital, an anonymous caller told the police that a speeding car had struck a truck on a road about two and a half miles east of the city and that the driver, who resembled Floyd, was being held. Chief Galliher and his men rushed to the scene but found nothing.[13]

The sheriff, police chief, and prosecutor interrogated Rose for several hours but learned nothing. After they allowed her to see her sister for almost an hour late in the evening, she was returned to the jail and questioned again.[14]

Miller's body was taken to a funeral home, where $750 was found in his pockets. Police asked those who had witnessed the holdups to view the body; a cashier from the Whitehouse bank identified Miller and Floyd as the bandits from a photo. Miller's two wives claimed his body, as did his mother. The latter won out, and Miller was buried with his "family of outlaws." His brother Grover said, "Well, they got him—he always said they would sooner or later, and he told me that if I didn't go straight the same thing would happen to me."[15]

Police, who found Floyd's car abandoned at an intersection, forced Rose to show them where the gang had hideouts. They surmised that Floyd had caught the bus for Chicago, Toledo, or Detroit after abandoning his car.[16]

Rose admitted she had helped in the Elliston, Kentucky, bank robbery after witnesses, who had seen her in the bank a few hours before the robbery, identified her. Farmer James Burroughs identified Floyd from a photo and said the gang had paid for a meal at his house after the robbery.

Shrugging her shoulders, Rose said, "Sure, I'll tell you about it. We were there."

Kansas City, Kansas, police came to Bowling Green to interview the sisters about the Ash killings. Rose denied any knowledge of it and said she had divorced William Ash long before she met Miller and Floyd.[17]

The sisters were turned over to the sheriff of Grant County, Kentucky, after Juanita made a miraculous recovery. Although the women, who received letters and financial assistance from Floyd while in prison, were sentenced to three years in the Kentucky State Penitentiary, they served only about ten months after an appeals court reversed their convictions.[18]

Castner died on April 22. After ballistic tests proved that it was Floyd's weapon that had killed him, the Wood County commissioners offered a five-hundred-dollar reward for his capture.[19] An intense manhunt that spread to every big city in the Midwest was fruitless. In the Detroit area a man whose description matched Floyd's claimed he was Frank Mitchell after stealing two taxis. Floyd was known to have friends in Detroit and Bay City, Michigan. The last clue was a sighting in Toledo, but he was not found there.[20]

Once more Pretty Boy Floyd had escaped.

Floyd fled to Kansas City. By now he was notorious, having finally won the respect of underworld leaders. They were eager to provide him with protection, for a big fee.

Some writers have claimed he became a killer for the Kansas City underworld, but this is unlikely; he was a freelance outlaw, not an organization man. According to another writer, he hid in the Toledo area during May and June 1931 with members of the Licavoli mob, whom he had met the previous winter through Bill Miller. Others insist he was a loner much of the time, only occasionally working with others on minor crimes. He was reported to have been the bodyguard for a bootlegger. Other unreliable reports say he robbed several banks in Oklahoma during this period.

Most likely the red-hot Floyd, with plenty of money from his bank jobs, just lay low in Kansas City. He was aware the Kansas City underworld would not tolerate criminals hiding out and pulling jobs in the city.[21]

Floyd hid out in one of the rooms above the Lusco-Noto Flower Shop at 1039 Independence Avenue. The rooms were comfortably furnished with radios and overstuffed furniture; some were joined to form suites with kitchens. Weapons—pistols, long-range rifles, pump guns, shotguns, and machine guns—were placed strategically in the rooms, ready for use.

The establishment was well known to police as a gangster hideout and a source of illegal liquor. Numerous crimes, such as murders, drug dealing, and extortion of gamblers, were planned here. Once officers had raided the place in search of killers reported to have driven there, but they had left by the time the police arrived.[22]

On the night of July 20, 1931, twenty-one plainclothes policemen and U.S. Prohibition agents led by Thad W. Rowden raided the flower shop for liquor in a well-planned operation. They were determined to put it out of existence permanently by collecting enough evidence.

At first, everything was going smoothly. But Floyd and John Calio were wanted for murder, and were not going to give up without a fight. Police believed Calio was hiding there but knew nothing of Floyd.

Calio, suspected of murdering a speakeasy owner a few days before, had been arrested many times on liquor charges and once for carrying concealed weapons.

First the agents ordered some liquor from the place and arrested the two Italian youths who delivered it. Next, they surrounded the building and some officers quietly entered it from the front and back. From a central hall upstairs the police made a thorough search of about twenty rooms. They arrested six Italian men and a black man.

Evidence of bootlegging, such as bottles, artificial whiskey flavoring, and stills, was found immediately. In one room was a weapons cache consisting of two rifles, a shotgun, five revolvers, and a large stock of ammunition.

Finally Rowden gathered all the officers and prisoners in a large room on the second floor and ordered some of the raiders to guard the prisoners. Others were to go in pairs to search the remaining rooms.

It appeared the raid was about over, without any problems. Agents were ordered not to draw their weapons, to avoid being labeled trigger-happy.[23]

Curtis C. Burks and Glenn Havens entered a dark little room in a far corner of the second floor.

They turned their flashlights on and saw Floyd sitting on a bed, with a .45 caliber revolver in his belt and much ammunition on the bed.

According to The *Kansas City Star*, there was the following dialogue:

"He's got a gun," yelled Burks.

"I've got it," said Havens, as he advanced into the room and took the .45 caliber weapon from Floyd's belt.

"Better look for another one," said Burks.

Floyd suddenly sprang from the bed, firing a second gun.

The flames spat in the darkness.

Havens asked, "Are you hit?"

Sinking to the floor, Burks responded, "He got me."

He had been hit in the abdomen and was paralyzed from the waist down.

Floyd raced out of the room and encountered Patrolman Clarence L. Reedy in the hall, where he was standing guard. He shot Reedy in the abdomen and the jaw. As he fled down the hall, he slightly wounded Prohibition Agent A. C. Anderson and another agent.

Floyd, supposedly surrounded, ran down the stairway to Independence Avenue, then spun around and fired as the agents came to the top of the stairs. They fired back, and a black man passing by was killed when he took a bullet in the head. The gangster jumped into a car and raced away.[24]

Agents rushed to help Burks, and someone called for an ambulance.

Lieutenant E. L. Nelson rushed to the building as soon as he heard about the shooting on the police radio. He ran into the building with a sawed-off shotgun and met the agents upstairs. They told him of the shooting. "Where was Calio?" he asked.

Nelson began an immediate search and entered the dark anteroom where Calio was hiding. There he saw a "spot of white" from a large box containing clothes.

"Get out of there," yelled Nelson, not sure anyone was actually in there, and poked his shotgun at the spot. When Calio grabbed the gun, Nelson fired point-blank, almost decapitating the gangster.

It had been a bloody affair: Prohibition Agent Curtis C. Burks had been mortally wounded, a patrolman seriously wounded, two other officers slightly wounded, a passerby killed by a wild bullet, and the gangster John Calio killed.

Charges of conspiracy to violate the liquor laws were filed against the seven criminals arrested. Lusco was beaten by police and had to be taken to the hospital.

"I am glad our agents did not shoot without full justification," said Colonel George H. Wark, Prohibition administrator of Missouri, Kansas, Oklahoma, and Arkansas.

They have been instructed to be cautious. However, their caution resulted in their injury from Calio last night.

The gang that has operated from this Independence Avenue nest shall be run down to the last man, and similar resorts in the North Side also will find the government agencies strong on their trail.

At first the police did not realize that Floyd was involved and assumed Calio had done all the shooting. Only later investigation revealed that Floyd was the actual killer.

Lazia was furious that a federal agent had been killed on mob property. To reduce the pressure on him, he ordered that the federal agents could have Floyd, because he was an out-of-towner, not an "organization" man, and therefore expendable. But Floyd had fled to a place where he felt safe—the Cookson Hills.[25]

4

The Phantom of the Ozarks

Pretty Boy Floyd committed at least half of all the bank robberies in Oklahoma during 1931 and 1932, according to some accounts.[1] He had teamed up with George Birdwell, an old acquaintance. Legend has it that Birdwell was a vicious killer who had slain ten men and robbed many banks. But in truth he had no police record; the only trouble he ever had was when a jealous husband shot him in the leg in 1913.

Birdwell, Floyd's "hatchet man," was a tall, very bony, Lincoln-esque, forty-year-old man with tight skin and a beak nose. In the past he had been a "Burning Busher" hill-country preacher who gave very emotional sermons until he became a drunk and lost his audience. However, he found work in the Earlsboro oil fields and was able to support his wife and four children until he lost that job sometime in 1931. Mrs. Birdwell was active in the PTA and her children excelled in school. Desperate to support his family, Birdwell decided to find Floyd in the Cookson Hills and beg him to consider him as his partner. Why would Floyd accept an inexperienced man with the reputation as a drunk? Somehow the former preacher persuaded the gangster to take him on.[2]

Floyd became known as "The Phantom of the Ozarks" and "The King of the Bank Robbers." His Robin Hood image, stealing from the rich and giving to the poor, came from his generosity to the poor hill people who helped him. Even today residents of Sallisaw and Akins believe that many of the bad reports about him are false. As far as they are concerned, he was generous to children and old people, and prevented corrupt bankers from stealing the land of poor farmers. He was reported to be feeding a dozen families.[3]

When he robbed the bank at Sallisaw, he did it because the bank President said Floyd was afraid to rob it, and to discredit the candidacy of Sheriff George Cheek, whom Floyd disliked—or so the story went. Then, without any interference from the law, he rode up and down the streets of Sallisaw, tossing money to the locals.

Floyd once wrote to the Sallisaw sheriff, "I'm coming to see my mother. If you're smart you won't try to stop me." The sheriff let him see his mother in peace.

When Birdwell's father died in a small Oklahoma town, the rumor spread that Floyd and Birdwell wanted to see the body. The local sheriff set a trap of five deputies, but Floyd and Birdwell managed to view the body and leave quietly. Some newspaper accounts say that event really happened in 1930, and Birdwell was alone.[4]

Some sheriffs left town when they heard that Pretty Boy was coming. It was said that sometimes Floyd announced in advance which bank would be his next target.[5]

Another story was that when Floyd went to Earlsboro to see some friends, his car was seized by the local sheriff. Floyd was said to have kidnapped a black man for a shield, have gone to the sheriff, and taken his car back.[6]

Floyd was often befriended by his black neighbors. In the summer of 1932, at a poor farm near the black community of Boley, Oklahoma, he and Birdwell were fed and given water for their car by a black woman. The gangsters gave her a twenty-dollar bill and she said nothing of the visit to local lawmen. Floyd was a close friend of Dock Hearn, a black neighbor of Birdwell's, whose house was occasionally a convenient hideout. After each robbery Floyd gave Hearn a dollar.[7]

The Floyd-Birdwell team had smooth sailing for several months. Their bank robbery technique was to steal a car and drive to the bank unmasked. Often they would lock everyone in the vault, and sometimes they took hostages.[8]

According to one account, "The steel-vested desperado is noted for the breakneck speed at which he drives and the machine guns which are always with him." Police were told that Floyd carried two machine guns in his car, and that he wore a steel jacket for protection. The bandits kept to the byroads, cut fences, went across fields; Floyd drove expertly and furiously.[9]

Of course there were numerous false reports of Floyd robbing banks, such as the fifty-thousand-dollar robbery of the Citizens State Bank of Strasburg, Ohio, on November 6, 1931.[10] Another bank that Floyd did not rob was in Inola, Oklahoma. A newspaper taunted him: "This Rogers County bank is a jinx for bandits. To date Pretty Boy Floyd has made no attempt to rob it." In the last five robberies four robbers had been caught, and one killed. Wisely, Floyd did not take the dare.[11]

On August 4, 1931, Floyd and Birdwell began their Oklahoma bank-robbing spree in Shamrock. Informers reported one of them stayed in the car while the other entered the institution and took four hundred dollars.[12]

They found the cashier atop a stool, winding a clock, when they entered the Morris State Bank, near Okmulgee, on September 8. He and two other employees were forced into the vault and locked in, but were able to release themselves within a few minutes. By then the robbers had escaped with all available cash, $1,745.30, and had vanished without a trace. At first others were blamed for this robbery.[13]

The next time out, the two outlaws did even better; they stole $3,849.28 from the Maud, Oklahoma, bank on September 29. Two employees and three customers were locked in a vault for about twenty minutes. The robbers fled in a small touring car; no trace was found of them. One of the robbers was said to be about twenty and the other middle-aged. Obviously, Floyd looked younger than he was.[14]

The following day the Sallisaw sheriff, George Cheek, received a wire from federal officers that Floyd and Birdwell were responsible for the Maud bank robbery and were planning to visit Sallisaw. He had all of Floyd's relatives' homes watched. Cheek and Otis Romans, a night watchman, staked out the home of one of Floyd's sisters, Mrs. Ruth Wofford, in Romans's car.

After the lawmen had driven past the Woffords' home, Floyd and Birdwell came up in a Ford coupe about eleven that night. The officers drove past the house again, this time with the two robbers following them. The coupe passed them at the corner, and the two lawmen followed close behind.

On the side of a hill on Hog Creek, a few miles northeast of Sallisaw, the gangsters' car stopped. The outlaws jumped out, and Floyd challenged the lawmen to "come out and shoot it out." Floyd and Birdwell emptied their guns. Four bullets tore through Romans's car. Sheriff Cheek responded once with his rifle and four times with his pistol, and Romans got off six pistol shots—to no avail. One newspaper wrote about Floyd, "If any of the shots had struck him, it is thought that they would have been harmless owing to the steel breast plate, which officers say he always wears."

After two deputies heard the gunfire and ran to the aid of the lawmen, the gangsters got into their car and raced toward Akins. They were seen going through the towns of Short and Van Buren, but then the trail was lost.[15]

The two robbers continued to increase their loot. On October 14, 1931, they hit the Earlsboro bank for $2,599 and left three bank employees and three customers locked in the vault. A neighboring merchant freed them.[16] On November 5, Floyd, Birdwell, and an unknown robber (possibly Fred Barker) took two thousand dollars from the bank at Konawa. One of the bandits manned a mounted machine gun in the car while the two others entered the bank shortly before noon. Covering four bank employees and two customers with pistols, they forced the employees to open the vault and hand over the cash. Meanwhile, a crowd gathered outside, but was held off by the machine gun. The two men forced the cashier to walk in front of them as a shield until they reached their car. A large posse failed to catch them, and bank officials failed to identify two suspects who were later arrested and released.[17]

On December 23, Floyd and Birdwell robbed the Morris bank of $1,162. The two entered the bank with Floyd carrying a machine gun; they forced two officials and five customers to lie on the floor, then proceeded to take all the cash in sight and marched the hostages out of the bank ahead of them to the sidewalk, where a crowd had gathered. Floyd held the crowd at bay with his machine gun, Birdwell leaped into the car, and they took off. Guards were placed on all surrounding highways and bridges, but the duo again managed to slip through.[18]

Around this time a government agent and a deputy sheriff visited several of Floyd's relatives, who told them they were totally unaware of Floyd's habits and hideouts. Floyd had refused to let his brothers join him in his criminal career. On January 5, 1932, one of Floyd's sisters, questioned in a Kansas City, Kansas, hotel room, said she had not seen him in "many months."

It was known that Bill Byrd (soon to be sheriff of Sequoyah County) was friendly to Floyd. Fred Green, the county attorney, was also a close friend of Floyd. Bert Cotton, police chief of Sallisaw, was suspected of being his enemy.[19]

On Saturday, January 2, 1932, two brothers, Harry and Jennings Young, were at the family farmhouse about seven miles west of Springfield, Missouri, when they were warned by a telephone call from their mother that their sisters had been arrested by the police and that they had "better be prepared." The brothers were former convicts, and Harry was wanted for the murder of the town marshal of Republic, Missouri, two years before.

A short time later two cars containing ten officers parked in front of the farmhouse. One officer fired tear gas through an upstairs front window. Nothing happened, so a sheriff said, "Let's kick the back door open." Three lawmen rushed the door and it burst open. Two shotgun charges from the kitchen killed two of them, and the third was seriously wounded. An intense gunfight followed. After the shooting was over, six officers were dead and three wounded.

The two killers escaped. Three days later, after a sensational manhunt, they were tracked to a house in Houston, Texas, where they killed each other rather than surrender to the law. At one point during the manhunt they had been missed by only five minutes.

The Young brothers had committed one of the worst killings of police in the history of American crime, even worse than the loss of five men in the Kansas City Massacre. The police refused to believe that only two men could have caused so much damage, and tried to implicate Floyd and Fred Barker. The Bowling Green, Ohio, sheriff told Springfield, Missouri, police he thought Floyd was involved. A Kansas

City tire shop proprietor identified Floyd and Harry Young as being to-gether. But by January 5 it was realized Floyd had nothing to do with the killings.[20]

Floyd hit the "big time" at the beginning of 1932. During January, stories about him appeared in the Oklahoma newspapers almost daily. He was reported to have said he would not be taken alive.[21]

The *Muskogee Daily Phoenix* was effusive:

With the partial identification of Charles Arthur Floyd, 28, as one of the band that killed six officers at Springfield, Mo. last Saturday night, the Oklahoma desperado steps into the rank of real "bad hombres" with the questionable honor of 11 men, all officers, to his credit.

The exploits of Billy the Kid, who plugged his officers by shooting them through their stars and of "Wild Bill" Hickock [*sic*], who drew his guns after a bullet had been fired into his brain, pale before the cool, monotonous killings of the fair haired "Pretty Boy" Floyd, who has introduced the submachine gun and the armored vest to the Oklahoma bad men.

Floyd was born and raised on a farm near Sallisaw, where his name bids fair to become as legendary as that of Jesse James, owing to his wild deeds, and his glamorous gun battles with the "law."[22]

On January 14, 1932, Floyd was reported to be the ringleader of bank robberies committed ten miles apart by different gangs at Paden and Castle, Oklahoma. He was accurately identified from pho-tographs as one of a trio that looted the State Bank of Castle of twenty-six hundred dollars. The gang forced two bank officials and two cus-tomers to go with them to the outskirts of the city as protection against gunfire, then released them unharmed.

About the same time three unmasked men robbed the First Na-tional Bank of Paden of twenty-five hundred dollars. The cashier and four customers were forced to lie on the floor by two of the bandits while the other collected the money. The customers were locked in the vault but got out immediately. Outside, meanwhile, a citizen tore the license tag from the getaway car. The cashier was taken as a hostage and released at Boley, six miles away. Two of the bandits were identified. Floyd had nothing to do with this robbery.[23]

O. P. Ray, assistant superintendent of the State Bureau of Identification, who ordered all available state agents to search for the bandits, said, "It is nothing unusual. They have been robbing in Oklahoma at the rate of two or three banks a week. Our information is that the two robberies were by two gangs."[24]

The banking establishment was outraged. Fifty-one banks had been robbed in Oklahoma during 1931. One headline read "Pretty Boy Pretty Bad, Says Banker." Floyd was Oklahoma's Public Enemy No. 1. The bankers demanded that Governor W. H. (Alfalfa Bill) Murray call out the National Guard to hunt down Floyd. Bank insurance rates were doubled on January 14, 1932. Banks in towns of less than five thousand population, where most of the robberies occurred, had to pay ten dollars per one thousand dollars of deposits. Rates were lower for larger towns.[25]

Eugene Gum, secretary of the Bankers' Association at Oklahoma City, said the governor should call out the Guard and "offer a big reward for capture of Floyd and his pals, who enforce their edicts with machine guns." Gum added, "As long as he stays down there and is protected as he is now, he will continue to attack banks."[26]

In Kansas City, Missouri, reporters asked Oklahoma Governor Murray, on a speaking tour, about the request for the National Guard. He said, "Who are these Floyds, anyhow?" The governor was not concerned, and said that the acting governor, Lieutenant Governor Robert Burns, could handle the situation. Murray thought using National Guard troops to hunt bank bandits was a bad idea. "What good would the soldiers do? All the troopers would do is make a lot of noise."[27]

The *Daily Oklahoman* wrote on January 16, 1932: "The mobilization of the national guards to suppress banditry in Oklahoma might stimulate the peace officers of the state to a greater effort to make Oklahoma unsafe for bank raiders, but it is doubtful if the guards themselves could do very much to suppress wholesale robbery."[28]

About twenty Oklahoma peace officers and Eugene Gum met with Acting Governor Burns and Adjutant General Charles F. Barrett in Barrett's office on January 15, 1932. Barrett said:

Rewards will be offered by the state and the Oklahoma Bankers' Association. The officers reached a mutual understanding and decided upon unity of action in the pursuit of Floyd. The National Guard will not be called out, but the equipment will be at the disposal of the officers. Automatic rifles, machine guns and other equipment will be furnished. If Floyd is found and resists, the guards will aid the local officers, if necessary, in his capture.[29]

The group thought Floyd had an "Al Capone" complex because, like Capone, he had never had a real test with the law. They agreed that Floyd must be captured—dead or alive. A central source of information was set up, and Birdwell and seven other gang members were listed as wanted.[30]

Burns offered a thousand-dollar reward, double the usual amount, and the Bankers' Association offered another thousand, dead or alive. Rewards totaled six thousand dollars.[31]

According to the *Daily Oklahoman:*

Officers say the desperado wears a steel vest and a few believe he has a metal skull cap. His small coupe is equipped with a machine gun and he carries a sub-machine gun with him in the robberies. The automobile, according to reports, is geared three-to-one, and equipped with bullet-proof glass, puncture-proof tubes in heavy duty tires, an auxiliary steel-plated gasoline tank and a bucket of heavy tacks. He darts through traffic at a speed of 70 miles an hour, officers say. . . . Sometimes he sleeps in his automobile.[32]

In a radio broadcast Burns said, "This is a desperate case. Floyd has terrorized the entire east central section of Oklahoma with his outlawry. Already six killings and at least 10 bank robberies have been charged to his gang. He must be stopped."[33]

During the middle of January 1932 eastern Oklahoma peace officers, aided by the State Bureau of Identification, hunted Floyd in the hills and oil fields with machine guns, automatic rifles, bombs, and steel vests supplied by the State Militia.[34]

The Oklahoma City police chief said, "Where a hundred fake tips might come in, one may be reliable. We are taking no chances."[35] An itemized list of Floyd's supposed activities is illuminating:

Jan. 13. Floyd held up a deputy passing through Wewoka and took his pistol.

Jan. 15. Floyd ate dinner in Henryetta, Oklahoma.

Jan. 15. Oklahoma City police received about 20 phone calls reporting Floyd sightings.

Jan. 17. Floyd reported near Wewoka, but the suspect was a salesman.

Jan. 20. Floyd hunted in the hill country of eastern Oklahoma. Also reported at Earlsboro and that night in Oklahoma City.

Jan. 21. Still reported in Oklahoma City. Man giving this information later was put in jail for investigation. Also, Floyd was reported to have robbed Dover bank.

Jan. 23. Reported in Texas.[36]

Acting Governor Burns received an unsigned letter from Floyd on January 20, 1932, from the southwestern Oklahoma town of Altus. He wrote, "Robert Burns, Acting Governor—you will either withdraw that $1,000 reward at once or suffer the consequences—no kidding. I have robbed no one but the monied men." After conferring with Adjutant General Barrett, who was directing the search, Burns turned the letter over to postal authorities. Handwriting analysts found it was genuine. Burns said the reward would stand.[37]

An editorial in the *Muskogee Daily Phoenix* read, "An attempt has just been made to scare Robert Burns, Acting Governor, into withdrawing a posted reward for the capture of 'Pretty Boy' Floyd. It is a cheap imitation, though none the less ominous, of the brazen flaunting of law by criminals of the big cities."[38]

According to the *Daily Oklahoman* that same day:

> When outlaws and relatives of outlaws seek to bargain with the state's chief executive for terms of surrender, we are approaching the outskirts of organized gangdom. The quest for "Pretty Boy" Floyd has become humorous, or less. He is reported seen at both ends of the state at once. Every town, every day, gets some report to his whereabouts, but he is not there when police arrive. . . .
>
> If this tiresome hunt goes on much longer the public will become convinced bank bandits escape either through tribute or through fear on the part of peace officers.[39]

Some people saw the humor in the Pretty Boy Floyd hunt. For example, he was made fun of at the Gridiron Press Show in Tulsa on February 3, 1932.[40] A humorous account entitled "Floyd Search is Oklahoma's, Rangers Claim," appeared in the *Daily Oklahoman*:

> All the cops and constables in Oklahoma still were searching for Charles "Pretty Boy" Floyd Monday night, but the teahound bad man could not be palmed off on Texas.
>
> Floyd, blamed with virtually every crime committed in Oklahoma this year, including the current translation of the Wickersham Commission's report and the new state income tax, has been seen in a couple of dozen places simultaneously, from Waukomis to Wapanucka, and unless some one captures him soon the late Al Spencer will have to surrender his laurels as "the phantom bandit.". . .
>
> Floyd has been "seen" in as many as three places at the same time, all of which is a physical impossibility as any amateur detective knows. Even the 70-mile-per-hour gait at which the "Pretty Boy" is reported to travel would not have been enough to get him around to all of the places where he is supposed to have left his calling card since January 1. . . .[41]

The *Tulsa Daily World*, in an editorial entitled "Ignoring the Recruits," wrote:

> Too much attention is being paid to Floyd. . . . The serious effect of this indirect adulation of such cattle as Kimes and Floyd is a public evil. It aids the recruiting. A certain glamor [*sic*] is built up about these louts; they are supposed to be courageous and daring and sometimes chivalrous. They are not. They are tough, selfish, lazy, spoiled, undisciplined, peevish boys. All such boys are in danger of going the gunshot, prison or electric chair route.[42]

While Floyd was being hunted, he decided to renew his relationship with Ruby and Jackie, although she had remarried and moved to Coffeyville, Kansas, just north of the Oklahoma line. After a heated argument with her new husband, Floyd persuaded Ruby and Jackie to go with him.[43]

They lived in Fort Smith, Arkansas, under the name of Mr. and Mrs. Douglas from September 11, 1931, to early January 1932. Jackie was enrolled in the local school. They paid their rent regularly, in advance and in cash. Birdwell and his wife often stayed with them.[44]

To Jackie his father was "just like any father." Years later the son reminisced:

> He was very generous. He would always put me to bed, ride me
> on his shoulders and play—a little rough, but very kind. . . . We
> wouldn't go out much, but once we went to see "Frankenstein."
> I was only 6 and it scared me. But he was holding me and telling
> me there was nothing to be scared of.[45]

Gifts to Jackie included two puppies, candy bars, many toys, and a big sack of coins. At Christmas in 1931 Charley and Ruby gave each other expensive rings.[46]

Neighbors, who were told he was a traveling salesman from Kansas City, rarely saw Floyd. Next door to the Floyds lived a deputy U.S. marshal "who would not have feared to meet the Pretty Boy in a gun duel at any time."[47]

Their landlady, Mrs. John Buell, who never had any doubts about the Douglases although "Mr. Douglas was never to be seen," and Ruby became close friends. Mrs. Buell loved Jackie and thought Ruby was nice and refined. When Floyd was home, Mrs. Buell never got to see him. Ruby's excuse was that he was sleeping because he had been out all night. She told her neighbors the same story.

Several months after the Floyd family had left Fort Smith, rumors spread that they had lived in Mrs. Buell's house. This fact was verified by a family photograph that turned up in 1934.[48]

Since Ruby did not like the Fort Smith schools, she convinced Floyd that they should move to Tulsa in early January 1932. Floyd stayed there for about six weeks; Ruby and Jackie lived there until the end of the school year in June. In the meantime, Floyd and Birdwell continued their bank robberies.[49]

The Floyds often rode a North Cincinnati Avenue bus downtown for shopping tours, but he was never recognized. They also went to a few movies, such as *Dracula*, at a downtown theater. Although the theater had a rule against young children seeing the picture because of its nature, Jackie went to the film with his parents. The ticket seller told the Floyds that it was not suitable for children. Floyd and Ruby at first thought they had been recognized, and Floyd started to go for his gun. There was a long line of people waiting to buy tickets, and rather than argue with the ticket seller or leave, Floyd and Ruby pushed Jackie ahead of them and went into the theater.

The couple lived in fear that officers were planning to kidnap Jackie in order to force Floyd to surrender. When Jackie went to classes, he was "tailed" by a friend of the family.[50]

In contrast to his cautious behavior in Fort Smith, Floyd was careless about hiding from his neighbors in Tulsa, and some of them recognized him. Once Floyd played with a group of small boys, flying kites at a vacant lot. One of the residents later said, "We hesitated to convey our information to police sooner for fear of retaliation from Floyd and his gang. They have been going into and out of the house at all hours of the night and early morning. They always drove a block or so before they turned on their lights."[51]

On January 31, 1932, Floyd attended services at a Shawnee church in the evening and gave a large contribution. A member of the congregation, A. M. Goodson, recognized Floyd after the services and spoke to him. The outlaw asked Goodson to "give my best wishes to the minister and tell him I want to be saved." Floyd then drove away.[52]

Finally, at the beginning of February some neighbors reported their suspicions to the local police, but the officers dismissed it as another false report.[53]

Early in February 1932 an informer gave the Tulsa police a description of the car Floyd and Birdwell were using, as well as a clue to the section of the city where they were hiding out.

Floyd was thought to be one of four men who tried to rob the downtown Kansas City Mercantile Trust Company on February 8; later it was determined he had nothing to do with it. Two Kansas City policemen had tried to prevent the bank robbery; one of them had been killed by machine gun slugs and the other wounded. "It looks like Charley 'Pretty Boy' Floyd was in on this," an unnamed federal agent told the United Press. Late that day police received a report that Floyd was headed toward Tulsa.[54]

Early the next morning, detectives George Stewart, Wilbur Wilson, Wade Foor, and Lon Elliott went looking for the two criminals. Soon the gangsters' car swerved in front of them on Peoria Avenue near Apache Street. When the officers ordered them to stop, they halted about fifty yards away and jumped out as the police car drew alongside.

A burst from Floyd's machine gun swept the top of the police car, smashing all of the glass and blowing part of the steering column away.

Foor and Elliott tumbled out of the back seat, and Stewart climbed out of the front seat as Wilson slumped down with a minor wound to his left arm.[55]

"I didn't have a chance to get my machine gun in action," Stewart said later. "The firing was so intense for a second it was impossible to do anything but take pot shots in the direction of the bandit car with sidearms."

Foor said he had put six shots into Floyd's back, to no effect. Floyd must have been wearing a bulletproof vest, but some people thought he must be immune to gunfire.[56]

When the gangsters hurried into their car and fled east off Peoria, Stewart reached into the police vehicle, pulled out the only machine gun owned by the Tulsa police, and fired. After two bursts of twelve shots each the gun was useless; there was no more ammunition.

As the other officers fired their revolvers, the two gangsters returned the fire. More than fifty shots were exchanged.

Although their car was almost impossible to steer, the officers tailed Floyd and Birdwell. The gangsters' vehicle staggered on two flat tires to Floyd's house and bumped to a halt as neighbors watched. Every available squad car rushed to the scene. No one was found.

"We are positive that it was Floyd," Lon Elliott said when he returned to headquarters.

For more than an hour the machine gun was out of commission while the officers hunted for ammunition. Stewart was then able to continue the search for Floyd.

Although Thomas I. Munroe, commissioner of fire and police, was reluctant to talk about the poor showing, he planned to buy six more machine guns with fifty-round clips. "We are going to fight fire with fire and next time will be prepared for any type of machine gunner. We have the men on the force to operate the guns and they [the guns] will be here within a few days."[57]

Two men were almost killed by police in Tulsa County in the hunt for gangsters. Chief of Police Nelson J. Moore called the events "unfortunate" but "easily understandable under the circumstances." The first near-victim was a Dr. B. H. Humphrey, whose car matched the description of Floyd's. The doctor later denied he was told to stop, and said he was fired on without warning as he was returning to Sperry from Tulsa, just north of Apache Street on Peoria Avenue.

> I was driving about 40 miles an hour going north, and the first thing I knew was when I heard the bullets from a machine gun rattling in the back of my car. I drove about 100 yards up the road, got a flashlight and got out to see where the bullets had come through. Three bullets hit the body and one or two had ruined one of my tires. Nobody came near me while I was stopped so I got back in, drove to Turley and reported the shooting to the Sheriff's office. I never saw the man who shot at me, although I think I saw a parked automobile near the filling station just before I heard the shots.

Harold Cullison, on a wolf hunt with a friend near Turley, was fired on by the police from an unmarked car about 2 A.M., after they had flagged his vehicle down and, fearing they were bandits, he had failed to obey a command to stop. After four bullets hit his car and two buckshot struck his nose, he ran into a ditch. The Tulsa police did not offer to help him pull his automobile back onto the road.[58]

Once again Floyd had disappeared, but he was believed to be hiding in the city. Numerous reports about bullet-riddled cars, including one owned by a Tulsa jailer, proved to be false. Detective Elliott said on February 10, "We . . . are still seeking the automobile used by the pair and believe it is stored in a private garage near here. The bandits . . . probably have abandoned the auto." City and county officers patrolled the highways into Tulsa without result. Several tips were received, but none had any merit.

At nine on the evening of February 10, two officers, Ray Moran and Homer Myers, drew up to a stop sign near Harvard Avenue on Fifth Street and noticed a car meeting the description of Floyd's with two men in it, but could not see their faces.

Floyd and Birdwell saw the officers and opened fire on them with pistols and a shotgun. As the policemen chased the gangsters at high speed, Moran shot at them with a pistol and a 12-gauge sawed-off shotgun while Myers drove. But Moran could not continue to spray buckshot because the extra shells they had were for a 20-gauge gun.

Moran fired fifteen shots from his pistol, and the gangsters about the same. No one was hurt, but the police car was pierced by eleven bullets and the two rear tires of the gangsters' car were flattened. Some of the buckshot pierced a slow-moving car on the road as the battle waged.

With only a thirty-five-yard lead, Floyd veered into a dead-end street. The officers thought they had them in a trap, but Floyd and Birdwell drove over a curb, up a steep embankment, and along a railway right-of-way. Abandoning the car on the tracks, they fled on foot. The police could not follow because their headlights had been shot out and the radiator emptied through bullet holes.

When the chase ended, the policemen called headquarters for reinforcements. An hour later the abandoned car was found. A license tag (the same one noted in the Konawa bank robbery) was found under a seat, the bullet holes filled and painted over. On the recently recharged battery there was a tag made out to Jack Hamilton of 513 Young Street. The officers guessed correctly that Hamilton was actually Floyd.[59]

At five the next morning, February 11, Detective Elliott led a squad of twenty officers equipped with machine guns, tear gas, and an armored transport truck to the house where Ruby and Jackie were living. As the armed squad, followed by the armored truck, came into view, Ruby and Jackie fled on foot and made their way to a bus station.

Five men went to guard the back of the house (one account says Elliott had concentrated all his men in front of the house, leaving the rear unguarded). The squad crept within firing distance of the house and fired a tear gas bomb through a window.

When Floyd and Birdwell fled from the rear of the house immediately afterward, the officers in the back let them walk through their midst to their car and made no effort to stop them from driving away. (A city police officer later made this charge anonymously.)

An operative of the American Bankers' Association told Elliott, "Two men, dressed in dark suits, wearing topcoats and grey hats, fled out of the rear door just after the tear gas was fired into the house." There was never any public report on how Floyd and Birdwell "walked" out of the house surrounded by police. The *Tulsa Daily World* called it "a spectacular and cool escape."

Local, county, and state police, as well as private detectives and agents of the Bankers' Protective Association, launched an intense manhunt. The roads leading out of the city were blocked, but somehow Floyd and Birdwell slipped through to the Cookson Hills.[60]

On February 14, 1932, the *Muskogee Daily Phoenix* published an editorial entitled "Floyd Scampers Away":

> Despite the fact that Tulsa officers must feel elated over finally obtaining proof that the man whom they twice have battled in running gun fights was Charles "Pretty Boy" Floyd, they must simultaneously feel chagrin, if not shame, over their failure to nab Floyd himself when he was literally within their grasp.
>
> Floyd's escape, if accounts of the affair are correct, was accomplished by the simple expedient of Floyd and his companion sneaking out the back door of a house while the officers clustered around the front door and tossed tear gas bombs. . . .[61]

A short time after the escape, Ruby and Jackie were picked up at the Union bus station in Tulsa and detained by the police. At the police station the boy pointed to a picture (an enlarged detective magazine likeness of the elusive outlaw found by officers at the house) and said, "That's my daddy." The police also had found several clippings about Floyd from Oklahoma newspapers and a photo of Floyd.

"Daddy and George Birdwell stayed all night at our house last night. They have been there for almost two weeks," Jackie said.

Ruby Floyd, sitting calmly in a cell in the women's quarters at the city jail, insisted she was Mrs. Ruby Hamilton. Although Jackie had said the picture was his "daddy," Ruby continued to insist that she did not know Floyd. She told reporters:

My name is Hamilton, Ruby Hamilton. I came here from Oklahoma City January 5 and rented the house on Young Street. My husband joined me three days later and remained there about two weeks. I have not seen him since. If I was married to Floyd, do you think for a minute I would admit it? Will you please get me the papers? All of them—Tulsa, Oklahoma City, Kansas City and St. Louis papers. I want to see if they are filled with a bunch of lies.

But Chief of Detectives Jack Bonham said she told him Floyd and Birdwell had been at the house. "She denied that there had been another man there," Bonham reported, "and said that Birdwell was always with him, that he was the only man he could trust."

Jackie played around the matron's quarters, apparently without a care in the world. The *Tulsa Daily World* wrote, "He is a tight-lipped, chubby-faced little blond. Smart as a whip, he skillfully evaded questions as though he had been well coached in the procedure."

Jackie said:

I go to school, I don't know what daddy does. He always reads the newspapers when he comes home with George Birdwell. He always has plenty of money and we have lots to eat and a radio. I am going to be an engineer or a doctor when I grow up. Daddy wants me to go to school. That's why we moved to Tulsa.

He described the numerous presents his father had given him but refused to admit his father was "Pretty Boy" Floyd.

Although the "taciturn and hard" Mrs. Floyd finally admitted her identity, she did not want to discuss her role as "Pretty Boy's" wife, or the wife of anyone. She denied that her father lived in Bixby and refused to give her maiden name. "It's no concern of yours, nor the newspapers," she shouted when asked if she knew her husband was the famous "Pretty Boy." "Go away. Take that photographer out of here and don't bother me." But shortly afterward she posed for a picture after the police had taken her picture. Mrs. Floyd, who claimed that this was her first arrest, called herself a housewife and told the police matrons a romantic story about her husband, a man from Georgia. "He was only 20 and I was but 16," she said.

Since the police were afraid that "Floyd might attempt something foolhardy" because he was known to idolize his ex-wife and child, several men were placed at the jail's entrances.[62]

Ruby and Jackie were released by city authorities on Saturday afternoon, February 13, 1932, after being held for investigation for thirty-six hours.[63]

She was helped by the police, who had turned her house topsy-turvy while searching for clues, in putting it back in order. A police guard had been removed the day before. Ruby said she would remain in the city, and her son would continue to go to the same school. She denied knowing where her husband was. By this time Tulsa police had given up looking for Floyd.[64]

That same day, on the front page of the *Oklahoma City Times*, the editor of the paper, Walter M. Harrison, made a heartfelt appeal:

Desperate killer though you may be, you remain a hero to one human being in this world. When Jackie, your 7-year-old son, identified your picture as "my daddy," he spoke with pride of possession. He knows your strong arms, your rough play. He tingles with happiness when he sees you coming, and he wonders why you go away so unceremoniously and stay so long.

He is innocently proud of you who have treated him so badly. With the blind devotion of every lad for his pater, Jackie now tries to walk like you, to talk like you. He has his hair combed like you comb yours and he is dreaming of the day when he can be a big man like you and go out into the big world after breakfast in the morning and never come back until suppertime.

This picture of your kid gave me a jolt. He is the stuff from which the future is made. He may have the making of a great merchant prince. But you have just about pitched his chances away.

Today you flee from the law. At the end of the trail for you, there is probably a little run in the open for the shelter of a thicket, the bark of a posseman's rifle and a lifeless fall. A pitiful end for the father of a fine son.[65]

This last paragraph was an uncanny prediction of events to come.

On Sunday hundreds of curiosity seekers drove past the house where the Floyd family had been living.[66]

On the night of February 23, the driver of a car that matched the description of Floyd's car aimed a machine gun at the Tulsa fire chief and a police captain as they drove past. No arrests were made in this incident.[67]

Floyd and Birdwell had vanished. False tips left the police busy but led nowhere.

It later became known that they paid twenty-five to fifty dollars for overnight visits to hill farmers, and they did not let anyone leave the house when they were there. When someone left, they also left. Sometimes the two slept in the car, where they had a supply of canned goods. This way they could stay in a hideout for days without being forced by hunger to go to town or to a farm. The duo traveled in small, light cars geared to high speed. Floyd said he liked tan cars because they were harder to see in the dust. Given a twenty-minute start, he could get away from anyone, he bragged. Sometimes Floyd posed as a sales "drummer."[68]

5

All I Know Is You'll Never Catch Him

Ruby said in February 1932, "I don't know anything about where Charlie hides, and I don't know anything about his plans. All I know is you'll never catch him. He can outsmart every copper in Oklahoma, and the Federal men, too. I know it!" Erv A. Kelley, former sheriff of McIntosh County, appointed by Oklahoma authorities as a special investigator to get Floyd, was not impressed. "I'm sorry, ma'am, but my job is to capture your husband, and I am to bring him in, dead or alive. It'll be either him or me and I'm not worrying about myself."[1]

Kelley, who had caught fourteen bank robbers and six murderers, and had been sheriff of McIntosh County for six years until his retirement in January 1932, worked ceaselessly to trap Floyd, Birdwell, and possibly Fred Barker.[2] Floyd became furious when he was told that Kelley had said he might take Jackie hostage to lure his father out of hiding.[3]

For the next several weeks the two gangsters eluded their pursuers, and Floyd visited his mother.[4]

Assuming correctly that the ones to watch were Ruby and Jackie, Kelley and William Counts, former Eufaula deputy sheriff and a close associate of Kelley, kept a watch on the Floyd home in Tulsa. On April 8, 1932, at four in the afternoon, the two lawmen saw Ruby and Jackie driving away from their house. They followed them to Bixby, hoping they were to meet Floyd.

Two farmers told Kelley and Counts that Ruby had parked her car at the Cecil Bennett farmhouse and had gone to a nearby two-room wooden house, the home of her father and two younger brothers.

Kelley called Crockett Long of Oklahoma City, a member of the State Bureau of Identification; A. B. Cooper, a private detective from Oklahoma City; Sheriff Jim Stormont of Okmulgee, and Tulsa detectives M. L. Lairmore and J. A. Smith. These lawmen met in Bixby at 8:30 that night and made plans to trap Floyd. The two local farmers were recruited and armed because they knew Floyd.

It seemed like a sure thing. Every conceivable avenue of approach and escape was sealed off by an officer. Kelley, armed with a machine gun with a silencer and a .38 caliber revolver, placed the men and chose the key place behind a chicken coop for himself. Eleven feet to his left was the open corral gate. Five hundred feet beyond the gate was the house. Nearby were the two farmers. Four machine gunners were placed along the sides of the road leading to the gate, with Kelley and the two farmers forming a roadblock. Counts was five hundred yards away at a schoolhouse, in the unlikely event the fugitives got through.

It was a long, very cold night, and it appeared that the outlaws might not show. At about 2:20 in the morning, four of the lawmen decided to go to Bixby to get some coffee. "Okay," said Kelley, "go get warmed up. I'll stay here alone—just to cover."

Five minutes later Floyd and Birdwell, driving at high speed without lights, turned onto a narrow lane and then drove slowly until they stopped at the open gate. Apparently they were suspicious, because farmers almost always closed their corral gates.

When Floyd turned the car's headlights on, Kelley left his hiding place, strode to within eight feet of the car, and called upon them to surrender.

Floyd fired seven shots from his .45 caliber revolver, hitting Kelley in each knee, his right arm, and twice in his left side.

Kelley managed to fire fourteen bullets from his machine gun's twenty-one-bullet clip. One bullet hit Floyd in his left ankle; another struck the automatic Floyd was wearing on his left side and shattered it. The other bullets made harmless holes in the dirt. The two farmers had trouble with the unfamiliar guns and could not or would not fire.

With Birdwell driving, the bandits' car backed up suddenly; crashed into a barbed-wire fence, pulling down part of it and a post; then turned around and drove off at a frantic pace. A couple of miles away the car careened off the dirt road into a ditch, but righted itself and raced on. Floyd, in great pain, was losing a fair amount of blood.

When Counts heard the shots, he jumped into his car and gave chase; before he had gone a hundred yards, he saw the receding taillights. He stopped to help the sheriff, who lay over his machine gun, surrounded by a pool of blood and holes in the dirt made by the machine-gun fire.

"When I got to the chief he was dead," Counts said later. "He gave them a break and Floyd got him. I'm sure of that. Kelley had been an officer 18 years and had never shot a man. He wanted to catch them alive."[5]

More than twenty-five hundred people would go to Kelley's funeral. He left a wife and four children, and Floyd lost many supporters because of the killing.[6]

The outlaws fled southwest to Earlsboro, to pick up Floyd's brother Bradley, who took them to a friendly doctor at Seminole. After treating Floyd's wounds and deciding to leave the bullet in his ankle, the doctor gave Floyd painkillers and some fresh dressings. He did not call the police. With Earlsboro being such an obvious hiding place, the bandits headed for a safer hideout in Muskogee County.[7]

The next day reporters came and asked questions of the locals. Cecil Bennett, who knew the Floyd family well, pretended he did not know them.

I was in bed asleep when I heard those shots, I thought maybe there was something wrong outside and then again I thought maybe it wasn't any of my business to see what was wrong so I just naturally stayed in bed and didn't bother to put my head out of the door.

"Pretty Boy" Floyd? No, I never saw him in my life. I wouldn't know him if he walked in now. Yes, a woman drove in yesterday asked if she could park her car here. I saw no reason why she couldn't. I didn't know her.

Over yonder? Sure that's Bill Hargraves's place. He works for me. A good farmer, too. You say he is Floyd's father-in-law. Well, that's something I never knew. Well, well.

The reporters also questioned Ruby. She said, "What happened there last night?"

"Your husband knocked off Erv Kelley."

"Well, that's fine." She smiled. "Did anyone else get killed?"

"No, no, no one else."

"Too bad."

"Did you know Kelley trailed Pretty Boy for three months before he caught up with him this morning?"

"Well, the son-of-a-bitch won't trail him any longer, will he?" She laughed.

Ruby denied planning to meet Floyd. She said she was asleep all night, hadn't heard any shots, and hadn't found out about it until later.

"Did you see that story they gave my husband in *Startling Detective Magazine*? That burned me up. They weren't even fair to him. They weren't honest about his life."[8]

Lawmen believed they had trailed Floyd to the vicinity of his brother Bradley's home at Earlsboro, and they concentrated their search there. Early the next night, three state officers headed the posses, armed with machine guns, sawed-off shotguns, and other weapons.

Tulsa Chief of Detectives Jack Bonham said, "We trailed the man we think was Floyd two miles south, and a mile east of the scene of the shooting, and from that point we have gotten nowhere. We know the automobile the killer used turned south, but that is all." The lawmen thought that Freddy Barker might be in Floyd's gang.[9]

The Tulsa County sheriff was angry that he had not been notified of the ambush, and the county attorney criticized the lack of cooperation.[10]

There was a report that Floyd, Birdwell, Barker, and an escaped convict, Frank Sawyer, seized a car from a youth and girl near Muskogee on April 12, 1932.[11]

Offers of aid in capturing Floyd flooded the Tulsa police. At least fifty amateur sleuths were looking for him. Chief Bonham told them, "Yes, we're working on the Floyd case, but can't use any help at present."[12]

Another detective said:

> Every section of Oklahoma has its quota of amateur detectives. But I believe we have a few more than average, that is judging by the letters and calls we receive offering aid in the bandit chase. The only thing which hinders many of the self-styled detectives from going out and bringing Floyd in dead or alive is the permission to carry a gun.

Many of the letters told of crimes solved by the writer and indicated degrees from correspondence schools. One letter said the writer had "solved many burglaries in his home town but had not yet taken on any heavy work. I would like to have a chance at Floyd and think I could make good. Could you send me all information available and a picture of the bandit."

A "reformed criminal" wrote that he "knew the Oklahoma bandit's hideouts and had met Floyd face to face many times." If the reward were promised, the writer had no doubts he could catch him.[13]

Bonham also received a letter addressed to him as "Chief of the Law" from a Kansas hopeful.

> I see in the paper where "Pretty Boy" Floyd had caused one of your men to be killed. I am asking your office to make me a sheriff and give me permission to carry two guns so I can look for Floyd and collect the $10,000 reward. I will help you look for him, that is if you will fix me up.[14]

Seventy-eight-year-old S. F. Lindsay, U.S. sheriff and peace officer in the old days, the killer of Jack Dalton, said Floyd was giving the officers the runaround. "You wouldn't have caught an old-time officer lugging around a machine gun even if we had them then. Machine guns are dangerous right up to one foot, but move back 20 feet and the average officer can't hit the side of a barn with one."[15]

Oklahoma Attorney General J. Berry King got a letter from Thomas E. Haines of Quebec, Canada, offering to get Floyd for the reward. He wrote, "Had I been there, he would have been in his grave long ago."[16]

During a car trip to Akins and Sallisaw in April 1932, a *Tulsa Daily World* reporter heard many stories of Floyd's activities. Many local residents said they had seen him dining recently at a local café. One deputy sheriff told him, "He's liable to do anything and be anywhere."

Floyd's mother and a sister, Mrs. Ruth Wofford, lived only half a block from the courthouse and city hall. His mother said:

> I don't know what to say. This is the first time I have ever discussed my boy's affairs with a stranger, with a newspaper reporter. The newspapers have been unfair with him. They've accused him of everything that's happened in the State.
>
> Certainly I'm worried. What mother wouldn't be worried over her boy.

She told the reporter that "personal affairs" were never discussed during their meetings, and she never asked him to justify his activities. "I've got faith in him."

Mrs. Floyd admitted her son had visited her recently, but refused to say when or under what circumstances. "I never want him caught because he wouldn't get a fair break." She did not know when she would see her son again.[17]

The restless Birdwell decided not to wait for Floyd to recover from his ankle wound at a Muskogee County hideout before he robbed again. A doctor had told Floyd that the bullet could not be removed for several days.[18]

On April 21, 1932, Prohibition enforcement officers, who had taken a large posse to the Cookson Hills after receiving a report that a man with a machine gun had been seen there, thought they had missed Floyd (actually C. C. Patterson, a member of the Floyd gang) and Birdwell by only twenty minutes. Patterson was a Kiowa, Oklahoma, outlaw who was wanted for the shooting of a Shawnee, Oklahoma, policeman. An informer in the Hills told them, "Floyd has just gone to rob a bank." They caught four moonshiners.[19]

On that day Patterson and Birdwell, armed with a machine gun and pistols, robbed the First State Bank of Stonewall in south-central Oklahoma of about six hundred dollars shortly before noon. They kidnapped two bank officers as a shield against a crowd of people, some of whom had guns. As the bandits fled in their car, they roughed up the two officers, then threw them out a short distance from Stonewall.

About half a mile down the Ada highway, the outlaws kidnapped Estle Henson, a twenty-year-old youth on a motorcycle. Police radio broadcasts quickly sent cars with heavily armed officers after them, but the trail was lost near Ada.

To prevent their escape across the southern end of the North Canadian River to a badlands strip that stretched from the river northeast through a series of hills that led to the Ozarks of Arkansas and Missouri, the posses guarded bridges and patrolled the dark river bottoms.

Famous round-the-world pilot Wiley Post led an "aerial posse" of two planes that took off from Oklahoma City with heavily armed officers searching for any sign of the bandits' car fleeing through the hills.

Officers encountered the getaway car three times and a gunfight ensued each time, but the best-manned and -equipped posses in recent Oklahoma history could not capture the fugitives.[20] The bandits were seen the next morning near Calvin, beyond the barrier lawmen had hoped would keep them from their hideouts.

Henson, who had been held for thirteen hours by the robbers before being released, wrongly identified a picture of Floyd and described Birdwell, for whom no pictures existed. The youth had not been afraid but "knew they meant business," and said the bandits "got a laugh" from the posses' effort to get them. One had said, "I guess those guys will learn it's no use trying to catch us."[21]

By the beginning of June 1932, Floyd had recovered from his wound, and he and Birdwell decided to rob the Stonewall bank. Sheriff L. E. Franklin of Pontotoc County, Oklahoma, received a hot tip early on June 5 that the Stonewall bank was going to be robbed again, this time by Floyd and Birdwell, on June 7, and that they would hide out on the farm of E. W. Echols, a mile north of Stonewall and twelve miles southeast of Ada.

Franklin asked for assistance from Oklahoma City. A party of five state officers headed by O. P. Ray joined the four Pontotoc County officers shortly before 5 P.M. on June 6 and went to the Echols' farm. Young Henson followed the heavily armed posse to be in on the capture.

Floyd and Birdwell arrived at the Echols' farm early the next day. (Echols later claimed he was afraid to tell officers they were there.) The officers saw the two gangsters as they reached the farm, parked their car behind a hedge, and entered a barn, which the officers surrounded immediately. One car was placed to block their route of escape, a driveway from the barn.

Franklin believed they had been warned of the trap, for the pair were heavily armed and thought to be wearing bulletproof vests and steel plates in their trouser legs, in their sleeves, and even under their hats.[22]

The sheriff said later, "They were making for their car when we opened fire and they retreated into the barn and hid behind baled hay in the loft, firing between cracks in the side of the building." No warning had been given. Only weeds offered protection for the officers, so they retreated behind the house or took refuge behind nearby trees.

As soon as the lawmen retreated, Floyd, with a revolver in each hand, and Birdwell, with a machine gun, made another rush for their car, dodging machine-gun fire from Franklin and state officer Reber and firing as they ran. Members of the posse on the other sides of the barn did not realize Floyd and Birdwell were attempting a run for it.

From a small elevation fifty yards from the lane of escape, Henson yelled at the pair. Birdwell leveled his machine gun at the youth and fired a spray of bullets at him, but then waved when he realized who he was.

Franklin and Reber emptied their machine guns at Floyd and Birdwell as the gangsters scrambled into their car; but the latter were shielded because the officers were on the far side of the vehicle. Two tires were flattened, and the windshield and rear window of the small sedan had been shattered.

As the gangsters chugged slowly up a muddy hill, the posse fired more than a hundred times at the fleeing men. The car that was to have been used as a blockade got stuck in the mud and failed to reach the lane before Floyd and Birdwell crept past.[23]

Both the outlaws and the officers continued to fire, but no one was wounded, although it was thought that one of the bandits was hurt.

Following in close pursuit, the lawmen believed the outlaws could be trailed easily, but they lost them about fifteen miles east of Ada.[24]

The next day the Stonewall bank had a sign in the front window reading "Notice to bank robbers: There is not enough cash in this bank to be worth the risk of robbing it." After four robberies it was felt desperate measures were needed. Only a limited amount of cash was kept on hand, and the bank put most of its money in bank vaults in nearby Ada. The president of the bank remarked that if the men had held it up that day, "They'd have had to borrow money to get out of town."[25]

Arkansas authorities mounted machine guns to protect three Fort Smith banks, and a bridge from Oklahoma was guarded when word was received Floyd was heading for Fort Smith on June 9.

Officers also received a false report that day that the Floyd gang had stolen a car from a black family near Warner, Oklahoma.[26]

The bullet-riddled car from Stonewall was found on June 11 in hilly country near Franks by the marshal of Stonewall.[27]

Five hundred men searched for Floyd and Birdwell. Assistant State Police Chief O. P. Ray said, "We might as well have it out with those boys."[28] The posses knew the outlaws would head for the Cookson Hills, so all roads leading into the Hills were blocked. Nevertheless, the felons somehow slipped past them. Even federal agents joined in the hunt, but to no avail. Whenever lawmen got close to the Hills, they received no help from the residents.[29] A *True Detective Magazine* reporter, Hubert Dail, told his readers what it was like to go with one of the posses:

Everywhere [we] received word that Floyd had been seen—a day, a week, or a month before. But in each case the inhabitants of the hillbilly country didn't know where the famous bandit was at that particular moment.

At one house, in a hollow, about two miles off the road, a posse advanced in a semicircle to confront a woman chopping wood. She paused, stared at the officers with hostile eyes. "What-dya want?" she demanded.

The deputies said they were looking for "Pretty Boy." A crafty glint came into the woman's eyes. "I reckon he's been here a hundred times," she said, "but I ain't seen him recently." She brought her ax down with a crash. "I'm scared of him."

This was a typical instance. Everywhere, the officers believed, people of the hills were refusing information about the outlaw, protecting him and his companions with tips as to the officers' movements.[30]

Finally the posse abandoned the search in disgust.

6

The Luckiest Bandit
That Ever Lived

In March 1932, Juanita and Rose were freed after ten months behind bars; their three-year sentence in Kentucky had been revoked on appeal. After release the sisters spent two weeks in Kansas City before Juanita went to Bradley Floyd's home at Earlsboro, where Floyd visited her from time to time. About six months later Rose saw Floyd near Earlsboro.[1]

When Floyd and Juanita visited Sallisaw and Akins, he introduced her to his friends and gave them pictures of the couple taken in 1929 in Kansas City. She was taught how to operate a machine gun, as the *Tulsa Daily World* put it, "with the same dexterity she handles Floyd."[2]

Ruby remained silent when news about Juanita broke. She talked little of Floyd. Of course Floyd did not take Juanita along when he saw Ruby. But when Ruby was shown a photo of Floyd and the girl with their arms around each other, she became enraged. At first she vowed vengeance, but soon became calm and said philosophically, "He's doing what he wants to do, I couldn't change him if I wanted to." She added, "I never want to see him again." Later it was rumored Juanita had borne his child, also called Charles Floyd, in 1933.

In June 1932, Ruby learned that Floyd had suffered a wound in his left ankle during the gunfight with Sheriff Kelley; she was also told that he had contracted a social disease and that a physician living in northeast Oklahoma was treating him surreptitiously.[3]

On July 28, Ruby and her son moved from Tulsa, where they had been living since the beginning of the year, to her father's home near Bixby.[4]

Birdwell, reported to have said "Trouble hangs on to a woman's skirt," did not like Juanita. Furthermore, he was drinking too much and was jealous of the attention paid to Floyd. Thus, the two men split up about this time.[5]

Floyd was inactive during the summer of 1932, and spent his time visiting Ruby and Jackie, Juanita, his mother, the Rings (Ruby's aunt and uncle, who lived near Boynton), and other relatives and friends. Lawmen would occasionally look for him at these places, and there were a few close calls. For example, twice he had to slip out the back of the Ring home when Muskogee County sheriff V. S. Cannon knocked at the front door.[6]

Of course there continued to be many rumors about him. One report indicated he was one of the robbers of the Fort Scott, Kansas, bank, where thirty-two thousand dollars was taken, on June 17. That same day eighteen police in Kansas City, Missouri, searched homes looking for Floyd but found nothing. Floyd was a suspect in a July 1 gunfight with police in Harrisburg, Illinois, in which one policeman was killed and another seriously wounded. At the same time officers were searching for Floyd at a Pontotoc County Fourth of July celebration, he was reported to be shaking hands with political candidates at a rodeo near Mulhall, Oklahoma.[7]

The most interesting rumor was that on the morning of August 3, Floyd was supposed to have kidnapped H. W. Nave, a former Tulsa policeman, stripped him of his clothing, and stolen his car about twenty miles from Oklahoma City. Nave went to the highway and made futile efforts to stop passing motorists. Finally a black farmer took him to the sheriff's office near Tulsa. But the incident was a hoax designed to cover up Nave's illegal sale of a mortgaged car to an Oklahoma City car dealer. Nave claimed one of the robbers had sold the car to the dealer. The *Tulsa Daily World* headline of the following day was "'Pretty Boy' Kidnaps Salesman."[8]

There were several reports that Floyd was wounded; among them was a story that he was suffering from four bullet wounds in the chest, courtesy of Sheriff Kelley, but had recovered sufficiently to travel. It was rumored he had been convalescing near relatives, living between Sallisaw and Akins.

In truth, Floyd had been wounded only in the left ankle and had received adequate medical attention near Okmulgee. In early September 1932, acquaintances around Seminole who had talked with him denied he was in bad shape. An Earlsboro barber reported on September 3 that he had shaved the outlaw that week: "Floyd is getting a great kick out of the numerous reports as to his condition and activities." Reports that he had been wounded at Stonewall never were verified.[9]

In the summer of 1932, Oklahoma authorities decided to take strong action against the epidemic of bank robberies, thirty of which were believed to have been committed by Floyd in the past eighteen months. Vigilante committees were formed in many larger towns, and the Oklahoma Bankers' Association posted a reward of a hundred dollars alive and five hundred dollars dead for any robber caught or killed in the act. The state had offered a two hundred and fifty dollar reward for information leading to the arrest and conviction of bank robbers. Burglar alarms were installed in banks.[10]

On July 29, Governor Murray posted rewards of one thousand dollars for the capture of either Floyd or Birdwell or fifteen hundred dollars for both, "dead or alive."[11]

Recently a friend of Floyd had gone to Murray about the outlaw's surrender, provided the governor not execute him. "I told him no," Murray said. "We'll capture Floyd sooner or later, dead or alive. If he's alive, we'll electrocute him." He reported that officers could have arrested Floyd recently in Arkansas but decided not to, because they would not have gotten any reward if they arrested him there.[12]

Arthur (Doc) Barker and his brother Fred (wanted for the murder the previous month of J. Earl Smith, a lawyer) joined Floyd after Doc was paroled on September 9. Fred was reported to be a member of the Floyd gang. The three were seen together in Sapulpa, Oklahoma, late in that month. They made threats against Claude Chambers, a Sapulpa master baker, who in 1921 had been a star witness against Doc Barker in a Tulsa murder trial that resulted in a life sentence for Barker, although he was actually innocent. Since September 10,

Chambers had received several anonymous telephone calls threatening his life. One Sunday late in September, he was awakened by the blowing of a car horn at his front door. When he looked out, he recognized Doc Barker in the car; an hour later Barker drove by the rear of Chambers's house. After Mrs. Chambers saw Doc Barker and Floyd together in a car near the business section of Sapulpa that afternoon, she and her husband moved not once, but three times. Police guards accompanied Chambers to and from work daily. A private investigator, who had arrested Barker for the murder, was asked to help in the investigation.[13]

Running low on funds, Floyd recruited a new gang. In early October 1932 a "good old boy" from Sapulpa, Aussie Elliott, joined the Floyd gang. He had once thought of a career as a baseball player and had been a crack shortstop in the minor leagues, but this had not worked out. So in 1930 he had robbed banks until apprehended for a Fort Gibson, Oklahoma, job. He was sent to the state prison but escaped. On August 28, 1932, Elliott had robbed a family near Ardmore, Oklahoma.[14] Floyd and Birdwell, separated since their escape at Stonewall in June, met on a weekend in late October 1932.[15]

The gang decided to rob Floyd's hometown bank at Sallisaw on November 1, 1932. Floyd came out of hiding in the Cookson Hills, traveled to Kansas City two weeks before the robbery, went to Tulsa ten days before, and visited his ex-wife and son the Sunday before the robbery.[16]

As planned, on November 1, at 11:30 in the morning, Floyd, Birdwell, and Elliott robbed the Sallisaw State Bank of $2,531.73. A few relatives and friends had been tipped off in advance and were waiting for Floyd. Farmer Bob Fitzsimmons, leaning against the bank door when the bandits' car came by on the wrong side of the road, recognized Floyd instantly. The outlaw, in a genial mood, called Fitzsimmons to his car, showed him his machine gun, and said, "This is a holdup."

Sallisaw Police Chief Bert Cotton was in his car just seventy-five feet away, around the corner. Only after the robbery did his friends tell him about it.

Floyd's seventy-two-year-old grandfather, also named Charles

Floyd, was sitting in front of the barbershop across the street. He boasted later that he turned his head and had not seen the robbery because his grandson worked so fast.

Otis Shipman was waiting to get a haircut, and Tom Trotter was in the chair, when Floyd came into the barbershop. Floyd greeted them, "Howdy, Oty," and "Howdy, Tom," then said, "We're going into this bank here and you lay off the telephone."

As the trio entered the bank, Floyd carried his machine gun in the crook of his left arm. He told Bob Riggs, the assistant cashier, who was alone, "You can keep your hands down but keep quiet. We don't want to kill anybody." Birdwell and Elliott then jumped over the cage and begun putting money into bags. They sent Riggs into the vault to pack the cash into a sack. As this was going on, several customers came into the bank and were ordered to get behind the cage, to keep quiet, and to keep their hands in the air. Within five minutes there were nine prisoners.

Floyd, grinning at his acquaintances, said, "It's a hold-up, all right. Don't hurt 'em, Bird, they're friends of mine." About one prisoner he said, "He's a friend of mine, he's all right." Another friend was called out of line and Floyd engaged him in conversation.

The robbers made Riggs come with them to their car and get on the left running board. "All right, hike it," Floyd ordered Elliott, who was driving.

The car door jammed, and six packages of nickels and half dollars spread over the sidewalk.

Five blocks from the bank, they let Riggs off. "Goodbye, old man, take care o' yourself," Floyd told him. Sheriff Cheek and two of his deputies chased them, but lost them five miles east of Sallisaw. When last seen, they were passing a filling station some twelve miles from Sallisaw, near Hanson. Some of the deputies thought the third robber was Freddy Barker. One reporter wrote, "It was like the hometown performance of a great actor who has made good on Broadway."[17]

Floyd was feeling so good about himself that he decided to have a newspaper interview with Vivian Brown, a reporter from the *Oklahoma News*, who had grown up in the hills and knew its people well. She had been told in early October to write a letter to Floyd and one of his friends would deliver it to him. A few days later he wrote back to her, to say he could not meet her. He told friends he would be glad to go to Vivian Brown's house, but they dissuaded him, arguing that a gunfight there might hurt innocent people.[18] The letter read:

Vivian Brown
   Dear Madam:
   I have been informed that you wanted an interview with me or had some questions you would like to ask me. I am sorry that I can't meet you in person. I will send this through a friend and you can publish it if you like but I want to ask you not to publish my picture cause as you know I have too much publicity now. In fact, I can't be hurt much, or I wouldn't be doing this but I haven't much to say as it is only a few words for Mr. Burns [C. A. Burns, chief of the State Crime Agency], the man that seems to know me so well and say so much. Well I can't say any thing about him as I don't know him but I do know him better than he knows me and I would like him better if he'd never abused my little boy [Jackie]. As low down as he says I am (maybe I am), but I would have been different with a child of his or any other child, because they are all innocent regardless who their father may be.
   I never saw this George Birdwell that I am suppose to know so well that I know of.
   And this stuff about me giving up is a lot of balanga [sic]. They say they will shoot me down on sight and no doubt some one will some day, but I will try to stay out of their way. Mr. Burns says that name that some one give me with is a joke, had went to my head and I am before the mirror. What guess he knows. And from what I hear about him he could get the gravy off of his coat and wash his neck once a year. Well I don't know if you will care for this or not. I am doing it for a personal friend. Excuse mistakes and writing.

Yours truly
Chas Floyd[19]

Later, Floyd changed his mind about seeing the reporter, or perhaps had written he would not see her as a ruse, so the police would not use Brown to bait a trap. Jess Ring, Ruby's uncle, made the arrangements. A friend of Floyd's took Brown to Pretty Boy's hideout, about thirty miles west of Muskogee in farm country, on the afternoon of November 4, 1932. They drove through a wooded area with thick underbrush until they came to the bank of a small stream that had cut a deep gully through the farmland, and pulled up alongside Floyd sitting in a car parked under a tree.

They all got out. Floyd was completely at ease and seemed to be in good shape, with no limp.

First they talked about the crops. Then Vivian Brown said to Floyd:

I think I have made it clear in my letter just what I want. I am really quite glad to meet you, for your name will live in the history of these country folk. Suppose you tell me just how and when you decided that a life of crime was the only thing you could do?

Floyd answered:

Well, that's a fair question, but you're not going to print anything that will lay a job on me, as long as it's going to hurt me.

As a kid growing up, I just loafed around like the rest of the kids. Then I got in that trouble at Akins about the post office and I thought I'd better tear out of the country and get me a job.

I did for a while, but when I landed up in St. Louis and pulled that job and, of course, they got me and took me back to serve my time up in Jeff City.

I was just a green country kid that got caught on a job, but I guess that was the job that put its mark on me and I could never shake it off. Yes, I tried.

After I got out of serving time in Jeff City, I really didn't figger to go on with life of that kind, but every place I went they picked me up.

I finally went to Colorado and was looking for a job in Pueblo when they picked me up as a vag and gave me 60 days.

When I got out I went to Kansas City and the second day there they got me again. Then I went to Ohio and was picked up in Akron and later in Toledo.

I couldn't shake those guys off not [sic] matter where I went. I went back to K. C. and met Bill Miller. By then, I decided I'd just as well get the goods as have the name, and once you get started in this game you can't turn back.

I guess after I went back to Kansas City I did go from bad to worse. I knew I could never live with my wife and kid and make a decent living, and that sure gets a fellow.

I guess I've been accused of everything that has happened except the kidnapping of the Lindbergh child.

And talking of children, the thing that makes me sore at this Burns and his laws are the way they treated Jackie up there in Tulsa last spring.

It ain't the names that they called me that makes me sore. Nothing gave them a right to tell that kid that he could never amount to anything as long as he has a father like me.

That kid can't help who his father is or what he does, but he does think the world of me and I sure think he's all right, too.

"What," Brown asked, "are the things you have done that you have been accused of, the things nearer the truth than anything else?" Floyd answered:

I guess I've done more bank holdups than anything else, together with holdup of pay rolls. It was all bonded money and no one ever lost anything except the big boys.

I never shot at a fellow in my life unless I was forced into it by some trap and then it was that or else.

Brown also asked him, "How many banks and pay rolls have you robbed up to this time?"

"I ain't gonna tell you that, but when I first went to Morris to pull that one, it was my 32nd. Here and in the east, too."

Later, Floyd said he had robbed an unlikely total of sixty banks and stolen a probably exaggerated half-million dollars.

Brown asked him, "What did you do with all that money?"

Floyd answered, "It wasn't all mine. I split it and in this game it ain't the money that counts, but the safety that money can help you get."

Brown and Floyd talked until dusk.[20]

Around the time of the interview, Floyd, Birdwell, and Elliott visited a speakeasy in the Cookson Hills. Floyd told the crowd, "You all know who I am. Now back up against the wall and let us do a little drinking." Everyone moved back. No one was allowed to leave. As the trio drank, they told funny stories about recent bank robberies. When they left, Floyd told the crowd, "Now, any of you that want to follow me, can try it, I'm Pretty Boy Floyd." This announcement was unnecessary, for his friends and acquaintances were in the crowd; some of them had been at the Sallisaw bank job. No one called the police. Business at the bar was good for a while because the infamous Pretty Boy Floyd had been there.[21]

The Floyd gang robbed the American State Bank in Henryetta, Oklahoma, on November 7, 1932. Elliott stayed in the car with the motor running, while Floyd and Birdwell entered the bank at 12:25 and drew their revolvers. As Birdwell lined up the three patrons against a wall, Floyd handed a sack to the bookkeeper and said, "If any of you give an alarm I'll kill you. Put all the money into that sack." They got $11,352.20, including $100 in nickels and dimes, in only two minutes; it was one of Floyd's biggest robberies. The gang took the two bank officers as hostages and made them stand on the running boards of the getaway car; once they had cleared the town, they dropped them off. They were more than a mile away before anyone sounded the alarm.[22]

The Oklahoma banking establishment was outraged by the Henryetta robbery. Instead of blaming local law enforcement officers, they now blamed Governor "Alfalfa Bill" Murray, who defended himself by insisting:

We would have had Floyd and Birdwell long ago if sheriffs and other officials in the hill country were not protecting them. Floyd has lots of friends in the Cherokee Hills. He has sent me word twice by relatives that if I would save him from the electric chair he would come in and surrender. I sent word back that I would not do it.

The bankers felt their property was more important than abstract justice. However, the governor would not change his mind. Nevertheless, state officials were hopeful. Eugene P. Gum, secretary of the Oklahoma Bankers' Association, told journalists, "Floyd has been the luckiest bandit that ever lived. Do not be surprised if you read, almost any day now, that Floyd and Birdwell have been slain."

Charles Burns, the chief law enforcement officer in the state, had his doubts. "This fellow Floyd is shrewd and slippery as an eel. In a general way we know where he is all the time. He never leaves the hill country except for a robbery."[23]

After the Henryetta job, Floyd and Birdwell discussed robbing the bank in Boley, Oklahoma, reportedly the largest all-black town in the country. It was a progressive town founded in 1903 by southern blacks, including many former slaves freed from their Indian masters.

But Birdwell had started to drink too much. Floyd also liked to drink, but he kept it under control. At first Floyd decided to rob the bank, but changed his mind when Birdwell could not stop drinking. Friends had warned Floyd the bank was too dangerous to rob. However, Birdwell was determined to go ahead without Floyd, who could not dissuade him.

Floyd and Birdwell had worked often with C. C. Patterson, and had used his Kiowa, Oklahoma, home as a hideout. Birdwell convinced Patterson and a black bandit named Johnny Glass from Earlsboro, who was familiar with Boley, to help him. But first Birdwell visited the bank and asked to cash a five-dollar personal check. As he expected, the teller told him they did not cash personal checks without proper verification. Birdwell simply said, "Forget it," and left. One night about a week later, Glass told Birdwell that the next day he would show him how a black man robbed a bank.

On November 23, 1932, the trio parked near the building. While Glass remained in the car, Birdwell and Patterson, whose long coat concealed his sawed-off shotgun, entered the front doors.

President D. J. Turner rose from his desk to help Birdwell. Also present were Treasurer W. W. Riley, Bookkeeper H. C. McCormick, and a customer. Birdwell pulled his Army .45 automatic and yelled, "We're robbin' this bank! Hand over the dough! Don't pull no alarm!"

McCormick slipped unnoticed into the vault, where there was a loaded 20-30 Winchester rifle.

Patterson took his shotgun from under his overcoat and pointed it at Riley, who pleaded, "Don't hurt nobody! Please!"

Patterson replied, "Shut up, you! Get your hands over your head!"

Turner gave Birdwell the money. But when the last bill in the drawer was removed, two electrodes rigged in the drawer came together and a loud alarm was sounded in the bank and in four local stores.

In the town's two hardware stores several men buying shotguns (it was the start of the bird season) put shells into them and ran to the bank.

Birdwell screamed at Turner, "You pulled the alarm? I'll kill ya for that, Goddamn you!"

He answered defiantly, "You bet I pulled it," as Birdwell shot him four times; Turner would die en route to the hospital.

Aiming the 20-30 Winchester rifle through the vault door's crack, McCormick fired at Birdwell. The shot struck Birdwell in the neck, blood spurting as he fell. "I'm shot. Hold me! I'm . . . ," he shouted, dropping the bag containing the seven hundred dollars collected; it was not picked up.

Patterson forced Riley and the customer to pull the barely alive Birdwell outside.

Glass, hearing the gunshots, ran to the bank to help his partners as they came outside. The two men dragging Birdwell dumped him forthwith and fled around the corner. Unattended, Birdwell died in a few moments.

The robbers could see men armed with shotguns and rifles running down Main Street toward them.

As Patterson and Glass stepped outside the bank, a rain of bullets met them and Patterson fell. Only the arrival of the sheriff put a stop to the "turkey shoot." With more then 450 birdshot wounds, Patterson would be crippled for life.

Miraculously, Glass fled to the car without being hit and drove some distance down the street before dozens of shots fired at him from all sides killed him. The car ran into the curb.[24]

Birdwell was considered by the law as a vicious killer and the "brains" of the Floyd gang. Burns said, "He is the man who planned their activities and he handled the machine gun in their raids. Without him Floyd's days will be few in the land."[25]

Lawmen believed Floyd would attend Birdwell's funeral and set a trap for him, but any chance of success was eliminated when the press told of the trap. A headline in the *Muskogee Daily Phoenix* read: "Birdwell's Bier Set as Trap for Elusive Pal, 'Pretty Boy.'"[26]

The night of the robbery, Ruby, who was recuperating from an emergency appendectomy paid for by Floyd, was surreptitiously removed from a Tulsa hospital by her father and Floyd, and taken to her father's home at Bixby.[27]

The *Muskogee Daily Phoenix* wrote, in an editorial entitled "Thanks to Boley":

> The state of Oklahoma owes a debt of sincere gratitude to the little town of Boley which made possible the permanent removal from its sordid bank robbery picture of one of the state's most active criminal menaces.
>
> In terminating the career of George Birdwell, killing an accomplice and wounding another, Boley has accomplished at least in part something that the law enforcement agencies have been attempting to do with no success whatever—break up the "Pretty Boy" Floyd bank robbing ring.
>
> Just how effective that break-up will prove remains, of course, to be seen. Floyd, unfortunately, was not present for the Boley "job.". . . But Birdwell is popularly credited with being the "brains" of Floyd's bank-robbing game. Without Birdwell, it may be that Floyd's robberies won't be so well planned or so precisely executed, and that the pretty one will blunder, just as Birdwell blundered into permitting matters to take the same happy course they took at Boley.[28]

Authorities, jubilant that Birdwell was dead, gave McCormick a five hundred dollar reward from the Oklahoma Bankers' Association and, in a special ceremony for him at the state capitol, made him an honorary major in the state militia. Another five hundred dollars was sent to the Boley Vigilance Committee for killing Glass. Governor Murray promised that the state would match the Association's rewards and in the future anyone who killed a bank robber would get five hundred dollars and anyone who killed the driver of a getaway car would get two hundred fifty dollars.[29]

Birdwell's body was taken to his hometown, where thousands attended his funeral. Some believed that Floyd attended the funeral dressed as a woman. McCormick went to the funeral with a protective group of Boley residents.[30]

Someone claiming to be Floyd threatened McCormick in a letter, telling him he would never live to see Christmas. It was an empty threat, but McCormick went about heavily guarded until the end of 1932. Oddly, in a way Birdwell did retaliate against his killer. McCormick had been carrying Birdwell's automatic in his hip pocket to protect himself from Floyd. But one day the gun accidentally went off, injuring his right leg. Immediately armed townspeople came to his aid.[31]

This was the peak of Floyd's "career." Several robbers declared themselves to be Pretty Boy Floyd.[32] Three national magazines would publish serial accounts of his life story, mostly fictional.[33] Floyd must have been pleased when the December 10, 1932, issue of a major national magazine, *The Literary Digest,* included an article called "Oklahoma's 'Bandit King'":

His name is Charles Arthur Floyd, and they call him "Pretty Boy."

But he's the "bandit king" of Oklahoma, the latest of that State's long line of outlaw chiefs.

He robs and laughs. Jeering the police, and even the Governor, he swoops down on a town, holds up a bank, and dashes away again by motor. In two years he has held up at least a score of banks. For his capture, dead or alive, there is an offer of a $3,000 reward.

But nobody has been able to bring him down. And this despite the tremendous risks he takes. That he is one of the luckiest bandits in criminal history is obvious from reading of his exploits.[34]

7

The Pretty Boy Floyd Gang

With the death of Birdwell, Floyd chose a new partner, Adam Richetti, a short, balding, thin man with liquid brown eyes.[1]

Richetti had been born at Strawn, Texas, on August 1, 1910. His family later moved to Lehigh, Oklahoma, where he finished the seventh grade. Then he worked as a painter.[2] He was known as a "good boy" with artistic ability. The only crimes he was known to have committed were the thefts of several typewriters from a high school and a prized baseball glove.[3]

On August 7, 1928, Richetti and another man had been arrested in Hammond, Indiana, for a mugging, in which they got a gold signet ring, valued at $6.00 and $3.75 in cash.[4]

He spent the next two years at the Pendleton (Indiana) State Reformatory and was released with one year's parole on October 2, 1930. The notorious John Dillinger was an inmate there at the same time.[5]

Floyd first met him in 1931, when Richetti was a Seminole oil field worker.[6]

Richetti and two other Oklahoma men, L. C. (Blackie) Smalley, with no previous record, and Fred Hammer, a former deputy sheriff of Seminole County, decided to form a gang.

On March 9, 1932, they attempted to rob the First National Bank of Mill Creek, Oklahoma. Richetti was the driver, and the other two entered the bank, where they got eight hundred dollars. But the Mill Creek Vigilante Committee became aware of the robbery and took positions around the bank before the bandits left. The robbers' lack of experience proved their undoing. Smalley and Hammer took no hostages for shields and backed out of the bank. The vigilantes fired a hail of bullets at them, killing Hammer and seriously wounding Smalley.

Richetti raced out of town, with intense gunfire directed at him. He made a temporary escape, but since he was wounded and his bullet-riddled car was disabled, he had to abandon the car just outside town and flee on foot through the fields. Two hours later the vigilantes caught him.[7]

He was sent to McAlester State Penitentiary on April 5, 1932, to await trial. After he was released on bond on August 25, he became a fugitive when he jumped bond and joined the Pretty Boy Floyd gang.[8]

There were reports that in 1932 Floyd went on a vacation with Richetti to New York City, where they stayed in a nice hotel and went to nightclubs and shows. They supposedly strutted down Fifth Avenue, recklessly spending money. It was reported that a sketch by Richetti showing Floyd robbing a bank was found in their hotel room by police.[9]

The following six months, Floyd changed tactics. Instead of personally robbing banks, he set up a bank-robbing gang. In return for planning and organizing the bank raids, he received part of the loot. The *Muskogee Daily Phoenix* of December 22, 1932, reported "Floydless holdups."[10]

According to FBI reports, the large, loosely organized gang consisted of Richetti (called "Rich"); Edgar Dunbar, who had served time in the Missouri State Penitentiary; Aussie Elliott; Fred Stone, an ex-convict from Minnesota; Ed Evans, a safe man and an ex-convict from Colorado who was wanted there; Coleman Rickerson; George Polk; Clarence Garatley; "Blackie" Smalley; Shine Rush, an Oklahoma bank robber; and others.

Floyd and his gang now had a hideout in a cave a few miles from Akins. People lived within a mile of it, but were friends of the Floyd gang. A six-foot cedar tree planted in a keg concealed the entrance to the cave, which opened up to a large room. It was here that Floyd brought John L. Moore, an old cellmate from the days at Jeff City, after he and Birdwell gave him a lift near Tulsa in June 1932. On the way, Floyd picked up one of his mother's cooked hams. After two days, Floyd drove Moore to Van Buren, Arkansas, gave him forty dollars to get home to Dyersburg, Tennessee, and told him that he could get in touch through his brother E. W. at Sallisaw.

At Dyersburg the local sheriff heard that Moore had told his friends he had been to Floyd's cave, and took Moore to Inspector Griffin of the Memphis Police Department, who in turn called in the Burns Detective Agency.

In November 1932, Moore met with A. B. Cooper, a Burns agent from Oklahoma City, and R. E. Delaney, a government agent at Fort Smith, and agreed to help capture Floyd.

They decided to raid Floyd's cave with the help of two Oklahoma City deputy sheriffs and Sheriff Jim Stormont of Okmulgee, Oklahoma, who brought along four of his men. Moore took them to the cave, but for some reason Stormont backed out and the raid was canceled.

Cooper and Delaney asked Moore to join up with Floyd and become an informer for them. He would keep in contact with a Burns Agency man at Memphis named Robinson and make daily reports. Moore agreed to do this, and wrote a letter to E. W. Floyd stating he was "hot" and wanted to get in touch with Charley. E. W. arranged to meet him at the Marion Rooms in Fort Smith.

After Moore met E. W. in early January 1933, E. W. took him to the home of his uncle Lee Hanty, an old one-story frame house with a log barn in the back, some seven miles from Sallisaw, where Charles was hiding out.

When the gang was there, the house was under constant guard. At night gang members would signal by turning a flashlight on and off three times when they approached the house.

Pretty Boy Floyd was there, sick in bed with the flu, guarded by Edgar Dunbar. During all the time Moore was a member of the gang, Floyd was ill and took painkillers.

Some gang members had doubts about Moore, but Floyd told them that he was sure they were mistaken because Moore had "celled with him and was O.K."

According to Moore, one of Floyd's main contacts was Fred Green, the prosecuting attorney at Sallisaw. The new sheriff of Sequoyah

County, Bill Byrd, was a good friend and never made any effort to arrest him. Elsewhere he had the support of the sheriffs and night marshals at Tahlequah and Grove, Oklahoma, and an Indian cattle buyer at Grove by the name of Coon. Moore also believed Floyd was friendly with many other officers in eastern Oklahoma. The only officer he was wary of was V. S. Cannon, the sheriff at Muskogee.

Floyd stayed close to Sallisaw, and when he committed a robbery, he ran for the Stilwell–Sallisaw road, where the local officers protected him.

Moore was told that while he was driving, Floyd sometimes wore women's clothes to conceal his identity.

Charles sent E. W. and Moore to Little, Oklahoma, where they delivered a package, contents unknown. "Tell that Constable to hurry up and get here, if he knows what's good for him," Floyd told E. W. Moore did not know who this constable was.

A day or two later, Floyd sent Moore, Ed Evans, Richetti, and Dunbar to Kansas City to get a machine gun from the infamous gangster Roger Touhy. Cecil Cooley, who had known Floyd at Jeff City and had a brother on the Kansas City police force who was an underworld informer, acted as middleman in the deal and gave the weapon to them. Floyd now had three machine guns, and Richetti was the gang's best man with that weapon.

All of the gang wore bulletproof vests; Floyd wore one that protected his back.

Moore had long talks with Floyd, who told him of his ambitious plans to rob banks in Greenwood, Arkansas; Fayetteville, Arkansas; Vian, Oklahoma; Tahlequah, Oklahoma; Vinita, Oklahoma; Clinton, Missouri; and Neosho, Missouri. But none of these banks was robbed.

Floyd also told Moore he was thinking seriously of getting into the kidnapping racket—perhaps kidnapping oilmen at Ponca City and Oklahoma City. Touhy was sending a man to him to teach him the tricks.

One of his associates had been the notorious Oklahoma outlaw Wilbur Underhill, but they had had a falling out, Floyd claimed. He had given Underhill's sister $1,000 to aid Underhill's escape from the Oklahoma State Penitentiary by bribing a captain of the guard. Moore believed Underhill and Floyd might get together again. Floyd also said he had an ex-convict friend, Herb Farmer, of Joplin, Missouri.

On January 12, 1933, Richetti, Dunbar, and Elliott robbed the Ash Grove, Missouri, bank near Springfield of $3,000, while Moore stayed in the getaway car. After the robbery they went to Richetti's brother Joseph's home at Bolivar, Missouri, and stayed the night. The next day they returned to Hanty's home and Richetti gave Floyd his share, adding that he had given his brother Joseph three hundred dollars. There was a false report that Floyd himself participated in the robbery.

About January 20 the gang went to Westville, Oklahoma. Then Moore and Elliott traveled to Fayetteville, Arkansas, to steal a car for the projected Fayetteville bank robbery. Moore was told to get a Chevrolet coupe with a rumble seat, but the car he hijacked from a woman did not have one. When he returned to Westville, Richetti threatened to kill him for not stealing the right kind of car. At Tulsa they stole a Cadillac roadster with a rumble seat.

Although Moore was able to tip off the officers that the Fayetteville bank was to be robbed, the robbery never happened.

After a little better than two weeks with the gang, Moore decided to leave because "Rich" continued to harass him; Floyd agreed to let him go.

From Fort Smith, Moore got in contact with Robinson at Memphis and told him he had left Floyd, but that he could direct him to Floyd's hideout. Robinson refused the offer and insisted that Moore continue to stay with Floyd, but Moore was afraid to do so.

Even though he had been promised immunity for crimes committed in Arkansas in return for spying on Floyd, Moore was arrested and sentenced to serve one year at the Arkansas State Penitentiary for stealing the car at Fayetteville. The officers had decided not to honor their commitment when he stopped informing on the outlaw.[11]

Floyd's ambitious plans were interrupted by the arrest or killing of several of his gang members. He may have planned the robbery of the bank at Comanche, Oklahoma, which three members of his gang (Rickerson, Garatley, and Rush) carried out on April 26, 1933. Leaving one man in their parked sedan, two men entered the bank and held seven persons at gunpoint while forcing the cashier to hand over two thousand dollars. After they had released five hostages, a posseman confronted them and was wounded in the hip in the gunfight that ensued. The robbers roared out of town and made a getaway.[12]

Three days later, Garatley was captured and Rickerson was killed when he refused to surrender at "Blackie" Smalley's farm. Farmer

Smalley and his wife were arrested, on the charge of harboring a criminal at a cabin behind their farmhouse. Previously Floyd himself had used this place as a hideout.[13]

Elliott and Edson Wilson had kidnapped two officers, wounding one, at Fort Smith on January 31, 1933, after stealing a car from a Tulsa rental company. In March they had a gunfight with Tom Rigner, city marshal at Depew, Oklahoma. Rigner was shot in the shoulder; Wilson was wounded, captured, and later taken to the Osage County jail at Pawhuska, but made his getaway in a stolen automobile.

On May 13, 1933, Elliott was captured after the sheriff of Creek County surprised him and another criminal at dawn in a vacant house near Sapulpa, after following a girl who was taking them breakfast. His companion was seriously wounded.[14]

Sixteen days later, Ford Bradshaw was acquitted of robbing the bank at Henryetta on November 7, 1932, because officials believed the Floyd gang had robbed it. Bradshaw later was acquitted on two murder charges. He had been arrested on December 10, 1932, at Vinita when a garage employee became suspicious of the arsenal that Bradshaw and his partner were carrying.[15]

On Memorial Day, May 30, 1933, eleven convicts at the Kansas State Prison, including Wilbur Underhill and Harvey Bailey, escaped and headed for the Cookson Hills. An intense manhunt was launched, making it harder for Floyd, who made no effort to join the escaped convicts, to hide in the region.[16]

The infamous outlaw was reported to have robbed banks from California to New York, to have sent death threats, to have committed many other crimes, and to have been seen all over North America. Several men were arrested because they looked like him. He was blamed for robberies committed by Francis McNeiley and George McKeever, who had physiques similar to Floyd and Richetti and also used hostages.[17]

At least twenty eyewitnesses, many of them leaders in the community, swore that Floyd robbed the Citizens' State Bank of Tupelo, Mississippi, of fifty thousand dollars on November 30, 1932. He supposedly was the author of a letter to the *Memphis Commercial Appeal* that indignantly denied that he or his gang had robbed the bank.[18]

It was also rumored that he had retired from being an outlaw and was living quietly in an eastern city under an assumed name.[19]

Also unconfirmed was a report that Floyd and Richetti had robbed a dance hall near Wewoka, Oklahoma, during this period. It was reported that he held a machine gun on three police officers while Richetti grabbed the cash in the ticket seller's booth.[20]

On May 29, 1933, Floyd's gang was rumored to have robbed the Rensselaer, New York, bank of two thousand dollars. During the robbery one policeman was killed and one wounded.[21]

That same day the Oklahoma Bankers' Association announced that so far only six banks had been robbed in 1933; by the same time the previous year, more than a score had been looted. After Birdwell's death, bank robbers had changed their tactics. For several months afterward, most bank robberies occurred at night. Therefore the Association eliminated the hundred-dollar reward for the capture of bank robbers alive and it reduced the bounty for killing one from five hundred to three hundred dollars, to be paid if the robber was killed in the act of robbing a bank or in the ensuing chase.[22]

Actually, Floyd had confined his movements to eastern Oklahoma during this time, except for infrequent visits to a relative in Fort Smith. Until the Kansas City Massacre in June 1933, he was often seen in Sequoyah County, where occasionally he went to Akins and watched, umpired, or played in baseball games. An uncle-in-law, V. H. Wofford, urged Floyd to leave the area, but the outlaw said he would be more secure in familiar surroundings.[23]

A. B. Cooper continued to hope that he could get Floyd when he visited his mother, and kept a close watch on her house, but friends warned Floyd and he avoided seeing her when the Burns men were there.[24]

In May 1933, on Mother's Day, Floyd visited his mother and they went to the Baptist church in Sallisaw, where they heard the Reverend Rockett give a sermon. Afterward they visited his father's grave near Akins and placed flowers on it. Floyd pointed to a spot nearby and said to his mother, "Right here is where you can put me. I expect to go down soon with lead in me—perhaps the sooner the better."[25]

Several newspapers turned down offers from Floyd's mother to "sell" them a story of her son's "actual life" since he had returned to Oklahoma. She denied reports of his crimes, but admitted that if he were cornered, there would be a battle to the death.[26]

In early June 1933, Floyd had E. W. arrange for Ruby and his son, who had left Bixby a month before and were staying with relatives near Akins, to meet him at the Smalley home near Seminole.

He was on his way to see them with Richetti on the early morning of June 3 when he stopped to help a Seminole County state legislator, C. L. Hill, fix a tire on the road near Wewoka. Three Seminole County deputy sheriffs passing by became suspicious, and when Floyd was asked for identification, he reached into his car, jerked out a machine gun, and snarled: "It's none of your business—you can go to hell! . . . Get away from here!" The terrified deputies jumped into their car and hurriedly went to Wewoka for reinforcements. Floyd and Richetti escaped in Hill's car. The *Tulsa Daily World* wrote, "a crew of officers managed to make the usual escape from Pretty Boy Floyd."[27]

Almost sixty officers with machine guns, tear gas bombs, and powerful rifles as well as side arms, headed by C. A. Burns, the State Police chief, joined in an intense hunt for Floyd, but as usual accomplished nothing. Burns said, "We believe we know where he is"—that is, near the Birdwell home outside Earlsboro.

Ruby and the wife of "Blackie" Smalley were arrested when they were caught pouring gasoline on a stolen car preparatory to burning it near Wewoka. Mrs. Eva Simpson, who was Mrs. Smalley's sister-in-law as well as Richetti's sister, was also arrested at the Smalley home.

After she was jailed, Ruby heatedly denied she had anything to do with car theft and claimed that one of the officers had arrested the two women when they had stopped their car to get water at a filling station.

> He threw a shotgun down on us. He made us get out of the car and searched us, and was so nervous we were afraid he would pull the trigger. He made us get back into the car and drive him to Wewoka where he locked us up.
>
> He is one of those smart laws who can't catch "Pretty Boy," so he picked on his old lady.
>
> I know positively that Charles could not have been implicated in the Rensselaer bank robbery for he hasn't been out of this state.

They were jailed at Wewoka and were arraigned late on June 3 for stealing the car; bond was set at two thousand dollars each. Floyd, Smalley, and Richetti also were charged with car theft.

Jackie was taken from the Smalley home to the jail, where he nonchalantly played marbles on the floor and told officers he had not seen his father in months. "I wish he'd hurry up and come home to play with me," the lad said. Meanwhile, Floyd's brother Bradley, Smalley, and Troy Keasee, brother-in-law of Representative Hill, were arrested at Bradley's home near Earlsboro and jailed at Seminole.

All the prisoners were soon released and all charges were later dropped.

Among the contraband taken by police from the Smalley home were a machine-gun stock, an automatic pistol, whiskey, and ammunition for a rifle like the one used by Coleman Rickerson in the Comanche robbery.

Hill denied he had had a rendezvous with the outlaw at Smalley's home. "The only time I was with the man reported to be Floyd either last night or early today was for a few minutes on the highway when he and companions helped me fix a tire."[28]

Considerable excitement prevailed in Oklahoma City and Seminole on June 4, 1933, when a rumor spread that Pretty Boy and Representative Hill were going to Oklahoma City, where the legislature was in session, to surrender Floyd. Oklahoma City newspapers and photographers kept a close lookout for the "big break" that never happened. When Hill went to the state legislature, he was subjected to wisecracks from his fellow representatives. The members roared with laughter after the speaker said, "'Pretty Boy' Floyd now is present."[29]

Just after his release from jail on June 5, "Blackie" Smalley delivered to Sheriff Frank Aldridge of Seminole County a written threat from Floyd, who had been at the Smalley home early that morning, that if Aldridge did not return the machine-gun stock and an automatic pistol taken from the Smalley home in three days, "I'll come and get you." Aldridge sent a message back by Smalley: "I've lived here all my life and intend to spend the rest of it here. You can find me any time of day or night, either at my office, on the highway or at my home."[30]

On the evening of June 8, Floyd and Richetti stole a 1933 Pontiac coupe owned by schoolteacher Joe Hudiburg from a garage belonging to the Excelsior school district, four miles north of Cromwell, Oklahoma. Hudiburg had driven his car into the garage and had locked it, but had neglected to secure the garage doors. It was a four-car garage with separate doors for each car, but there were no partitions, so that once someone was inside, all cars were accessible. Somewhat later the two men entered the garage and picked the lock to Hudiburg's car.

Meanwhile, Hudiburg went to his house and played bridge with friends, who left about 11:30 P.M. He then went out to lock all doors to the garage, trapping Floyd and Richetti inside, and went back into the house. The two outlaws had no choice but to force their way out with the stolen car.

About ten minutes later the noise of the car breaking through the locked door brought Hudiburg and several others running out to investigate. The outlaws were driving away, accompanied by a second car (stolen in Maud, Oklahoma).

Hudiburg and some of his neighbors pursued the thieves in the bright moonlight, but they never came close enough to recognize them. They lost them when the two criminals abandoned the second car and continued on in Hudiburg's. A gun found in the abandoned car was turned over to Sheriff Aldridge.

When Hudiburg's car, covered with scratches and dents, was picked up in Bolivar, Missouri, it looked as though it had been driven through thick woods. Later Richetti told Sheriff John Killingsworth that "he would teach some fellows not to lock a man in a garage any more."[31]

On June 14 the Pretty Boy Floyd gang was reported to have robbed the Farmers and Merchants Bank of Mexico, Missouri, of $1,628. Later that day a Missouri highway patrolman and the sheriff of Boone County were killed by three men after the lawmen had staked out the highway leading from Mexico. Since Floyd and Richetti were in the area, they were suspected of the murders. A woman eyewitness reported it was Floyd, but she was too far away for a positive identification. Later, others confessed to the murders.[32]

In the June 1933 issue of its publication, the National Sheriffs and Police Association offered a hundred-dollar reward for the outlaw's capture, describing him as a "thief, cop killer, bank robber and cold-blooded killer, who shot police officers on sight and who shoots to kill."[33]

On the morning of June 16, 1933, the heavily armed Floyd and Richetti, with more guns in their car trunk, went to Bitzer's Garage in Bolivar, Missouri, where Richetti's brother Joe was a mechanic, to have a bent fender repaired. The very pleasant Floyd and the owner, Ernest Bitzer, who recognized Floyd and knew Richetti, sat down on a bench. Floyd asked him about the latest news, the local law, and the town's characteristics.

Shortly after 7 A.M., Sheriff Killingsworth of Polk County, who had served only six months in office, came in to visit and get gas, leaving his gun in his car. Killingsworth later remarked, "I saw this man and Ernest Bitzer sitting on a bench, talking, and I knew from Bitzer's face that something was wrong. I took a second look, and I knew what it was."

Richetti knew the sheriff and yelled, "There's the law." The outlaws drew their guns, but couldn't prevent a man behind Killingsworth from slipping out and calling the police.

They lined up the six people in the garage at the point of revolvers while Joe fixed their car. "This is life and death with us. We have to do it, they would kill us if they could," Floyd told the prisoners. "Line up against the wall. If you try to get away we'll kill you." Floyd apologized to Bitzer for holding the men in the garage.

Meanwhile, Richetti loaded a machine gun and cursed the lined-up men. Floyd cooled him down. "That liquor is getting the best of you," he observed.

They decided to take Joe Richetti's car. It was a full ten minutes before they filled the gas tank and drove off, but still no one had interfered with them.

After forcing the sheriff into the backseat of the car next to Richetti, Floyd took the wheel and yelled, "You can have my car, Joe!" They quickly traveled northwest.

The men in the garage fled in all directions. A few minutes later, officers finally came and gave chase. Sometimes the posse got as close as a mile, but at Warsaw, Missouri, the trail was lost.[34]

More than three hundred policemen, including highway patrolmen, Kansas City officers, and deputy sheriffs, hunted them. Hundreds of farmers throughout western Missouri were armed. It was believed, correctly, that they were headed for Kansas City. Police in the area supposedly guarded all roads into the city, riding in cars with bulletproof glass and carrying rifles and riot guns.

Sheriff Jack Killingsworth later described to the press what had happened:

Floyd seemed as clean a fellow as I ever ran into, outside his record. He treated me nicer than I ever expected. . . . Floyd, I saw right away, was a right nice fellow. He would kill a man, but not unless he had to. These men are killers, they told me I would be safe if I would direct them to safety. We wandered over roads I knew would be hard to follow. Then the highway patrol got right behind us. They stuck a gun in my side, and told me to wave them back—I was more than willing. What worried me from the start was the boys would try to help me out.

Killingsworth even gave advice to the outlaws. He suggested that since their car was hot, it would be best to get rid of it and get another one. They abandoned their car in Deepwater, Missouri, where it was found the next day.

Floyd forced Killingsworth to flag down a new Pontiac driven by Walter Griffith of Clinton, a real estate man. After he stopped and his car was seized, Griffith was seated in front with Floyd, while Killingsworth and Richetti got in back. Both outlaws used marijuana; Richetti drank moonshine whiskey from a fruit jar and became surly.

Griffith, upset that Floyd was driving too fast, asked him not to scratch the paint on his new car. He had no idea who his captors were. Only after Richetti made threats on his life when they stopped at a wooded ravine near Ottawa, Kansas, to wait for darkness, was Griffith quiet.

Depressed, Floyd, with a pistol at his belt and a machine gun nearby, said:

They'll get me. Sooner or later I'll go down full of lead. That's how it will end.

How would you like to be hunted day and night? How would you like to sleep with this thing [the machine gun] across your knees?

I have a son. Maybe you think I wouldn't like to see him.

Finally Floyd said, "Well, . . . I guess it's time to go."

They got to Kansas City about eleven in the evening, stopping in the central industrial district. Floyd went into a building to make a phone call and then returned to the car.

He drove to Ninth Street and Hickory, where he ordered Killingsworth and Griffith, who thought they might be killed, to get out. Floyd told them, "You wait here for five minutes, and then walk down and get into this car. You then drive home and don't call no one because we will be watching."

After Floyd drove a short distance and stopped, he and Richetti got into a waiting car, taking their guns with them, and headed downtown.

A few minutes later Killingsworth and Griffith walked up to the Pontiac and drove off. Killingsworth later said, "Floyd told me to take the golf bags he left in the car they abandoned at the garage to remember him by. But I told him I wouldn't need anything to remember him by."

Only much later did the men call the police. The sheriff's justification for not informing the police immediately after his release was "I promised Floyd I wouldn't tell. My action is what any man with sense ought to do. They might come back some time, and I am not going to take chances."[35]

PART 2

Public Enemy No. 1

Machine Gun Challenge to the Nation

On June 16, 1933, the same day that Floyd and Richetti kidnapped Sheriff Killingsworth, something happened in Hot Springs, Arkansas, that would lead to one of the worst massacres of lawmen in American history.

The local chief of police, Joseph Wakelin, and his chief of detectives were on friendly terms with the underworld. Consequently criminals used Hot Springs as a "cooling-off joint," for a good fee. In fact, the two policemen were criminals themselves, being actively involved in a stolen car ring, and Wekelin's mistress ran a local brothel.

At noon that day Frank Nash, one of the most wanted criminals in the country, was at the White Front Cigar Store.[1]

Nash had been born in Indiana. When he was still a child, his family moved to Hobart, in southwest Oklahoma, where he started his career as a small-time thief. His first really serious run-in with the law did not occur until 1913, when he and a companion pulled off a theft of almost a thousand dollars from a Sapulpa, Oklahoma, store; Nash murdered his partner and took all the loot.

Nash was caught a couple of hours later and was given a life sentence at the Oklahoma State Penitentiary. While there, he became friends with Herbert "Deafy" Farmer, who would play an important role in the events of mid-June 1933. The smooth-talking Nash convinced the authorities to let him out of prison in 1918 so he could join the army to fight in World War I; instead, he resumed his criminal career.

In 1920 he was sent back to the penitentiary for twenty-five years, for safecracking; his sentence was reduced to five years after he became a trusty. Nash, who kept insisting he had "urgent business" to take care of on the outside, was let out in only two years.

After his release, Nash joined one of the last gangs in the Old West tradition, the notorious Al Spencer gang; among its members was the deadly Wilbur Underhill.

Spencer had a big ego and wanted to do something that would make him famous. Although the day of the train robbery was past, on August 20, 1923, the gang robbed the Katy Limited at Okesa, Oklahoma, and stole twenty thousand dollars in Liberty Bonds. This was a federal offense.

After a ten thousand-dollar reward was offered, a U.S. marshal soon tracked down the perpetrators. On September 20, 1923, Spencer was killed in a gunfight near Bartlesville, Oklahoma. The other members of the gang were rounded up quickly—except for Nash.

He had fled to Mexico with a two thousand-dollar reward on his head. Unfortunately for him, an El Paso policeman traveling in Mexico recognized him. Nash was arrested at a ranch near El Paso after the police received a tip he had business there. On March 1, 1924, he and other gang members were each given twenty-five years for mail robbery and were sent to the federal prison at Leavenworth, Kansas.

Nash simply walked away from Leavenworth Prison on October 19, 1930, after becoming a trusty and stealing a set of Shakespearean plays. He made his way to Chicago, where he met Verne Miller and joined up with two escapees from Leavenworth: Francis Keating and Thomas Holden. To disguise himself, Nash wore a toupee that covered his bald spot, grew a mustache, and put on weight.

The next few years were busy ones for Nash. He organized a prison break from Leavenworth in December 1931, ran an illegal beer parlor, managed slot machines, and robbed banks with the Barker-Karpis Gang. He also married a pretty woman named Frances Luce.[2]

There was a close call for Nash at the Old Mission Country Club golf course in Kansas City on July 7, 1932, when Holden, Keating, and

Harvey Bailey were arrested by the FBI while playing golf. Nash, who was with them, was unnoticed and managed to slip away.[3]

In Hot Springs, Arkansas, where Nash was "vacationing" in June 1933, he was known as a wealthy and generous businessman from Chicago who called himself "George" and talked about his membership in the Masons. Around noon on June 16, Nash was at the White Front Cigar Store talking with several men and drinking beer.

Two FBI agents from Oklahoma City, Joe Lackey and Frank Smith, accompanied by Otto Reed, the chief of police of McAlester, Oklahoma (who was in the raiding party because he knew Nash), acting on a tip from an FBI informer who had been given five hundred dollars, pulled up in their car in front of the store and waited until Nash was by himself. Then they rushed him with guns drawn.[4]

"Put your beer down and come on," one of them said, and the trio escorted Nash to their car. They took off his hat and his toupee; sure enough, it was the famous bald bank robber, Frank "Jelly" Nash.

To confuse anyone attempting to intercept them, they decided to take their prisoner by an indirect route to Leavenworth. Nash offered FBI Agent Frank Smith his hundred-dollar toupee and his Masonic card as souvenirs, but they were refused.[5]

Back at the White Front Cigar Store, Dick Galatas, who managed a horse-racing and baseball book there, had witnessed the incident; he told the local police that a Chicago businessman named George had just been kidnapped.[6]

The police sent a notice to all surrounding police departments to be on the lookout. At Benton, Arkansas, the lawmen had to prove they were federal agents who had captured a notorious criminal.[7]

Galatas rushed to Nash's wife, Frances, who was at a tourist camp with her young daughter from a previous marriage. She became greatly upset when Galatas told her of the "kidnapping" and could not understand why anyone would do so, although she suspected her husband was a bootlegger.

Galatas said that he decided to help Nash only because he was a brother Mason. The three of them went to Galatas's home, where Galatas called Nash's friend Doc Stacci at the O. P. Inn near Chicago and told him about Nash's capture.[8]

There followed a series of underworld long-distance phone calls about Nash, including calls by Stacci to Verne Miller and to Frank B. "Fritz" Mulloy in Kansas City.[9] Galatas also called the Little Rock police, who told him they had stopped the car and had learned Nash was being taken back to Leavenworth by way of the Joplin Road.[10]

After the lawmen left Little Rock, they stopped at a café in Russellville, Arkansas. It was obvious that their efforts to be unobserved were a joke, but they continued on to Fort Smith, where they would decide what to do next.

At Fort Smith they called the special agent in charge at Oklahoma City, R. H. Colvin, who instructed them to leave their car at Fort Smith and take the train to Kansas City, where they would meet reinforcements. It would be safer that way.

At 8 P.M. the lawmen took their prisoner to a stateroom on the Missouri Pacific train bound for Kansas City.[11] A deputy sheriff and a newspaper reporter saw them, and one of them (or perhaps both) called the Hot Springs police, who then called Galatas.[12]

Meanwhile, Galatas decided Herbert "Deafy" Farmer of Joplin, Missouri, an ex-con man, pickpocket, and gambler, might be able to help them, especially since he was a friend of Nash. He operated a hideout for criminals and one of the best underworld post offices in the country. Galatas and Mrs. Nash went to the local airport to catch a flight to Joplin to see Farmer. The operator of the airport wanted a hundred dollars for the trip of two hundred air miles; Mrs. Nash insisted on fifty dollars, but she finally agreed to the higher figure. Since Mrs. Nash was afraid to fly, she demanded that Galatas come with her.

Farmer met them in Joplin and drove them in his Cadillac to his farm six miles from town. Late that day they called Verne Miller, a close friend of Nash, and told him about Nash's arrest. Mrs. Nash was tearful, and Miller said, "Don't take it so bad." He assured her he would try to do something.

After Miller learned Nash was going to be taken to Kansas City by train and then on to Leavenworth by car, he called his associates in New York and Chicago, but it was too short notice. He also called the Barkers in St. Paul, but they were busy with the kidnapping of wealthy St. Paul brewer William A. Hamm, Jr.[13]

The big-time gangster Miller had given no indication of criminality in his younger days. He had had several odd jobs, such as county fair parachute jumper, wrestler, and boxer. In fact, he was a World War I hero, having shown a great ability with machine guns. Like many war heroes, he ran for public office, and was elected sheriff of his native Beadle County, South Dakota. He was very popular until he served a short prison sentence for embezzlement. After his release he became a bootlegger in Huron, the Beadle county seat, running his liquor in from Canada. Once again he was caught, but jumped bond and left South Dakota. Being good with guns and fast with cars, he was sometimes hired as a torpedo or as a driver by the Chicago or Detroit underworld. Miller also became a bank robber with the Barker-Karpis gang.

The conservatively dressed Miller was five-feet-eight, weighed 160 pounds, and had blue eyes and blond hair. Known as a "lady killer," he had a beautiful girlfriend named Vivian Mathias.

Although he was a vicious criminal who drank too much, he was convincing when he played the part of a respectable, wealthy oilman. He even belonged to the best country clubs of Asheville, North Carolina, and Kansas City, where he loved to play golf.

Miller joined the Tommy Holden and Francis Keating gang of St. Paul, where he was first distrusted because of his background as a sheriff. One story is that to prove his loyalty, he broke all of the fingers of a hood the Holden-Keating gang disliked.

One of their major robberies was the Kraft State Bank at Menomonie, Wisconsin. Among the seven robbers were Miller, Nash, Keating, Harvey J. Bailey, Frank Weber, and Charlie Harmon. The gang was outraged when Weber and Harmon killed the bank president's son; they executed their two associates as punishment.[14]

Seeking help from the local underworld, Miller went to Club Paris, a gangster hangout in Kansas City. It was a Friday night and the club was crowded, but he spotted Johnny Lazia, the local crime boss, with one of his lieutenants, James "Jimmy Needles" LaCapra. Miller told them of Nash's arrest and said that he intended to free him the next morning. Three men with machine guns could easily overcome lawmen armed with shotguns and revolvers. He said he needed two men. But Lazia didn't want any of his local boys involved. Then the ganglord remembered that two top guns, Floyd and Richetti, who had been driven to a nearby whorehouse on Holmes Street after they had released Sheriff Killingsworth and Griffith, were in town. Maybe they could be enlisted.[15]

Miller, Lazia, and LaCapra went to see the two men at the whorehouse. Miller said he would pay them a lot of money (one account was that it was ten thousand dollars) if they would help him free Nash the next morning. It was a good deal all around. Miller got the men he needed, Lazia avoided being directly involved, and Floyd and Richetti not only would get the money they desperately needed but also would be friendly with the powerful mob boss in Kansas City.[16]

To make sure the police had no machine guns, Lazia called police headquarters and persuaded officials to move the department's machine guns to the North Side Democratic Club.[17]

Miller and his two new associates made plans for the following morning. He drove them to Union Station, where he checked the train arrivals from Fort Smith and called Mrs. Nash at the Farmer home in Joplin. She started to cry and said she "couldn't do that" when he asked her to go to her mother's. Miller replied, "Don't carry on so. You'll see Jelly again." He finally hung up when she could not stop sobbing.[18]

Then the three men drove to Miller's home. Miller went into the bedroom where Vivian was sleeping, woke her up, and told her to bring her daughter Betty to spend the night with her, because he needed Betty's room for two friends.

Settled in, the gangsters slept for only a short time before they went out into the fresh morning and headed toward the Union Station in Miller's dark-green 1933 Chevrolet coupe. Vivian and Betty were still asleep.[19]

It was a beautiful, bright morning, with the temperature a pleasant seventy-one degrees, that Saturday, June 17, 1933, when the gangsters parked in front of the huge front doors of the station.

Pretty Boy Floyd entered Union Station and sat down on a chair in the deserted office of the Travelers Aid Society, near the Fred Harvey Restaurant in the concourse.

At about 6:45 Mrs. Lottie West, a caseworker for the Travelers Aid Society, went into her office and saw a man sitting there. He was immaculately dressed in a well-cut blue serge suit, a Panama hat she later described as "beautiful," and two-tone shoes.

"Is there something I can do for you?" she asked. When the man said nothing, Mrs. West thought he was very rude. He got up and went out the station's east gate and across the plaza.[20]

There was the normal station din: the click of heels on the marble floors, announcements of train arrivals, noises from the Fred Harvey Restaurant, cab starters' whistles, and the constant movement of cabs and cars.[21]

The Little Rock Flyer came in at 7:15 A.M. After Smith, Lackey, and Reed got off the train with Nash, they hurried toward the stairwell to the lobby. Waiting at the top of the stairs were two of the honest detectives of the corrupt Kansas City police force—less than half the force was believed to be honest—Frank Hermanson, a veteran of thirteen years, and W. J. "Red" Grooms, with only one year on the force. Also there were two special agents from the Kansas City FBI office, Raymond J. Caffrey and Special Agent in Charge R. E. Vetterli.

About 7:20 A.M., Nash and his escort of seven lawmen walked in a fan-shaped formation through the station. In the middle of the group was Nash, his handcuffs poorly covered by a handkerchief. Reed and Lackey carried sawed-off shotguns, while the others had pistols. Reed also had a .38. One officer kept his hand on his hip, ready to draw his revolver.[22]

Mrs. West remarked to the Harvey manager, "He must be pretty bad. Maybe he is Pretty Boy Floyd." She had a good view of the massacre that followed.[23]

The lawmen exited the station and crossed the plaza toward Caffrey's two-door Chevrolet, which they had decided to use (instead of an official vehicle) to avoid attention. Four agents and Chief Reed were to drive Nash to Leavenworth in the unmarked car; Hermanson and Grooms were to follow in another car.

The gangsters were watching as the lawmen grouped themselves closely around the prisoner. Only twenty-five feet away Miller and Richetti were on the running board of Mrs. West's Oakland. Floyd hid behind a lamppost.

After Caffrey unlocked the Chevy's right door, Nash started to climb in the back, but Caffrey insisted that he get in the front. Joe Lackey, Otto Reed, and Frank Smith quickly piled into the back, with

Smith in the middle, where prisoners normally sat. As Grooms and Hermanson stood with Vetterli near the right side of the hood, Caffrey went around the back of the car and started to open the driver's door.[24]

Suddenly, from the left behind the lawmen, Pretty Boy Floyd moved from his hiding place, raised his machine gun, and shouted, "Put 'em up! Up! Up!" At about the same time Miller and Richetti stepped out from behind Mrs. West's car.[25]

For a second the lawmen could not believe what was happening. Then Grooms drew his pistol and fired two quick shots at Floyd, wounding him in the left shoulder.[26]

Miller yelled, "Let 'em have it! Let the bastards have it!"[27]

As the gangsters blazed away with two machine guns and a sawed-off shotgun, the first men to fall dead were Hermanson, whose head was half blown away by a shotgun blast, and Grooms, killed by machine-gun fire. They lay on their backs on the pavement, their bodies touching.[28]

After Vetterli received a flesh wound in the left arm, he ducked down. Then he scrambled around the rear of Caffrey's car to the left-hand side, where he hoped he would be better protected and could shoot at the gangsters. But at this point shots were coming from all directions. Vetterli panicked—or, as he later put it—"It being apparent that we were in a trap, and there was nothing to do, I decided to make a break for the station to put in a riot call." As he ran, shots whistled by his head and lodged in windows and bricks of Union Station.[29]

Special Agent Ray Caffrey fell to the ground, mortally wounded by a shotgun slug in his right temple; he would die on the way to the hospital.[30]

The four men inside Caffrey's vehicle were helpless as the windshield was shattered by gunfire.

Nash, immediately aware he was being freed, started to slide toward the driver's side. "For God's sake don't kill me!" he yelled. Floyd and Richetti had never met him, and they probably took Nash for a lawman because he sat in the front. Nash died instantly from machine-gun fire. His head snapped back, his blood splattering the back seat and his toupee askew.[31]

Lackey dropped to the floor after he was shot, then was hit again a few seconds later. His revolver's handle on his hip was splintered and saved his life. With two machine-gun bullets at the base of his spine and a revolver bullet in his pelvis, he was in terrible pain. He survived, but would have to retire.[32]

Frank Smith drew his gun after the firing began. As he looked out, he saw the flame of a machine gun, heard bullets hitting, and felt the heat of the firing; he decided not to play the hero and dropped to the floor, hoping to be thought dead. He was unwounded, perhaps because the gangsters may have believed he was Nash.[33]

Chief Reed fell on him, killed by machine-gun fire.[34]

Pretty Boy Floyd and Miller examined Caffrey's bullet-riddled auto. As Floyd looked inside, he said, "He's dead. They're all dead."[35]

Mrs. West saw Mike Fanning, a motorcycle patrolman assigned to the station, running through the station doors. "There he is, Mike, get him!" she shouted, pointing to the big gunman (Floyd). "Shoot the fat man, Mike."

Fanning fired three shots. The big man dropped to the ground; Mrs. West assumed he was hit and ran back into the station. Thus she failed to see how the killers escaped.[36]

About ninety seconds had passed since the shooting began, and about a hundred shots had been fired.[37] Bullets pockmarked the wall of Union Station. Terrified bystanders fled in every direction. Cab drivers ducked to the floors of their cabs. Cars collided. A man in a wheelchair was pushed by a redcap at frantic speed. Mrs. West called to six Catholic nuns to run out of danger. Four did, but the other two stood paralyzed with fear. Someone yelled what many thought: "My God, is this Chicago?"[38]

The three gangsters made a quick getaway, with Miller at the wheel, onto Pershing and left onto Broadway, just missing a trolley car whose passengers were disembarking. They left skid marks as they ran a red light.[39]

By the time Vetterli had put in a riot call to police headquarters and rushed back to the scene, the assassins were gone.[40]

Dead were Nash, Reed, Caffrey, Grooms, and Hermanson. Lackey and Vetterli were wounded. Only Smith was unhurt.[41] Floyd had been hit in the left shoulder, and Miller had a slight wound on his right little finger.[42]

When Miller got home about 9 A.M., he awakened Vivian and told her that his friend Fritz Mulloy was coming to pick up her and Betty.

Vivian knew something was wrong, but asked no questions. She saw no one but Verne. But the door leading to the other bedroom was closed. Mulloy arrived, and drove Vivian and Betty to his house, where they had breakfast. After breakfast Miller called and asked Vivian to come home, but to leave Betty at Mulloy's house. He told Mulloy that they would be leaving the area and asked him to take care of their furniture and other possessions for the time being. Vivian took a taxi home; during the ride the driver told her about the shootout at Union Station.

On arriving home, Vivian found Miller and two men she had never seen before. Miller told her one of the men was named Floyd. (Later she identified Floyd and Richetti from photos.) Floyd was lying on the bed, a wound in his left shoulder.

A deeply shaken Miller told Vivian they had been to the station to get Frank Nash; there had been some shooting; Frank had been killed, and Floyd had been wounded.

Vivian prepared breakfast, but none of them wanted anything to eat. Miller and Richetti drank some coffee, and Vivian took a cup to Floyd.

Floyd and Richetti remained in the bedroom all day, except when Richetti came out a second time for coffee. Vivian also took coffee to Floyd a second time. She said nothing to either Floyd or Richetti about what had happened, and they, too, were silent. Sometime during the day Miller said that his car had been used for the trip to and from the Union Station.

After the daily newspaper was delivered to the house, Miller read an account of the shooting that said five or six men had been involved.

"That's what the newspapers can do," he said.[43]

Sometime after dark Miller left the house by himself to look for Johnny Lazia; finally he located him at the scene of the massacre. The ganglord was having a late supper with James LaCapra and other friends at the Fred Harvey Restaurant in Union Station.

Miller asked Lazia for medical attention for Floyd and a safe escort out of town for Floyd and Richetti. He added that he was leaving town himself in a few hours.[44]

After Miller returned home, Vivian heard someone walk onto the porch, whereupon she was sent to the bedroom. When she came into the living room about twenty minutes later, Floyd and Richetti were gone.[45]

The next day Miller, Vivian, and Betty fled to the apartment of Volney Davis in Maywood, Illinois. Miller told him he had tried to free Nash and had secured the help "of a good man"—Charley Floyd. Although he was reluctant to talk about the massacre, he said that the delivery would have been successful had not one of the officers reached for his gun; that when he saw the officer make a move to shoot, he decided it would be either his death or the officer's, and that he (Miller) and his companion then opened fire. Richetti was not mentioned. Miller then caught a plane to New York City; Vivian and Betty went to Vivian's parents' home in Brainerd, Minnesota.[46]

Lazia brought medical aid to Floyd in his new hideout. Then some of Lazia's men asked Floyd if he could travel, even though he had lost a lot of blood. Floyd grabbed his machine gun, raised it into firing position, and declared, "I can handle this baby."

"Eddie and I are gonna get out of here and lay low for a while," Floyd then said.

"Eddie" Richetti added, "Yeah, all we need now is a car."

Late on Monday evening, June 19, Lazia arranged for an escort to take them in a Buick sedan safely out of Kansas City, onto Highway 40 and east toward St. Louis. They had no trouble getting through the police net surrounding the city.[47]

The Kansas City Massacre outraged the public. Throughout the country editorials angrily demanded that something be done to combat the new crime wave. The *Boston Transcript* asked, "In what other civilized country could such a thing happen? Right in the center of a large city, in front of a union station?"

Attorney General Homer Cummings thundered, "The gauntlet has been thrown down. The murder of a Department of Justice agent is an open challenge to the government of this nation. The entire department has been ordered to assist in this case."

And something *was* done. There were new laws and increasing support for law enforcement. J. Edgar Hoover would become a public hero, and it was the beginning of the rise of the FBI to a powerful national police force.[48]

9

The War Against Crime

Even today there are many unanswered questions about the Kansas City Massacre: who committed the murders; whether some of the deaths were caused by lawmen involved in the event; and what weapons were used. Although there were at least twenty-five eyewitnesses, estimates of the number of gunmen ranged from two to six.

The FBI launched what it liked to call an intense "scientific investigation." Hoover reinforced the Kansas City office with top agents Gus Jones, Harold Andersen, and E. E. "Ted" Conroy. The FBI did not trust the corrupt Kansas City police, who leaked stories to the press. The well-respected Sheriff Tom Bash worked closely with the FBI.[1]

The Bureau, which feared for the safety of its agents and informers, was shocked when one of its informers in Hot Springs was killed on July 5, 1933, by the underworld. Another informer, who had helped the FBI's Oklahoma City office find Nash, told an agent there that Dick Galatas had said he intended to kill whoever had betrayed Nash. Moreover, the special agents who had survived the Massacre might be killed to eliminate witnesses. The threat was taken seriously.[2] The wounded Joe Lackey was housed at a Kansas City apartment house under a false name for his protection.[3]

With the help of Floyd's archenemy Burt Haycock, who had become the security officer of Southwestern Bell Telephone Company,
the FBI traced long-distance calls in the region made on June 16, 1933,
the day before the Massacre. These included one from Herb Farmer's
farm near Joplin to Verne Miller in Kansas City and others from Hot
Springs to an underworld hangout, Doc Stacci's O. P. Inn in Melrose
Park, near Chicago. The Bureau was also able to verify those from the
inn to the Kansas City homes of Verne Miller and Fritz Mulloy, as well
as one from a pay phone at Union Station to Herb Farmer's home.[4]

Not until several months later was the Bureau sure that Floyd,
Miller, and Richetti were the killers. On June 29, 1933, the FBI had
searched Miller's home and found beer bottles there with fingerprints
on them, but had neglected to check them out until they were sent to
the FBI lab on February 13, 1934. On March 14 the fingerprints were
identified as those of Richetti. Where Richetti was, Floyd must have
been.[5]

Interestingly, ballistic tests, one of the most important aspects of
the scientific police work, were not done for the most part by the FBI
lab, but by a forensic ballistics expert in Kansas City, Merle A. Gill.[6]

Major John Halvey, who later became chief of detectives for the
Kansas City police, believed that

> The mystery of Detective Hermanson's wounds was never even
> brought to the public's attention. I was one of the first patrol-
> men to arrive on the scene and the entire side of Hermanson's
> head had been blown off. Only a shotgun could have inflicted
> that type of wound. Chief Reed carried a shotgun when escort-
> ing prisoners, and we wondered if in the shooting the gun had
> not accidentally been discharged. But the FBI covered up so
> many facts about the case, we never really knew much.[7]

Mrs. West reported that Floyd had a machine gun and the two others had a shotgun and another machine gun.[8] Ballistic tests confirmed
that a shotgun was used in the slayings, but the FBI insisted it was a
different gauge from the lawmen's shotguns. But how did Lackey get
hit by a revolver bullet if only the officers were carrying revolvers?[9]

Gill made the important discovery that the firing pin of the machine gun that killed Lazia on July 10, 1934, had been used in the

Massacre. Later the FBI lab examined the gun and came to the conclusion that the gun itself also had been used.[10]

Gill also thought that the .45 Floyd had in his right hand at the time of his killing had been fired in Kansas City and that a shell from Floyd's gun was identical to a shell found at the scene of the Massacre. But the FBI lab disagreed, based on photographs of the shell.[11]

Hoover, upset over the disputes the FBI had with Gill, wrote, "Well it serves us right for ever having dealt with Gill. I always opposed it & never approved the turning over of the evidence." And again, "This sustains the opinion which I have had of Gill all along. It proves what a grievous error it was to turn over to him for examination our evidence. We had a laboratory of our own & I never have understand [sic] why we dealt with this man."

Hoover denounced Gill as having a "lack of ethics" and "certainly would never recommend this man Gill for anything. Tell the Criminal Division that in view of our experience with him we could not conscientiously concur in any recommendation where his veracity or integrity is involved." And finally, "We will have nothing to do with Gill."[12]

The evidence is overwhelming that Floyd, Richetti, and Miller were involved in the killings.[13] At first Mrs. West said Floyd was not one of the killers when she was shown a picture of him. Later she changed her mind and never again recanted.[14] But she was an unreliable eyewitness. For example, on May 7, 1936, she phoned the FBI's Kansas City office to tell them she thought a criminal named William Dainard, whom she had seen in a newspaper photo, was the suspicious-looking man she had seen at the Kansas City Massacre. There was no evidence to support this.[15]

Several lawmen, such as Sheriff Tom Bash, were sure Floyd and Richetti were the killers. Both Kansas City, Missouri, papers ran stories naming Floyd as the killer, but the FBI would not comment.[16]

During late June 1933, the FBI in Kansas City was notified by agent Melvin Purvis of Chicago that a confidential informant of the Chicago office of the Burns Detective Agency had made several trips to Kansas City immediately after the Massacre and through his local sources had heard that Floyd and Richetti were the killers. He also had heard that they were hidden by Lazia, and that Floyd and Richetti had left Kansas City about eight hours after the Massacre. But this information was ignored by the Bureau.[17]

Floyd himself denied the crime. He wrote to Kansas City Detective Captain Thomas J. Higgins on a plain business postcard, postmarked Springfield, Missouri, on June 21, that read:

Dear Sirs:
    I—Charles Floyd—want it made known that I did not participate in the massacre of officers at Kansas City.
Charles Floyd[18]

William Gordon, chief of the Bureau of Identification, examined the handwriting and announced it was Floyd's.[19]

An ex-convict named Blackie Audett claimed in a book, *Rap Sheet*, published in 1954, that he had seen Miller and three gangsters other than Floyd and Richetti actually do the killing. But Audett was a prisoner at Leavenworth (from 1928 to July 1933) at the time of the Massacre. During the original FBI investigation he had said other gangsters had done the killings.[20]

City Manager Henry F. McElroy gave a statement to the press defending the local underworld: "It has been definitely established that no Kansas City gangster had anything to do with the shooting at the Union Station this morning." Kansas City Director of Police Eugene C. Reppert and the *Kansas City Times* named Miller and William Weissman, brother of a local gambler and racketeer named Solly Weissman (who had been shot and killed in Kansas City several years earlier), as the killers. But William Weissman was cleared soon after. In fact, almost all major criminals were accused of the Massacre.[21]

Finally on July 6, 1933, the Justice Department ordered Floyd's arrest. Also named for complicity in the killings were Verne Miller, Harry J. Garner, Bernard Phillips, and William Weissman, as well as the five convicts who had escaped from the Kansas State Penitentiary on Memorial Day—Harvey Bailey, Wilbur Underhill, Ed Davis, James Clark, and Robert G. Brady.[22]

The theory of Gus Jones, special agent in charge at San Antonio, was that Harvey Bailey was the killer. Agent Ray Suron disagreed.

Bailey wrote a letter to Sheriff Bash that on June 16 he had robbed the Black Rock, Arkansas, bank with two companions, so there was no way he could have committed the crime. Fingerprints on the letter matched those found at the bank.[23]

After Jones arrested Bailey on August 12, 1933, at the Shannon farm in Texas, he told the press that the arrest solved "the Union Station Massacre and the Urschel kidnapping." What about Pretty Boy, a reporter asked. Jones answered, "He had nothing at all to do with the Union Station job. Nor the Urschel kidnapping."

Other lawmen, such as Sheriff Jack Killingsworth and Kansas City Chief of Detectives Thomas J. Higgins, also believed neither Floyd or Richetti had committed the murders.[24] As late as January 29, 1934, the special agent in charge of the FBI's Kansas City office, J. M. Keith, believed that Floyd had not been involved in the Massacre.[25]

About two weeks after the Massacre, the Buick used by Floyd and Richetti to escape Kansas City was recovered near Cleveland. There was the charred body of a man in the burned-out vehicle.[26]

Frances Nash did not attend the funeral of her husband. Instead, she fled to relatives in Wenona, Illinois, with her young daughter. The FBI followed her there, arrested her, and took her to Chicago for questioning, and then to Kansas City on July 12. The next day they charged her with conspiracy to obstruct justice. She pleaded not guilty and was allowed to stay with her parents in Aurora, Minnesota, until the date of the trial.[27]

She inherited her husband's possessions, including his toupee. Hoover had wanted the hairpiece for the FBI exhibit, but he was told that there was no way the FBI could get it for display. "Why did they ever release this?" Hoover wrote. Even as late as July 1935, during Richetti's trial, the FBI director asked for it, without success.[28]

Galatas and his wife, Elizabeth, disappeared from Hot Springs, fleeing to California and then to New Orleans. Hoover told his agents not to release a picture of Galatas to the press and magazines before further efforts to locate him. There followed an intense investigation for over a year. Finally the September 15, 1934, issue of *Liberty* Magazine had a feature article about the "mad dogs" still remaining that showed a picture of Galatas. In a few days two informers reported him for the thousand-dollar reward, and he was arrested on September 22, 1934, in New Orleans, where he had a business selling cellophane products.[29]

Since Miller and Nash were friendly, the FBI showed pictures of "Moore" (Miller's alias) to his associates and neighbors, who identified him as Miller. They had thought he was "a nice guy."[30]

During the search of Miller's home on June 29, 1933, bloodsoaked sheets and a cot were found in the attic, as well as some beer bottles with fingerprints on them. In April 1933 Earl Christman, a Barker-Karpis gang member, had died there.[31]

Miller fled first to Volney Davis's apartment in Maywood, Illinois, and then caught a plane to New York City, where he hoped to get work from Louis "Lepke" Buchalter. But Miller was red-hot, and Buchalter did not want his visitor. By now the FBI suspected Buchalter and other northeastern gangsters of helping Miller, and they shadowed them. Police told Buchalter that they would cause problems for him so long as they thought he was helping Miller. Special Agent Andersen led a team who kept a close watch on visitors to Atlantic City over the Labor Day weekend because of a rumor that Miller might be in the area.

In fact, Miller was hanging out with Longie Zwillman's gang in Newark. He was drinking heavily; it was rumored on the street that he had killed one of Zwillman's boys in a drunken brawl.[32]

As a cover, Miller pretended to be Stephen J. Gross, Jr., a salesman of optometrical supplies. This name was printed on letterheads, prescription blanks, and cards, and he had acquired suitable paraphernalia.[33]

Then he fled again to his Chicago apartment, where Vi Mathias and her friend Bobbie Moore were staying. "Lepke" had provided money for Vi to move around to avoid the FBI.

But the Bureau and police were waiting for Miller. They had rented an apartment nearby, where agents were placed, and others surrounded his apartment building. Two agents who knew Miller kept constant watch. For a long time he stayed out of sight. Finally they made their move, but Miller suspected something, and instead of taking the elevator, which would have meant his certain capture, he ran down one flight of stairs and escaped in a waiting car driven by Bobbie

Moore. Somehow the men on the outside were not signaled quickly enough. A policeman fired seventeen shots from a machine gun at the fleeing car, but missed Miller and Moore. Miller fired back with his automatic, but no one was hurt. Abandoning the vehicle a few blocks away, he and Bobbie fled in different directions and escaped. Bobbie Moore later surrendered; she had not seen Miller since the escape.

But Miller's luck was running out. It was rumored that four underworld executioners had surprised him steaming in a Louisville bathtub, had killed him there, and had taken his naked body hundreds of miles by car to a drainage ditch near Detroit, where they dumped his body, which was found on November 29, 1933. It was more than a routine gangland execution: clothesline bound his arms and legs; his skull had been crushed by blows with a blunt instrument; his tongue and cheeks had been punctured with ice picks; and he had burn scars on his body.

Why was Miller executed? Was it because he was suspected of killing Gus "Big Mike" Winkler, a Chicago mob leader? Were Detroit mobsters retaliating for other recent killings? Was it in revenge for killing one of Zwillman's boys? Or simply because he was too hot?[34]

Johnny Lazia was in big trouble. Not only was the FBI suspicious of him, but the Joe Lusco mob, especially Ferris Anthon, was interfering with his operations.

Early on the morning of Saturday, August 12, 1933, Anthon was shot and killed at the front entrance to his home, the Cavalier Apartments in Kansas City. Under protection at the same apartment building was FBI Agent Joe Lackey, one of the survivors of the Kansas City Massacre, who thought the gunfire was a warning for him to keep silent.

Sheriff Tom Bash, his wife, a fourteen-year-old neighbor girl, and a deputy sheriff, driving home from an ice cream social, happened to pass the scene of the shooting. They heard the gunfire, and the driver jammed on the brakes while Bash reached for a riot gun. Bash and the deputy, armed with a revolver, sprang out to the sidewalk.

"Halt! Don't move," Bash shouted.

Two gunmen attempted to flee. Bash fired two shots that killed them instantly as their vehicle careened into the front of the sheriff's car.

Another gunman came out shooting at Bash until his pistol was empty. Each shot missed. "Don't shoot me—Don't shoot me!" the gunman then yelled as he was arrested by Bash.

The deputy chased a fourth gunman but lost him.

The captured gunman was a Lazia thug, Charles Gargotta. The two dead gangsters were nightclub operators Sam Scola and Gus Fascone.

Things got worse for Lazia. First, one of his top men, James LaCapra (alias Jimmy Needles) became his enemy. A bomb expert, he had thrown one of his creations from an auto into the front of Lazia's North Side Democratic Club. The entire front of the building had collapsed.

Another top lieutenant, Gargotta, was in jail for attempting to kill Sheriff Bash. Early in 1934 Lazia was convicted of income tax evasion and was sentenced to a year in jail and a five thousand-dollar fine. He still was the underworld boss in Kansas City, but his days were numbered.

Early in the morning of July 10, 1934, Lazia, his wife, and his bodyguard-chauffeur were attacked by two gunmen in front of their home, the Park Central Hotel. The seriously wounded Lazia was rushed to a hospital.

Special Agent Harold Andersen hurried to the hospital, hoping to get a confession from the ganglord before he died. He asked a priest to tell him if Lazia made a confession, but Lazia died about half an hour later without talking.[35]

Ballistic tests found the machine gun used in the Lazia shooting had been used in the Kansas City Massacre. Now there was a definite link between the Massacre and the Kansas City mob.[36]

The local police suspected members of Joe Lusco's mob, but others believed it was the work of James LaCapra because of his split from Lazia. LaCapra insisted that he "had nothing to do with Lazia's killing," but it did no good.

The first attempt to kill LaCapra occurred one morning in downtown Kansas City when a carload of thugs tried to gun him down. He saved himself by running inside a post office.

LaCapra fled west in August 1934, but Lazia's men followed him. Near Argonia, Kansas, they fired on LaCapra's car and forced him off the road. Once again he survived.

LaCapra was arrested and taken in for questioning at Wellington, Kansas, and then moved to a Wichita jail for safekeeping.

Kansas City FBI special agents Harold Andersen and Walter Trainor thought they could get the real story about the Kansas City Massacre out of LaCapra. After all, he had been close to Lazia, was believed to be willing to talk for revenge against those who were trying to kill him, and was looking for protection.

LaCapra told Andersen, "They shoot at me on the city streets, they shoot at me on the country roads, there's no place to be safe, especially for something I had nothing to do with." The Kansas City police were planning to come to Wichita for him with a fake warrant, and he believed he would never reach Kansas City alive.

Andersen promised LaCapra that he would receive protection in return for telling the story of the Union Station Massacre.[37] LaCapra agreed to do so, and told a grand jury in Kansas City that he was with Lazia when Verne Miller asked for help in freeing his pal Frank Nash on the Friday night before the Massacre. At first Lazia refused, but then decided Floyd and Richetti might be willing to help Miller. LaCapra said, "Pretty Boy Floyd and Adam Richetti had just got into town a short while before, and Floyd had got in touch with Johnny Lazia to let him know where he was. Johnny told Miller that Pretty Boy Floyd was the person Verne needed, and Lazia said he would get them together."

LaCapra also told the grand jury that he, Lazia, and Miller had gone to a Holmes Street whorehouse, where Lazia made the introductions and Floyd agreed to help free Nash. Miller then took Floyd and Richetti to his home. Afterward, Lazia called police headquarters and asked them to remove the machine guns from an armored police car and take them to his North Side Democratic Club.

LaCapra related that the evening after the Massacre, Miller found him, Lazia, and two others eating dinner at the Union Station's Fred Harvey Restaurant. Miller demanded a doctor for Floyd, a car for himself, and a safe escort for Floyd and Richetti out of the city.

"Johnny promised everything—a doctor for Floyd, a car for Miller, and he said he would see that Floyd and Richetti got away," LaCapra said. "He took care of everything, and Floyd and Richetti left on Monday night. Some of the boys gave them a safe escort out to Highway 40."[38]

U.S. District Attorney Maurice Milligan and the FBI now were certain there was no longer any serious doubt who were the killers. They had eyewitnesses and fingerprint evidence, and no one doubted Floyd and Richetti had been in Kansas City at the time. Now they had an inside report on what actually happened. On September 30, 1934, Vivian Mathias finally had agreed to tell what she knew about the comings and goings of Miller, Floyd, and Richetti. But, fearing for her life, she refused to testify before the grand jury. The special agent in charge at Kansas City, M. C. Spear, thought the recent inactivity of Floyd and Richetti indicated guilt.[39] On October 10, 1934, the attorney general issued a statement to the press that the Kansas City Massacre killers were now known—Pretty Boy Floyd, Miller, and Richetti.[40]

The FBI grew in power and size after several incidents, including the Kansas City Massacre, had shocked the country and the public made angry demands that something be done about the crime menace. A short time after the Massacre, Charles F. Urschel, a wealthy Oklahoma City oilman, was kidnapped from his home by Alfred Bates and George "Machine Gun" Kelly. John Dillinger, released from prison in May 1933, robbed numerous banks, helped friends escape from prison, led raids on police stations, and made two sensational jailbreaks in a bloody fourteen-month crime wave. A member of his gang, Baby Face Nelson, escaped from prison and murdered several people, including three Bureau agents, before being killed in a shootout with the FBI. In April 1934 there was the FBI fiasco at Little Bohemia Lodge in Wisconsin with the Dillinger gang, who escaped after an FBI agent and a local resident were killed and four others were wounded, none of them criminals. Clyde Barrow and Bonnie Parker spread terror throughout the Midwest. Also in the Midwest the Barker-Karpis gang, led by Ma Barker, her sons, and Alvin "Old Creepy" Karpis, was notorious for its bank robberies, murders of policemen, and kidnappings of wealthy businessmen.

Congress reacted to the public demand and in May 1934 passed legislation greatly expanding the Bureau's jurisdiction over interstate crimes. The Fugitive Felon Act made escape across state lines to avoid prosecution a federal crime. Other laws gave the Bureau increased enforcement powers and protection for its agents. Severe penalties were enacted for killing or assaulting federal officers. Agents were finally given the authority to carry firearms and full arrest power for offenses against the United States. The FBI was also authorized to give up to twenty-five thousand dollars in rewards. The Lindbergh Law, which had been passed after the kidnap-murder of the son of the famous flyer, was amended to create a presumption of interstate transportation of the victim, to cover cases where there was no ransom demand, and to provide for the death penalty. The following now became federal offenses: to extort money or other valuables by telephone; to rob any national bank or member bank of the Federal Reserve System, or to engage in interstate transportation of stolen property worth more than five thousand dollars.

While Floyd was in deep hiding, other major freelance criminals were hunted down. In 1933, kidnap victim Urschel having been returned safely, Machine Gun Kelly was arrested in Memphis and members of his gang were soon in custody. On May 23, 1934, Bonnie and Clyde were killed in an ambush on a Louisiana road. In Chicago, on July 22, 1934, Dillinger was killed outside the Biograph movie theater by the FBI.[41]

The major figure in the Dillinger case, FBI superagent Melvin Purvis, special agent in charge of the Chicago office, was a national hero who rivaled even the mythical J. Edgar Hoover. He was a small man who, like Floyd, enjoyed wearing good clothes. The polite and pleasant Purvis often changed his shirt three times a day. He came in eighth in a 1934 *Literary Digest* poll to determine the most important people in the world. He was involved in the major FBI cases of the time and was lionized by the press, although at times he was severely criticized.

In spite of his fame, Purvis's years at the FBI from 1927 to 1935 were rocky. (Before that he had been a lawyer in his native South Carolina.) He had constant conflicts with Hoover over his occasional mistakes, and Hoover thought that Purvis's ego was too big and that he sought too much publicity. Purvis even replaced Hoover's name with his own on press releases; he was the only special agent in charge in the history of the FBI to do so.

Conflict increased when Purvis was appointed special agent in charge at Chicago in 1932. Part of his success was due to being in Chicago, the major center of organized crime. One of his big mistakes was his harassment of Roger Touhy, who was innocent of many of the crimes Purvis accused him of. Purvis also blundered at Little Bohemia. But he had great personal courage and was a competent and popular leader, although he tended to get overexcited.[42]

In Floyd's home territory, on Memorial Day 1933, some convicts, led by Wilbur Underhill and Harvey Bailey, who had escaped from the Kansas State Penitentiary headed for the Cookson Hills.[43] In September two of the escapees, Bob Brady and Jim Clark, fled from the Hills, but they did not last long. Clark was captured at Tucumcari, New Mexico, on October 7, and police killed Brady on January 19, 1934, at Paola, Kansas.[44]

Wilbur Underhill and Ford Bradshaw had formed a gang based in the Hills that raided banks in Helena, Kansas; Stuttgart, Arkansas; Coalgate, Oklahoma; and Okmulgee, Oklahoma (where they took thirteen thousand dollars). Underhill had several narrow escapes from the law, and his downfall came at the end of the year after he had married his sweetheart, Hazel Hudson. Federal agents, led by R. H. Colvin, paid an informer five hundred dollars to reveal the location of the "Tri-State Terror." Although he was seriously wounded after a terrific gun battle at the bungalow where he was honeymooning with his bride, Underhill fled to a Shawnee furniture store, where he was captured. He was taken to a hospital in critical condition. But the FBI was afraid that Floyd or others would try to rescue him, so they made the controversial decision to take him to the McAlester State Prison hospital, although there was doubt that he could survive the journey. He died there on January 6, 1934, after saying, "Tell the boys I'm coming home."[45]

Ford Bradshaw was upset about Underhill's capture, so he harassed the town of Vian the following night in revenge. In response the authorities routed Aussie Elliott and Raymond Moore from a hideout near Marble City. (Elliott had escaped from jail on October 28, 1933.) The two were killed by officers near Sapulpa in early February 1934; the chief of police and a patrolman also lost their lives.[46]

Soon after, Ed Newt Clanton died in a gunfight in which Deputy Sheriff Earl Powell also was killed. Clanton, a member of Bradshaw's gang in the Cookson Hills, had fought in the so-called "Battle of Braggs

Mountain," in which three officers and three outlaws were killed. One witness said, "You couldn't see the trees for the lead flying."[47]

Something had to be done to end the lawlessness. On February 17, 1934, a thousand men based in Tahlequah, Muskogee, Stilwell, and Sallisaw raided sites in the Cookson Hills. It was a fiasco; only a few minor criminals were caught, although it had been hoped that the major outlaws, such as Floyd, Bradshaw, and the Barrow gang, would be flushed out.[48]

On March 3 the end came for Bradshaw, who was riddled by bullets fired by Deputy Sheriff Will Harper at Arkoma, Oklahoma, just across the state line from Fort Smith, Arkansas. Bradshaw was an associate of Floyd whose cruelty shocked even the hardened Floyd.[49]

Floyd's reputed uncle, Lonnie Poe, lost an appeal of a fifteen-year sentence for the four thousand-dollar robbery of the State Bank of Cyril, Oklahoma, on May 11, 1934.[50] On July 28, 1934, Richetti's sister, Eva Simpson, and Thelma O'Connell, Floyd's sister-in-law, were arrested in Texas for taking a stolen car across state lines. Their bonds were the highest ever in the Eastern Federal District of Texas for such an offense.[51]

But where was Floyd?

Although he had faded from the headlines, he had been reported seen in almost every state in the Union. The arrest of Frank Delmar by state and federal officers on a highway near Claremore on August 11, 1934, left Floyd the only major outlaw still at large in Oklahoma.[52]

10

We Are Going to Kill
Him, If We Catch Him

Newspaper reports on Pretty Boy Floyd declined after the Kansas City Massacre, and the exploits of other notorious criminals, such as Dillinger and Bonnie and Clyde, captured the headlines. Among the stories floating about that summer of 1933 were that Floyd had dyed his hair red, that he was dead, that he had lost a leg, that he was in South America, and that he wanted to kill Sheriff Tom Bash. There was even a rumor that Floyd was a general in the Chinese army.[1]

The word was out that he was trying to sell his story to Hollywood. Lurid details of a plot to kidnap a movie star came from the West Coast. Guards were placed around the Malibu Colony after a Texas aviator told the Los Angeles FBI office that he had met Floyd and two other men in San Diego, and had agreed to join them as a pilot in a plot to kidnap an actress who was filming a feature movie. She was to be seized from her Malibu home at midnight on July 30 and flown to an isolated mountain region in Mexico; a quarter of a million dollars would be demanded as ransom from her movie producers. A trap was laid where the flyer said he was to meet Floyd and his gang near Malibu Beach—but the gangsters never appeared.[2] Floyd was also suspected in the attempted kidnapping of Oklahoma oil ty-coon Frank Phillips in September 1933.[3]

Some claimed that Alvin Karpis and Fred Barker, who were re-ported to have murdered Lazia, were being harbored by Floyd in the Ozarks.[4] Other stories had Floyd and Wilbur Underhill working to-gether. On August 7, 1933, the day that Underhill was married (under his own name) in Coalgate, Oklahoma, officers spotted him eating in a café, accompanied by Floyd, Bob Brady, and four other outlaws. Floyd rose, paid the bill, and left unmolested. Another time a lone of-ficer found Pretty Boy and his gang at a Kiowa, Oklahoma, hideout, but the group was long gone when reinforcements arrived.[5]

On June 24, 1934, in Branson, Missouri, sixty state and federal agents with machine guns raided an Ozarks ranch after a tip that Dillinger and Pretty Boy Floyd had been brought there by an ambu-lance the night of June 22, with one of them badly hurt. They found nothing. Floyd was also suspected of joining the Dillinger gang to rob a South Bend, Indiana, bank on June 30.[6]

Another unsuccessful raid to capture Floyd made headlines on Au-gust 13, 1934, at Tulsa.[7]

According to several accounts, which were believed by Dwight Brantley, special agent in charge (SAC) at Oklahoma City, after the Massacre, Floyd and Richetti first went to Cleveland, where they were denied help, and then to Akron, where they also were turned away by underworld contacts. The two men reportedly fled to the only place they felt secure—deep into the Cookson Hills, where they avoided friends, subsisting on field corn and sorghum, and sleeping in abandoned farmhouses.[8]

In mid-February 1934 Clyde Barrow and others were seen going into the Hills just after the Eastham prison break in Texas. It was common knowledge that Floyd disliked the Barrow gang. He did not want the hill people to give them aid or supplies; if they stayed around more than twenty-four hours, he wanted the people to get word to the Tahlequah sheriff. On February 17 a thousand-man "comb-out" of the Cookson Hills forced the Barrow gang and, it was thought, Floyd to flee. Only a few minor criminals were caught, but things got better for law officers when a road was built through the Cookson Hills soon after.[9] Floyd and Richetti were believed to have fled to Toledo, where they paid protection money to the Licavoli mob.[10]

Many rumors also existed about Adam Richetti. He and a man named Shine Rush were reported to have robbed the Whitesboro, Texas, bank in May 1934 and to have purchased a car with the loot.[11]

Sometimes people were hurt in the hysteria and confusion. At Prescott, Arkansas, on the night of November 3, 1933, two women in a car that fit the description given by a filling station operator of a car supposedly driven by Floyd were slightly injured by broken glass and taken to a hospital after the police fired on them. The women had tried to evade a blockade because they thought the officers were robbers.[12] One man from McAlester, Oklahoma, was questioned in three different cities as to whether he was Pretty Boy Floyd. At a café and at a barbershop large crowds gathered and stared at him, thinking he was the famous bandit.[13]

Headlines in 1934 incorrectly reported rewards for Floyd. For example, in May the *St. Louis Globe-Democrat* stated that there were rewards totaling ten thousand dollars for Floyd.[14] In June the *Muskogee Daily Phoenix* had the headline, "Want $50,000? Bring Them In." It noted that Dillinger and Baby Face Nelson had rewards of ten thousand dollars, and Alvin Karpis, Arthur Barker, Homer Van Meter, and Floyd had rewards of five thousand dollars. It continued:

Uncle Sam is letting everybody in on the ground floor of an opportunity to make a lot of money, more or less easily. All that is necessary to collect from $1000 to $50,000 under Uncle Sam's newest plan for relieving unemployment and poverty, is to nab or cause the capture of one of the sextet pictured above.[15]

After H. G. Cross of Waupun, Wisconsin, wired Dillinger's father an offer of ten thousand dollars for Dillinger's body, he received an unsigned letter postmarked Dallas, July 25, telling Cross to put an ad in the *Dallas Morning News* on August 1 if he was interested in the body of Public Enemy No. 1 of the Southwest (Floyd) for five thousand dollars.[16]

In an article entitled "Watch for These Mad Dogs!" in the September 15 issue of *Liberty*, Floyd was included, but Baby Face Nelson was listed as Public Enemy No. 1 and the Department of Justice's "most wanted man." This article led to the capture of Richard Galatas—as *Liberty* put it, "Another Mad Dog Captured."[17]

The November 3 issue of *Liberty* also mentioned Floyd:

John Dillinger is dead—shot down in the street in Chicago like the mad dog he was.

One of his rabid ex-associates, Homer Van Meter, has also been killed.

But three others, three as vicious, as murderous, as diabolically "lucky" in escaping capture as Dillinger himself was, are still at large. [Nelson, John Hamilton, and Floyd] . . .

They are being hunted—but who knows that at this moment some or all of them are not prowling, armed, through the streets of American cities? . . . Nobody is safe while these confederates of his and other killers of their stamp are running loose. . . . The public should join in the hunt. Everyone should take a hand in the effort to rid the country of mad dogs like these.

Therefore, *Liberty* is offering a reward of $1,000 . . . dead or alive.

. . . Pretty Boy Floyd is a Western bad man and ruthless killer. Floyd, when surrounded by cops, has actually made friends of small-town merchants and others—by flattery, by gallantry, by gifts of money. These friends have aided him to escape.

Like Dillinger himself, each of the three has repeatedly slipped through cordons of village, city, county, state, and federal police forces.

But they cannot elude all the people of the country!

If you happen to see one of them, communicate at once with the nearest policeman. . . .

Liberty is more than willing to pay $3,000 to rid the nation of three such mad dogs.

Study their pictures carefully. Read their records. Then keep your eyes open![18]

Actually, the thousand-dollar reward of the Oklahoma Bankers' Association had been withdrawn in July 1933, after Floyd's FBI identification order had been issued. The governor of Oklahoma's reward of a thousand dollars had been good for only six months. But the thousand-dollar reward from Ohio still was in effect.[19]

The FBI at first did not want any big amount offered for Floyd. In April 1934 the FBI reward for the gangster was only five hundred dollars. Two months later it had doubled for Floyd and was $250 for Richetti.[20]

Late on the night of December 3, 1933, Ruby, a male friend named Bob Carney, and a female cousin of Floyd's were injured in a car accident near Charleston, Arkansas, when the driver crashed into a bridge and was killed. They were taken to a hospital, where Carney, who had a broken leg, was thought to be an exact double for Floyd. He was arrested after he tried to leave the hospital before officers could arrive.

Ruby's former Fort Smith landlady, Mrs. Buell, was called to the hospital. She was surprised to find that "Mrs. Douglas" was actually "Mrs. Floyd," who started to cry when she saw Mrs. Buell.

"I quieted her," Mrs. Buell later said, "and told her that she meant as much to me as she ever did."

"You haven't done a thing," Mrs. Buell said. "Why should you cry?"

She asked Ruby, "Why doesn't your husband quit his way of living? I am sure he is a smart man. He easily could make an honest living."

"How can he quit? The whole world is against him now," Ruby answered.

Mrs. Buell also asked her, "Have I ever seen him?"

"You have seen him many times. He has bought groceries right in your store many times," Mrs. Floyd responded.

Mrs. Buell later said, "I understand, however, that he was an expert at disguise."[21]

Seminole County officers who were searching for Underhill got a tip that Floyd was in the area on "personal business" regarding his ex-wife's car accident.[22]

On March 1, 1934, the grocer in Floyd's Tulsa neighborhood got a judgment of $58.02 against the gangster and Ruby for groceries purchased but never paid for. He decided to keep the document as a souvenir.[23]

When Ruby and Jackie visited St. Louis in May 1934, Jackie told reporters he wanted to be a lawyer when he grew up. He added, "I don't like to hear the bad things people say about my daddy. I don't believe those things they say about him."

Ruby said she was certain Floyd had "led a straight life for the last two years. No matter what you hear my husband has done nothing wrong during that time."[24]

While in St. Louis, Ruby met "Professor" Glenn Condon, who was hoping to make money with a "Crime Does Not Pay" show that would go to the Chicago World's Fair; they agreed to a five-year contract. Condon, from Tulsa, had been a newsboy, reporter, city editor, legislator, evangelist, marine, press agent, soapbox orator, advertising director for an oil company, and the discoverer of Walter Winchell while he was the editor of *Vaudeville News*. He had been trying to distribute a film on a nudist colony, but he had been arrested by the St. Louis authorities.

Condon told the press the Floyd show was "a natural. . . . It's tremendous, that's what it is. A living sermon on lawlessness is what we intend making out of it." He said he would emphasize Floyd's murders as well as his many bank robberies. To him the wages of sin were death or at least the penitentiary.

To begin with, Condon gave Ruby an Indian costume and Jackie a cowboy suit. He wanted Ruby to be an Indian princess.

"What I wouldn't give to have the Pretty Boy himself in the show!" he said.

"The moral of our show will be that crime doesn't pay," declared the "professor." "We should clean up in Chicago."[25]

As part of the show, Ruby and Condon decided to have Jackie baptized at the First Baptist Church of Fort Worth by the charismatic minister J. Frank Norris on the night of Father's Day, June 17, 1934, and to have the event filmed.[26]

Dr. Norris, minister of the largest congregation in Texas, had been a force in religion and politics for many years. Although he had been charged with, and later acquitted of, murder, and had been accused of burning his church for the insurance, Norris railed against crime and vice. Nevertheless, many criminals and shady people joined his church. A sensationalist showman eager for publicity, Norris often attacked public officials on his radio show.[27]

It was common knowledge that Floyd wanted the baptism because he did not want his son to follow in his footsteps; he wanted him to go to church and school, and become a lawyer.

On Father's Day five thousand persons watched the ceremony, and movie cameras recorded the baptism while it was being broadcast on the radio. Ruby claimed Floyd had heard the broadcast.[28]

Hoping to exhibit the motion picture of Jackie being baptized in her show, Ruby arranged for O. V. Black, a Ponca City businessman, to become a guardian for Jackie.[29]

An ex-convict, E. Edison Beach, was the manager of Ruby's theatrical venture. He had allegorical pictorial charts printed to illustrate "Crime Does Not Pay" that were to be a warning and lesson to every father, mother, and youth. Ruby, Beach, and an Oklahoma film concern, Silverton and Condon, signed the contract. There was even a report that the contract had been signed by Charles Floyd.

The approximately four-minute-long film showed views of Pretty Boy with his son, Dr. Norris reading a letter from Ruby asking for the baptism, and the baptism itself. After the film Jackie told the audience he was nine years old and that he wanted to be a lawyer or a preacher. Mrs. Floyd then gave a two-minute speech that crime does not pay.

Beach wanted to film Floyd's surrender to Dr. Norris, his confession of faith, and his reception into the church. But the FBI would not allow it.[30]

On July 2, 1934, the show premiered in the Star Theater in Sallisaw, then traveled to several midwestern cities. But the venture was apparently a failure, and it did not make it to the World's Fair.[31]

The show was denounced in an editorial entitled "Making Crime Pay" in the *Kansas City Journal-Post:*

> The wife of "Pretty Boy" Floyd, notorious killer and bandit, is capitalizing on the criminal record of the outlaw on the stages of the Liberty and Regent theaters this week.
>
> This offense to decency and good morals is all the more pronounced because her 9-year-old son appears on the stage with her.
>
> The excuse for the exploitation of the criminal reputation of Floyd is contained in a few trite lines to the effect that "crime never pays," which are uttered by Mrs. Floyd.
>
> But, as pointed out in a subjoined article, Mrs. Floyd's appearance would indicate that she has made it pay.
>
> And Ed Dubinsky, operator of the theaters, is making it pay.

Perhaps after all it is upon him that censure should fall. He primarily is responsible for the disgraceful exhibition, which the law enforcement agencies ought to stop.[32]

On the following day the *Journal-Post* printed numerous public comments on the show by club women, ministers, and others. Mrs. J. Howard Hart, president of the Kansas City Council of Parent-Teachers Associations, said, "It is truly a great injustice to childhood and such a performance is demoralizing in its effect on adolescent youth." Dr. Joseph Myers of the Community Church said the show was "one of the thousand current illustrations of the mad greed for profits." He thought it was nothing more than

> . . . cheap and blatant sensationalism. Anybody interested in the development of decent values of the community should deplore such an exhibition.
>
> It is a decidedly bad reflection upon the community which allows such a thing to exist. When the exploitation of womanhood and childhood is based on crime, it is the most vicious exploitation which profit-mad humans can devise.

Nat Spencer, secretary of the Citizens' League of Kansas City, said, "Exploitation of crime and the criminal is unwholesome and detrimental to public morals."[33]

While performing in Kansas City, Ruby told newspaper reporters that Floyd would never let a woman put him "on the spot. He wouldn't make love to or become involved with anyone else, I know that."

She was asked if he was involved in the Kansas City Massacre. Ruby angrily replied, "I know he wasn't."

"How do you know?" reporters asked her.

"Never you mind: I know he was not in on that shooting."

"Do you think Floyd will ever give himself up or allow himself to be taken alive?"

"I wouldn't know," was her noncommittal reply.[34]

Exploitation of the Floyd legend spread. The Great Western Movie Company of Chicago produced sheet music for a song entitled "Pretty Boy Floyd—the Phantom Terror." It had a gory red cover, with a sketch of Floyd on an emaciated horse. The outlaw was shown gripping a pistol strapped to his right side. In the western background were sagebrush and cacti. The lyrics went as follows:

> Pretty Boy Floyd, God gave you a beautiful face.
> To think of it makes me sad.
> You might have been a man worthwhile.
> Instead of a lousy rat![35]

The hunt for Floyd and Richetti intensified after March 14, 1934, when a fingerprint found at Verne Miller's home was identified as belonging to Richetti. But the FBI at this time was concentrating most of its energy on the search for Dillinger.[36]

FBI and other law enforcement officials believed, correctly, that the two gangsters and their molls, Juanita and Rose, were traveling together.[37]

The FBI director himself felt there was no reliable information that Floyd had been wounded or that he had been seen since the Kansas City Massacre, and he wrongly believed the gangster "has been in and around Oklahoma, Arkansas, and Texas. . . . There seems to be but little doubt that he is in one of the three states mentioned."[38] But E. E. Conroy, SAC of Kansas City, thought there was no recent information that Floyd or Richetti was in the region.[39]

Until February 8, 1934, when a warrant issued secretly at Kansas City, charging Floyd with conspiracy to assist in the escape of a federal prisoner and obstructing justice (which carried a two-year sentence), the only federal process was an FBI identification order issued on June 22, 1933, for questioning in the Kansas City Massacre.[40] On July 3, 1934, the FBI secretly filed a complaint before the U.S. commissioner at Kansas City, charging Floyd and Richetti under the National Motor Vehicle Theft Act for having stolen a car near Deepwater, Missouri, and driven it to Kansas City, Kansas, at the time of the Killingsworth kidnapping in June 1933. A warrant was issued.[41]

On June 6, 1934, SAC Brantley of Oklahoma City said Adam Richetti would be captured soon.[42] There was no identification order or publicity on him until shortly before his indictment in the Kansas City Massacre on October 22, on the theory it would be easier to catch him if it was not known he was being sought actively.[43]

A boyfriend of Richetti's sister Eva was paroled from Leavenworth Prison early at the request of the FBI, and was used as an informer.[44]

By June 1934, SAC Dwight Brantley had assigned two agents, one of them Frank Smith, to the Floyd case exclusively, but found he could not follow up on all the rumors. According to one FBI report, "Mr. Brantley stated that there are numerous rumors received by his office as to the whereabouts of Floyd. Sometimes they place him in three different localities at once."[45]

Hoover wrote, "I do not believe that mail covers alone will produce the desired results and, therefore, suggest that agents become acquainted with all relatives of both subjects in your district so that they can be personally observed at frequent intervals."[46] In particular, Hoover thought such expedients as a telephone tap and mail cover on Floyd's mother should be tried.[47] But since the homes of Floyd's and Richetti's relatives were in isolated rural communities, surveillance could not be maintained.[48] The FBI bugged a St. Louis hotel room when Ruby, her son, and a cousin were there in May, but nothing of value was discovered.[49]

FBI Agent Frank Smith, with his headquarters at Muskogee, developed a number of informants, two of whom were in almost daily contact with members of the Floyd family. The informants, a gambler and his woman, were living in the same house as the Floyd family, which included Floyd's mother, her daughter Mary and her children, and E. W. Floyd and his wife.[50]

There were numerous reports that Floyd sent emissaries with offers of surrender if his life would be spared, but Governor Murray turned them down. The Oklahoma governor himself spread some false rumors. On October 17, 1933, he announced that Floyd had been wounded in a gunfight with state officers:

> He is wounded all right. I know that much. He was shot several weeks ago near Coalgate. He was shot through the right leg and right shoulder. They shot him in the wrong side. If they had shot him on the other side, it would have been near the heart.
>
> The officers searched a house he had been in. The people admitted he had been there. They could smell the medicine.

A man was in here recently. He offered to turn "Pretty Boy" in if I would agree that he wouldn't have to pay the death penalty.

I told him I wouldn't do it. He said that "Pretty Boy" would give himself up.

I couldn't make a deal like that. The only way it could be done would be by clemency if he were given a death penalty in court. If he took life imprisonment, it would be with the idea of getting out. We'll get him.

The governor scoffed at reports that Floyd was hiding out on the west coast. Instead, he was certain he was in the southeastern Oklahoma hill country. O. P. Ray, assistant superintendent of the State Police, refused to comment on the governor's statement that Floyd had been shot by state officers. Local officers knew nothing about it.[51]

During May and June 1934, Hoover gave serious consideration to two surrender negotiations. Ruby's theatrical manager, E. Edison Beach, along with his father-in-law, A. K. Comstock, a lawyer from Pawhuska, Oklahoma, and Floyd's family were involved in the first negotiations. On May 16, Comstock discussed the surrender offer with the FBI. Although Comstock had wanted a reward of seven thousand dollars Hoover was willing to offer him only five hundred dollars.[52]

Ruby wrote to Dr. Norris, who thought Floyd was in poor medical condition, asking him to arrange a surrender.[53]

The FBI agreed to only two conditions: if Floyd surrendered, he would not be killed; and Floyd would be taken to Fort Leavenworth, where he would get medical attention. It would not guarantee that there would not be a death sentence.[54]

There was some public sentiment for sparing Floyd's life if he surrendered. For example, on May 7, Isaac D. Dalton of Collinsville, Illinois, wrote to Attorney General Homer S. Cummings:

Dear Attorney General:
    Could you or our Grand President, Franklin D. Roosevelt, find it in your heart to send out a statement to Charles [Pretty Boy Floyd] that you would save him from the death penalty if he [Floyd] will surrender, plead guilty and take a life sentence.
    He is nothing to me, just a bad criminal but the statement of

his wife in the *St. Louis Globe Democrat* about their boy is really pathetic. Then I think that act would have an incentive that would cause other desperadoes to take their eyes off the mountain that they are fleeing to and cause them to reflect and change their course.[55]

Jackie's guardian, O. V. Black, suggested that Floyd might surrender upon the condition that any reward money would be for the boy's education. But Hoover wrote, ". . . we cannot be put in the position of paying a man to surrender."[56]

SAC Blake of the Dallas FBI office, who thought Floyd was hiding not far from Dallas on June 23, 1934, told Dr. Norris he had forty-eight hours to produce. If he did not, the negotiations would be broken off on June 27.[57]

Hoover was impatient. In late June he "wanted to discontinue the foolishness of trying to get Floyd to surrender, and . . . I desire steps be taken to really effect his apprehension." He thought Floyd "has been giving us the 'run-around' in the fake offers of surrender."[58]

SAC Brantley wired to Hoover, "If Floyd surrendered, won't be killed, but does not surrender would be killed on sight," on May 18 and June 23.[59]

Also in late June, Hoover, "getting weary of the 'fishing' that the Floyd crowd was doing," agreed, and in effect ordered the summary execution of Floyd. For example, on June 28 he told Brantley by phone

to inform Comstock that the Division has just about concluded its negotations [*sic*] of this kind and that Floyd could be informed that . . . orders are now for a concentrated drive on Floyd and that we are going to kill him if we catch him; that we are tired of this negotiating and if he wants to come in and surrender he had better do it immediately or he will be killed.

The FBI director also wrote:

. . . it would be very important for Floyd to surrender, because if he does not, he will surely be killed. . . . orders are out to kill Floyd on sight, and if he doesn't surrender in short time, he will no doubt be killed by our men; in other words, . . . we are closely on his trail, and if we once catch up with him, we won't take any chance of his surrendering.[60]

To be fair to Hoover, he did on one occasion in late June moderate his tone when he stated to the SAC of Dallas, ". . . of course we desired to take Floyd alive in order to gain information relative to the Kansas City Massacre."[61]

Other FBI officials also were ruthless, such as E. A. Tamm, who wrote to the director on July 28, "I also told Mr. Soucy [of the New York FBI office] to take no chances but if he could knock off Floyd, it would be a fine thing."[62]

The FBI director reorganized the Bureau for an all-out hunt for Floyd. He ordered SAC Brantley to "spend any money necessary" on June 6.[63]

On June 23, Hoover assigned the Floyd case to Assistant FBI Director Harold Nathan for his exclusive attention, and sent him to Oklahoma City. Nathan had a feeling Floyd was in the narcotics racket, but he had little to base it on.[64] He told the press, "Let the government worry about Floyd. He's like a fumbled football, some day we'll drop on him."[65]

On June 28, SAC Blake and SAC Brantley were ordered to concentrate on capturing Floyd "and let everything else be sidetracked."[66]

Dillinger was killed by the FBI on July 22, 1934. On the following day Hoover announced to the press that Baby Face Nelson was the man now most wanted by the Justice Department. (Baby Face finally had the no. 1 status he craved.)

"We're going to get that fellow. Now that Dillinger is gone we're going to concentrate on all members of his mob that are still left and on 'Baby Face' in particular. Nobody can kill one of our men and get away with it."[67]

A reward of five thousand dollars was offered for Nelson's capture and twenty-five hundred dollars for information leading to his capture. Hoover also mentioned John Hamilton, Homer Van Meter, and Richard Galatas, as well as Floyd. The headline of the *Tulsa Daily World* of July 24 was "'Pretty Boy' Floyd Is Included on U.S. List for Death."[68]

Who should inherit Dillinger's title of Public Enemy No. 1 was hotly debated. The term was not official, being a newspaper creation. Oklahoma authorities of course thought of Floyd as the ace of desperadoes, but others believed Baby Face Nelson deserved the dubious honor.[69]

It was considered likely that federal rewards would be offered for Hamilton, Van Meter, and Floyd. But Nelson at this time was definitely the prime target of the FBI.[70]

Hoover became increasingly frustrated with the Floyd case. On August 18 he wrote, "Our men should stop the watchful waiting policy & do some aggressive work toward getting him."[71]

Two days later he wrote:

I am disgusted at the attitude of lethargy which is being assumed in this case, it appearing to be the idea of the various special agents in charge that all that it is necessary for them [to do] is to wait for something to happen in some other district which will develop leads in their district. . . . I desire that appropriate contacts be made to assure . . . reliable information concerning Floyd's whereabouts . . . that mail covers, telegraphic covers and telephone taps . . . be utilized."[72]

E. A. Tamm reported on August 25, "The Director is virtually disgusted with the fact that we have been looking for that fellow for months and months and we do not know whether he is in Alaska or Florida." However, by this time FBI officials believed Floyd and Richetti were not in Oklahoma.[73]

By September, Hoover decided to make Floyd the nation's most wanted hoodlum—Public Enemy No. 1—and thousands of wanted posters were distributed throughout the nation.

S. P. Cowley was put in charge of the major FBI cases—the Dillinger case, the Bremer kidnapping case, and the Kansas City Massacre case, on September 6.[74]

"I have a feeling that the pursuit of Floyd, in the Oklahoma, Arkansas, and Kansas City districts has been rather lackadaisical," Hoover wrote on October 1.[75]

One FBI report said, "the Director is very anxious to get this fellow as quickly as possible."[76]

The Floyd family, ca. 1918. Seated left to right: Emma, Mamie, Mary, Walter. Standing: Charles, E. W., Ruby, Bradley, Ruth. Reprinted with permission from *The History of Sequoyah County, 1828–1975* (Sallisaw, Okla.: Sequoyah County Historical Society, 1976).

This police photo of Charles Floyd was taken May 6, 1929, in Kansas City, Kansas. Courtesy of AP/Wide World Photos.

Charles Floyd, his son Jackie, and his ex-wife Ruby, at Fort Smith, Arkansas, in 1931. Courtesy of Bettmann Archive.

Ex-wife Ruby, Charles Floyd, and Bessie Mayberry (Ruby's aunt) at Tulsa, Oklahoma, in 1932. Courtesy of the FBI.

Charles Floyd *(left)* and Jess Ring *(right)* in rural Muskogee County, Oklahoma, in early 1933. Courtesy of the FBI.

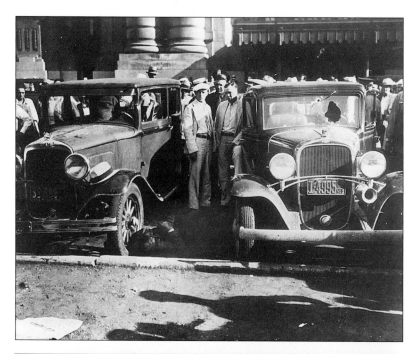

Scene at Union Station following the Kansas City Massacre, June 17, 1933.
Courtesy of the FBI.

DEPARTMENT OF JUSTICE
WASHINGTON, D. C.

23 L 1 U 000 19
L 1 U 000

WANTED

CHARLES ARTHUR FLOYD, aliases
FRANK MITCHELL, "PRETTY BOY SMITH"

DESCRIPTION

Age, 26 years
Height, 5 feet, 8½ inches
Weight, 155 pounds
Hair, dark
Eyes, gray
Complexion, medium
Nationality, American
Scars and marks, 1 Vac. cic.
(tattoo Nurse in Rose)

CRIMINAL RECORD

As Charles Arthur Floyd, No. 22318, arrested police department, St. Louis, Missouri, September 16, 1925; charge, highway robbery.
As Charles Floyd, No. 29078, received S.P., Jefferson City, Missouri, December 18, 1925, from St. Louis; crime, robbery, first degree; sentence, 5 years.
As Charles A. Floyd, No. 16950, arrested police department,
Kansas City, Missouri, March 9, 1929; charge, investigation.
As Charles Floyd, No. 3999, arrested police department, Kansas City, Kansas, May 6, 1929; charge, vagrancy and suspicion - highway robbery; released May 7, 1929.
As Charles Floyd, No. 887, arrested police department, Pueblo, Colorado, May 9, 1929; charge, vagrancy; fined $50 and sentenced to serve 60 days in jail.
As Frank Mitchell, No. 19983, arrested police department, Akron, Ohio, March 8, 1930; charge, investigation.
As Charles Arthur Floyd, No. 21458, arrested police department, Toledo, Ohio, May 20, 1930; charge, suspicion.
As Charles Arthur Floyd, sentenced November 24, 1930, to serve from 12 to 15 years in Ohio State Penitentiary (bank robbery, Sylvania, Ohio); escaped enroute to penitentiary.

Charles Arthur Floyd is wanted in connection with the murder of Otto Reed, Chief of Police of McAlester, Oklahoma, William J. Groome and Frank E. Hermanson, police officers of Kansas City, Missouri, Raymond J. Caffrey, Special Agent of the United States Bureau of Investigation, and their prisoner, Frank Nash, at Kansas City, Missouri, on June 17, 1933.

Law enforcement agencies kindly transmit any additional information or criminal record to nearest office, United States Bureau of Investigation.

If apprehended, please notify Special Agent in Charge, United States Bureau of Investigation, 905 Federal Reserve Bank Building, Kansas City, Missouri, and the Director, United States Bureau of Investigation, Department of Justice, Washington, D. C.

An FBI "Wanted" poster was issued on June 22, 1933. Courtesy of the National Archives.

Melvin Purvis and J. Edgar Hoover in 1934. Courtesy of the National Archives.

Rose Baird *(left)*, companion of Adam Richetti, and Beulah Baird *(right)*, companion of Charles Floyd. Courtesy of the FBI.

Adam Richetti *(left)* and Wellsville (Ohio) Police chief John Fultz *(right)* following Richetti's capture. Courtesy of the East Liverpool Historical Society.

A posse was organized at Wellsville, Ohio, on October 21, 1934, to round up Pretty Boy Floyd. Top photo courtesy of AP/Wide World Photos; bottom photo courtesy of the Wellsville Historical Society.

Ellen Conkle poses in her kitchen with the utensils and dishes used in Charles Floyd's final meal. Courtesy of the East Liverpool Historical Society.

Curious onlooks file past the body of Pretty Boy Floyd at the East Liverpool, Ohio, Sturgis Funeral Home on October 22, 1934. Courtesy of the FBI.

Chester Smith, the police officer who claimed that he brought down Charles Floyd, takes Pretty Boy's fingerprints at East Liverpool, Ohio, on October 22, 1934. Courtesy of the FBI.

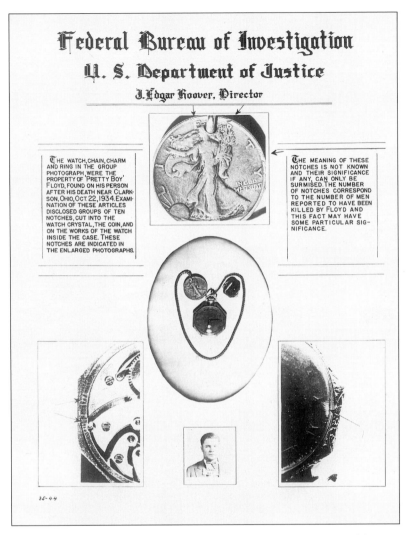

After Floyd's death the FBI found ten notches on his watch. Courtesy of the FBI.

The FBI marches on. Courtesy of *The Plain Dealer*.

On October 5, Hoover increased the reward for Floyd to three thousand dollars and the reward for Richetti to two thousand dollars, but these were not to be publicly advertised or authorized. Finally, Hoover planned to place several undercover agents in Oklahoma and Arkansas that day, although he had rejected the suggestion that an undercover agent be placed at Sallisaw two months before.[77]

The arrest of a few minor criminals by the FBI gave the impression something was being done; Dick Galatas in New Orleans on September 22, Kansas City gangster Dominio Binaggio in St. Louis on October 4, and Shine Rush, a pal of Floyd and Richetti, in Oklahoma on October 12.[78]

On October 10, 1934, the FBI announced that the Kansas City Massacre case was solved. The guilty parties were Floyd, Miller, and Richetti, and the federal government planned to begin a grand jury investigation of the multiple killings on October 22 at Kansas City.[79]

Newspaper headlines incorrectly reported that Floyd had been flushed from an Iowa farm by two peace officers on October 11. In fact, it was three minor thieves who jumped into a car and led the police on a wild chase to an empty house on a dead-end road. They turned around, attacked the police with a machine gun and automatic rifles, and successfully shot their way out.

A general alarm from Kansas City was broadcast at once. Highway junctions and bridges were barricaded and guarded. All major roads in the region were patrolled by officers. A National Guard plane from St. Louis with a two-way radio and a machine gun hunted the trio. The fugitives were reported to be in Minnesota, Iowa, and Missouri.[80]

Near Mexico, Missouri, a salesman was forced at gunpoint to push a stalled car, and he identified Floyd as the driver. Twenty-five officers beat their way through a cornfield in a hunt for the gangsters a few miles south, but found nothing. A woman near Moberly, Missouri, reported that three men had asked her for soap and water. They told her one of them had cut his finger and asked her if she had any guns that would take .32 or .38 caliber cartridges, then left. An hour later a garage owner said a man gave him five hundred-dollar bills for a new car, but fled in his old car when he started to look at the bills suspiciously. The police believed Floyd was determined to make his way to the safety of his favorite haven, the Cookson Hills.[81]

Tulsa filed another charge against Floyd—parking overtime in the business section in 1931![82]

Floyd's mother was questioned by the press on October 12. Bitterly she said:

> I know Charles couldn't do all they've accused him of. We hear all kinds of reports—Charles is in a holdup in one state one day and in another state the next—or two or three states away. He couldn't be everywhere at once. I get so mad at what they say about him I could fight. But I don't believe what they say any more.

She also said her elusive son was "ready to settle down if they'd give him half a chance. I don't believe Charles is dead. I know they say he is and I haven't heard from him in a long time. The officers claimed they wounded him in a gun battle at Stonewall. I don't believe he was even there."

She recalled that at his father's funeral in 1929, "Charles wasn't in trouble then. The law kept after him and he couldn't stop."[83] Mrs. Floyd kept her porch light on because she believed her son was coming home.[84]

To reporters the embittered FBI Agent Frank Smith said, "I don't even know there is a Charlie Floyd." He complained that his own life "isn't worth a nickel" so long as he was tracking down the phantom bandit. He also said, "As sure as his name is Charlie Floyd," the gangster's demise was inevitable.[85]

The press was confident that the efficient FBI would get the outlaw soon. An editorial in the *El Paso Morning Times* entitled, "It Won't Be Long Now," predicted Floyd's demise:

> For 18 months hardly a word had appeared concerning the robber and murderer, "Pretty Boy" Floyd. . . . But the other day the United States Department of Justice nominated Floyd as "Public Enemy No. 1.". . . Now that the title has been fastened upon Floyd . . . we may be sure that a small army of federal agents will trail him until they get him.

Already they have disposed of the myth of his death or flight from the country. They found his hiding place on a farm in northern Iowa. He escaped in a hail of bullets, and may have found cover again. But the federal officers will stay after him until they get him.

Under the direction of Attorney General Cummings and J. Edgar Hoover, head of the Enforcement Division of the Department of Justice, more real progress is being made in running down criminals than at any previous time in this generation. This department is becoming one of the most efficient branches of our government.[86]

FBI investigations showed that the hunt for Floyd and Richetti in the Midwest was a wild goose chase, but Bureau officials still were optimistic that they would be caught soon, although lawmen had no idea where the outlaws were.[87]

On the Lam

After the Kansas City Massacre, Floyd and Richetti were pariahs to most of the underworld. It was simply too dangerous to help the notorious gangsters, and their former hideouts were now closed to them.

But after fleeing to St. Louis and then to Cleveland in June 1933, they were able to persuade a member of the Lepke gang, the wily and cunning Moe Davis, a dapper Jewish gangster in his early thirties, to arrange hideouts for them—after they agreed to pay generously for the protection.

Davis, a well-known fence, was connected with the Club Mayfair, a Cleveland nightclub owned and operated by Harry Proper. He also operated a bookie joint in downtown Cleveland and was the "big boss" of the Arrowhead Inn near Cincinnati. He had never been arrested, although he had been suspected, but cleared, of the murder of a man near Cleveland in 1930. Since Prohibition, Davis had engaged in smuggling, gambling, and narcotics. By 1930 he was a "big-shot" bootlegger in Cleveland and had many connections outside that city, especially in Detroit, Chicago, and New York.[1]

Floyd and Richetti asked Moe to contact Verne Miller for them. It is not certain that they were paid for the Massacre, but the gangster James

LaCapra said that during the summer of 1933, Floyd "proceeded east [from Cleveland] where he picked up some money with Verne Miller."[2]

About two weeks after the Massacre, the Buick used by Floyd and Richetti in escaping from Kansas City was found burned near Cleveland with the charred body of a man in it. Moe Davis was a suspect in the murder.[3] The cautious Floyd isolated himself from friends and acquaintances, and stopped sending money to Ruby and Jackie.

In mid-September, Floyd and Richetti decided their hiding places in Cleveland and Detroit, known underworld centers, were unsafe. They met Juanita and Rose in Toledo and fled to a quiet middle-class neighborhood in Buffalo, a city not known for its criminal activity. There they hoped they could hide safely and avoid any payoffs to the mob.[4]

Floyd made one final defiant gesture before going into deep hiding by sending a crudely typed thank-you note from Canfield, Ohio, to J. R. Scott, a staff artist at an Ohio newspaper who had compared Floyd's exploits to those of Jesse James:

> Thanks for the compliments and the pictures of me in your paper.
> I'll be gone when you get this.
> Jesse James was no punk himself.
> I'm not as bad as they say I am.
> They just wouldn't leave me alone after I got out.
> Yorus [sic] truly
> Chas. A. Floyd[5]

Floyd and Juanita used the alias of Mr. and Mrs. George Sanders, and Richetti and Rose called themselves Mr. and Mrs. Edward Brennan. They moved to number 821 at the Amiantus Apartments, a furnished second-floor, five-room apartment with a bath, located at 8 18th Street. They stayed there from September 21, 1933, to October 18, 1934. The owner of the Amiantus Apartments didn't ask for references, and the rent of forty-five dollars a month was always paid in cash and on time.[6]

The chief of police of Nunda, New York, thought he saw Pretty Boy Floyd and Juanita at a Rochester, New York, restaurant on October 13, 1933.

Four days later, an FBI agent went to the largest city in the region,

Buffalo, on the hunch they might be hiding there and conferred with city police officials. Several photos of Floyd and Juanita were given to detectives, with instructions to make an exhaustive inquiry to see if they had come to the city or were in hiding there. No trace was found, but Buffalo police promised they would continue to watch for them.[7]

During the time the fugitives were in Buffalo, they led a circumspect existence, staying in the apartment practically all the time. There were never any disturbances, loud talking, or arguments.

They had many of their meals brought in. Only once did they eat out. There was no heavy drinking, no nightclubbing, no moviegoing. They managed without a telephone or a car and were never seen hailing a taxi.[8]

They played cards, kept the radio on much of the time, and they subscribed to the local newspaper.

The women also subscribed to *Photoplay*, *Woman's Home Companion*, *True Romances*, and *True Story*; the men subscribed to *American Detective* and *Master Detective*. Once Floyd said while reading a detective magazine, "My God! A lot of guys sure get bum raps in the world."[9]

When the fugitives read about Verne Miller's murder in November 1933, Richetti sneered, "Crazy fool should have stayed hid."[10]

Whenever anyone came to the apartment, such as the janitors, Floyd and Richetti retreated to another room. One of the young women usually answered the door. Occasionally one of the men paid the paper boy.

No mail came from friends or relatives, nor did they correspond with anyone. The letters that came were mostly the result of the women's responses to ads.

Juanita and Rose, who claimed later that the men never talked of their activities, such as the Kansas City Massacre, knew better than to ask any questions.

The women made infrequent, hurried trips to the beauty shop and the grocery store. All of them went walking at night, but usually the couples left at different times.

Richetti, who was known to Juanita and Rose only as "Eddie," talked very little, spending his time reading or sitting alone. "Eddie" never mentioned his jobs, and he usually sat with his head down, saying nothing. He sometimes lay on his bed, moaning.[11]

Floyd, more pleasant and talkative, paced about the apartment for hours, walking back and forth like a caged animal. He put on weight, and he eventually wore a path through the carpet. Through the glazed glass door the apartment's engineer saw a figure who walked back and forth continuously, and seldom left the apartment. He thought something was "wrong" with the man and the other occupants.[12]

As far as was known, none of the occupants worked. The neighbors were told by the women that the men were "bookies." Juanita also said her husband had been a truck driver.

The two couples were friendly with the neighborhood children and often threw money to them from the window, telling them to buy candy. Parents thought it was perhaps unwise to let their children visit them, but no one notified the police.[13]

During the summer of 1934, the sisters became friends with an Italian family named Lettieri, who lived in a house behind the apartment building. They went there for beauty treatments from Lucy and occasionally visited with her husband, Victor, who could not speak much English, and their baby. Rose and Juanita suggested that the Lettieris call on them, as their husbands would like to see the baby. On one occasion they were invited to the apartment for dinner, and afterward they played cards.[14]

The group also became friends with Joe Sanfratello, the owner of a butcher shop. Many times his son Mike delivered meat to their apartment and saw them there. On a couple of occasions he was invited to have a drink with them.

In July 1934, Mike saw all of them outside of the Fifty-Fifty Grille when it opened. The two gangsters were rather hesitant about going into the restaurant, and one of the women refused to enter. After Mike came along and suggested they accompany him inside, they all entered and Mike procured a table. But when they were joined by another couple, they became very nervous and stayed only a short time. This was the only time they all went out together.[15]

Two associates of Floyd's sought him out in Buffalo and gave him $250 a month. When he got this money, the group would have a friendly poker game, which Floyd usually won.[16]

A local hood, Chuck Connors, was suspected of knowing Floyd and Richetti, because a car that fit the description of his Packard sedan was seen occasionally at the apartment house. Outside racketeers were known to look up Connors when they came to Buffalo.[17]

C. L. Henderson, a customs officer who lived directly over their apartment, and William F. Coughlin, resident of the penthouse in the apartment building, both saw a Packard sedan calling for Floyd and Richetti late at night every few weeks. The two gangsters would leave, then return several hours later.

Henderson considered them suspicious characters and told a fellow customs officer, as well as the owner of the apartments, but no one alerted the police.[18]

Once Coughlin saw Floyd with a tall, athletic man in the apartment hall. But he did not recognize Connors's photo when it was shown to him by the FBI. Coughlin's ten-year-old daughter, Flora, often visited the apartment and frequently saw Floyd and Richetti.[19]

The two men went on a few trips together. They would leave at night and be gone from one day to three weeks. Juanita and Rose later claimed that they did not know where they were going, nor did they know of any crimes committed during their Buffalo stay.[20]

In May 1934, Floyd and Richetti traveled to Floyd's hometown, and on Mother's Day, May 13, Floyd visited his mother at a farm near Akins, slipping in before dawn and spending three hours there. The gangster told his mother he knew he was doomed. He would surrender and accept life if there were no death sentence and he would not be shot to death.

The *Tulsa Daily World* of May 15, 1934, reported the visit and surmised he was hiding out in eastern Oklahoma and in the Arkansas hill country. There were many sightings of the two gangsters at this time and place. For example, a man in a secondhand clothing store in Sallisaw saw Floyd and Richetti in his store, and recognized them from photos. The Floyd family later told the FBI that Floyd had visited his relatives in May, and his brother Bradley told the press of the visit after Floyd's death.[21]

The family also told the FBI that Floyd had seen Bonnie and Clyde, whom he disliked because he thought they were too trigger-happy, during his visit. Barrow told Floyd that the recent killing of a patrolman was a mistake and was done by Bonnie. Bradley Floyd also said Bonnie, Clyde, and Henry Methvin stayed two or three days at his place. They asked for Charles for a big job and partied while there.[22]

Methvin, who offered to turn in Floyd, confirmed this and told the

FBI that Bonnie and Clyde had seen Floyd about three weeks before their deaths.

Later, however, Methvin changed his story, and said that about a month before Bonnie and Clyde were killed, Barrow's mother received a letter from Floyd making arrangements for the meeting about five miles from Earlsboro. He claimed they had expected to make contact through Bradley, but they never saw Floyd.[23]

A few months before Floyd's death, Floyd and Richetti saw Alvin Karpis in the parking lot of the Harvard Club near Cleveland. They drove up in a new Ford coupe and sent somebody to get Karpis to come out to them, because they felt it would be safer that way. Karpis "wasn't too happy about them knowing where I was," but the two gangsters wanted to pull a job with him. Karpis had enough troubles of his own, however, and would not join them. Floyd and Richetti told Karpis that if he changed his mind, to get in touch with a contact in Canton, Ohio.[24]

In June 1934, underworld rumors of a Floyd-Dillinger merger were common. On June 30, five men robbed the Merchants National Bank at South Bend, Indiana. Dillinger, Baby Face Nelson, and Homer Van Meter were easy to identify. Floyd was identified by Perry Stahly, bank director, and Delos Coen, the cashier. But no one had any idea who the fifth "fat man" was.[25] Several authorities do not believe that the Dillinger gang robbed the South Bend bank.[26] However, according to Joseph Raymond "Fatso" Negri, an associate of Baby Face Nelson, it was indeed the Dillinger gang at South Bend.

Negri also thought Pretty Boy Floyd was one of the robbers. On the night of the robbery, the gangsters argued about getting a doctor for the wounded Van Meter. Although "Fatso" never saw the face of the stranger, from the conversation he suspected that it was Floyd. Dillinger and another gangster referred to "a good friend of Richetti." Later Nelson implied he had met Floyd.[27]

Van Meter had told Dillinger they should get at least a hundred thousand dollars from the bank. Nelson got a wheelman and a torpedo. The morning of the robbery, Saturday, June 30, was a beautiful day, warm and clear. By 11:30 A.M. the downtown section was crowded. At the Merchants National Bank twenty-five customers waited in line. Across from the bank, the State Theater was showing

Stolen Sweets with Sally Blane and Charles Starrett. A twenty-nine-year-old policeman, Howard Wagner, was directing traffic at the intersection where the bank was located.

Seventy-nine hundred dollars had been deposited in the bank from the post office. Two city detectives, Edward McCormick and his partner, had trailed the assistant postmaster taking the money to the bank because of a tip the post office was to be robbed. The two detectives were now eating pork chop sandwiches in a nearby restaurant.

A brown Hudson double-parked next to the bank and four men got out. In the automobile beside the getaway car a young man named Alex Slaby saw that the men had guns and realized they must be going to rob the bank.

Dillinger pointed a gun at Slaby, telling him quietly, "You'd better scram." Slaby left his car and headed for the bandits' car. Its motor was running and the car radio was playing a popular song. As he started to reach for the ignition keys, Baby Face Nelson, who was watching the car, yelled at him, "What're you doing?"

Slaby answered, "Nothing." He walked away, planning to call the police, and Nelson, who had trouble concealing his machine gun under his coat, did not try to stop him.

Van Meter stood guard with a .351 rifle next to the front of the bank. His outfit of straw hat and overalls caused some passersby to think he was just a clown, even with his rifle.

Floyd and Dillinger were joined by an unknown fat man who had come to South Bend in another car. When the trio stepped through the bank's front doors, Dillinger yelled, "This is a holdup."

As the terrified customers crowded together at the far end of the bank, Dillinger and the fat man gathered up the loot from the cages.

Without warning, the smiling Floyd fired his machine gun at the ceiling. The crowd panicked and rushed to the directors' room. Still smiling, Floyd looked directly at Delos Coen, the cashier, who was standing at his desk next to a director of the bank, Perry Stahly. They both thought the man staring at them was without doubt Pretty Boy Floyd.

Outside, most people did not pay much attention to the gunfire, thinking it might have something to do with the Fourth of July. But Patrolman Wagner took it seriously and crossed the trolley tracks toward the bank. Rifle fire from Van Meter cut him down and he fell, mortally wounded. He died shortly after he got to the hospital.

Meanwhile, Baby Face Nelson was having a bad time. He began firing his machine gun indiscriminately after a jeweler, Harry Berg, came out of his shop and fired at him with his revolver; Nelson's bulletproof vest saved his life. Berg was able to run back to his shop unharmed, but one man suffered leg and stomach wounds and another was hurt by shattered glass from the windshield of the car he was driving. Berg would keep his shop open in spite of a broken plate-glass window. He later placed a sign on his shop, "Not hurt. Open for business." A high school student, Joseph Pawlowski, ran up to the bank after he heard the shooting. He saw Nelson firing wildly, thought someone had to stop him, and leaped on the gangster's back. Nelson fought fiercely and finally flung the boy through a plate-glass window and fired at him from only ten feet away. When a bullet passed through the palm of his right hand and penetrated the window behind him, Pawlowski passed out.

After word about the robbery reached the local police, four officers headed for the bank. Machine-gun fire from Nelson passed over the heads of Patrolman Sylvester Zell and another officer, striking the State Theater's canopy. A man shouted, "Look out, Zell. It's a holdup!" Cautiously they continued to head for the bank.

Detective McCormick and his partner left the restaurant after hearing about the robbery over the restaurant's radio. But the traffic was terrible, so McCormick decided to go on foot and took along a shotgun.

He saw Dillinger, Floyd, and the fat man come out with three hostages—Coen, Stahly, and a man named Bruce Bouchard—but could not use the shotgun because he might hit an innocent person. He thought with disgust that if he had had a rifle, he could have hit all of the gangsters.

In fact, other lawmen accidentally hit Coen in the left leg, Bouchard in both legs, and Stahly in his side. Floyd kept punching Stahly with a gun and cursed him out as he ordered, "Keep going." It was a wild scene; the gangsters were scrambling to get into their car as they exchanged shots with the officers.

Detective McCormick told someone in his way, "Get the hell out of there!"

"To hell with you too!"

McCormick fired his shotgun and the bystander screamed, "Oh, my God," and fled into a clothing store.

Floyd jabbed Stahly in the back with his gun and took his arm when they got to the getaway car. "You're going with us," the gangster insisted. But Stahly jerked out of his grip and told Floyd, "You've got your money. Make your getaway."

"Come on, get in here!" yelled the fat driver of the getaway car, as Floyd spun around and fired at Stahly's head, close to his left ear.

Van Meter was helped along by Dillinger after he took a bullet in the right side of his head. The bullet-riddled Hudson nearly was in a collision but was soon far ahead of the pursuing police cars.

Instead of the hoped-for twenty thousand dollars, the take was only a disappointing forty-eight hundred dollars for each of the bandits.

A policeman had been killed, and six citizens and a gangster had been wounded.[28]

On July 22, 1934, Dillinger was killed by FBI agents in Chicago. Floyd was upset that Hoover had told the nation afterward that Pretty Boy was one of the remaining major public enemies the FBI was determined to get.[29]

About thirty days before his death, Floyd left the Buffalo apartment with Richetti and remained away a short while. When they came back, they had more money than they had previously.[30] The manager of the South Side office of the Toledo Trust Company thought Floyd might have been one of the participants in an attempted holdup on September 18, 1934, and he requested a picture of Richetti from the FBI.[31]

The two couples grew increasingly bored and restless. When Floyd and Richetti saw their pictures and read about their indictment at Kansas City on October 11, they made no comment but looked grim.

Until this time the women did not know Richetti's real name. Rose asked Floyd about this and he said, "Ask no questions."[32]

Rose and Juanita were pleased when the "boys" told them they were going home to the Oklahoma hills, and asked Floyd if they were going to see their mother. He replied with his usual "Ask no questions."

Floyd planned to get saddle horses and use them to visit friends and relatives and later retire to Mexico, where his gangster associates would join him. The sisters had a cover story that they were going to Chicago to visit the World's Fair.[33]

12

Death Hunt

Using aliases and false addresses, Juanita and Rose bought a Ford V-8 coach for $325 in cash in Buffalo on October 18, 1934. Late the next day the foursome left the apartment. Richetti was driving and Floyd sat in back, a machine gun close at hand. Floyd took a turn at the wheel as they went southwest along Lake Erie and then south into Ohio, in fog so thick they could hardly see the road. About three o'clock on the morning of Saturday, October 20, after they had traveled some three hundred miles, Floyd ran into a telephone pole near Wellsville, Ohio, a small town on the Ohio River.

Nobody was hurt, but since the car was damaged, it was decided the women would walk to the nearby town of East Liverpool and send back a wrecker; Floyd and Richetti would hide nearby in a rural area. The men carried blankets with them, as well as the machine gun.

After the women found an all-night garage, a wrecker came and took the car to make the necessary repairs. Juanita and Rose went along, planning to return with the automobile in several hours.[1]

The placid Wellsville area was a sparsely settled farming region with very rough roads and steep wooded hillsides. Four miles north was East Liverpool, and beyond it was the city of Youngstown.

It was a beautiful autumn day, with multicolored leaves in great abundance.[2]

At ten in the morning a local man, Joe Fryman, was talking to his son-in-law about hauling a load of coal when he happened to look up an adjacent hill and see two strangers lying there.

Fryman decided to investigate, with the excuse of looking for pears to pick. Richetti, who was lying on a blanket, and Floyd, who was sitting, said they were taking pictures (although there were no cameras to be seen) and were waiting for two girls to return.

Fryman thought it odd that they had so much "stuff"—blankets, overcoats, and cushions.

"Dave, let's look at the pears and see if they are hurt," Fryman said to his son-in-law.

Floyd asked, "Do you live right down there?"

"No, I live on up the road," Fryman answered.

As Fryman and his son-in-law started down the hill, Floyd hollered, "If you see a couple of girls down there on the street, tell them to come on up, we are waiting for them."

They went to the house of farmer Lon Israel and told him what had happened. Israel said, "It looks kind of fishy to me. Why would they be wanting to take pictures with all that junk?"

They all agreed it was suspicious and that the Wellsville police chief, John H. Fultz, should be told. Since Israel did not have a phone, he called the chief from a store about 10:30 A.M. and told him he had seen "suspicious" men near the intersection of State 7 and the Pennsylvania Railroad tracks. Fultz replied he would be there soon.

The chief of the two-man police force thought perhaps these men were the same ones who had robbed the Tiltonsville bank the day before. Armed with a .38 revolver, he took two unarmed special officers with him, Grover Potts and William Irwin. All three were in civilian clothes.

Israel joined the three policemen on the main road and agreed to guide them.

They stepped off the road and started up the path. Fultz was in front, with Potts behind him, then Israel, and then Irwin.

After they had gone about twenty-five feet, just as Fultz was rounding a clump of bushes, a man came toward them, seemingly out of nowhere.

Immediately Floyd asked, "What do you want?" He jerked his gun out and said, "Stick them up."

Fultz told him he would not stick them up.

"I said put them up!" the gangster insisted.

"I am going down to the brickyard to work, and I don't see why I should put my hands up."

"Don't come another inch, fellow, or I will pump you," Floyd replied.

"You wouldn't shoot a working man. Fellow, you don't need to think we are crazy."

The police chief kept walking toward Floyd as the gangster kept saying, "Stick up your hands." Fultz answered stubbornly, "I won't do it." He advanced until Floyd's gun was in his stomach.

Allowing Fultz to walk past him, Floyd stepped to the right while keeping his gun on the police chief.

Fultz thought the gunman would try to frisk him and he would get a chance to hit him, but Floyd continued to stand to the right of all of the men and let them pass.

A ploy of turning away from the gangster so he could not see Fultz as he went for his gun in his pocket failed when Floyd told him, "Keep your hands there and don't run."

Fultz attempted to get some distance between them so he would have an equal chance to shoot it out with Floyd, but every time he would try to get a little ahead of him, Floyd would tell him, "Don't go so fast. If you start to run, I will shoot you."

"Nobody's going to run, nobody's done anything to run for."

But Fultz kept trying to get some space between them.

Suddenly, off to the side he spied a man stretched out on a blanket and leaning on his left elbow. He hailed him, "Hello, buddy, how are you, you seem to be taking it pretty easy."

Richetti replied, "Yes," and smiled.

"Don't let him kid you. Shoot him, he's an officer!" Floyd yelled.

As Richetti twisted around with an automatic in his hand, he began shooting at Fultz.

The chief pulled his gun, and as he whirled around, he yelled at Floyd, less than ten feet away, "You big yellow son-of-a-bitch," and fired. He thought he had hit Floyd in the stomach, but Floyd was, once more, miraculously unharmed.

Floyd leaped behind the three men trailing the chief as Fultz turned his gun on Richetti, firing three shots. He then aimed a last shot at Floyd before reloading two shells and firing once at Richetti.

The two gangsters now turned their backs on the three unarmed locals and aimed at the chief as he fled down the hill.

Floyd picked up the machine gun and fired it, but after a few seconds the gun's grip broke and it came apart. The gangster cursed and threw it down.

Israel, Potts, and Irwin took this opportunity to flee back to the house.

Fultz had a slight wound in his foot. All of the other shots had missed.

Richetti, his gun empty, ran through the tangled bushes as the chief chased him for about a hundred feet, until the gangster jumped over a fence and fled to a house. Just as he was about to burst through the door, Fultz landed a bullet in the door just above his shoulder.

Richetti raised his hands and pleaded, "I give up. For God's sake, don't shoot me, don't kill me. I am done." With Richetti a few feet away, Fultz said, "Don't come any closer. Turn your back to me." While Richetti was doing this, Fultz, who did not know what had become of Richetti's gun, reloaded his own weapon.

After frisking him, Fultz hustled Richetti to his car and took him to the Wellsville jail, where Richetti was able to flush the bullets in his pockets down the cell toilet.

Meanwhile, Israel gave Potts and Irwin each a double-barreled 12-gauge shotgun and shells. As they left to rejoin the fight, Israel stayed behind, looking for another shotgun.

When Irwin and Potts came out, they saw Floyd going up the hill and crossing a narrow road about a hundred feet ahead.

Floyd looked around, saw the two, and fired, hitting Potts in the right shoulder.

Irwin fired one barrel of his shotgun, and Potts emptied both barrels at the gangster, who crouched in a ditch before dashing up the hill through the brush and disappearing into the woods.

When Israel, who thought the chief had probably gotten killed and the two thugs were coming after him, found another shotgun and was loading it, he heard the blasts of shotguns. He ran out ready to fight, but saw only the two policemen.

Israel and Irwin gave up on Floyd so they could take care of the wounded Potts.

The gunfight was over. Richetti had been taken prisoner by a small-time police chief, and Floyd had deserted him. It was a humiliating experience—they had been outwitted by an officer they had the drop on and had outgunned!

Floyd had escaped without any injuries, so his chances were good. It would be hours before the area would be sealed off. Probably no one yet knew who he was. If he could get a car, he could be in Youngstown in less than an hour. There he could seek sanctuary with a friend.[3]

At about 12:15 in the afternoon, Floyd descended a hill to a road near the Peterson place, where two brothers, Theodore and William Peterson, and their friend, a twenty-five-year-old unemployed youth named George MacMillen, were working on a car. Floyd was dirty and roughed up a bit, but they thought he was well-dressed.

The gangster offered them five dollars if they would take him to Youngstown. When MacMillen asked the other boys if they wanted to do it, they hesitated.

Floyd increased the offer, "I will give you $10 if you fellows would be interested enough to drive me. My car is broke down in hollow, and I will appreciate it very much if you will drive me. I went up past the brick works in a car hunting duck and went over the hill and broke the machine."

The Peterson brothers asked if they could fix it for him. Floyd told them he had broken the front axle, walked over to the car they were working on, and put his foot up on the axle to point out the damage.

As the boys were backing their car out and Floyd was getting in, their mother came out and asked them what they were doing. Because she was wary of the dirty stranger, she said, "You can't go."

"Sorry, buddy, but I can't go," one of the boys told Floyd.

But since MacMillen was unemployed and broke, he agreed to drive Floyd in his model T for the ten dollars. His friends told him to go ahead.[4]

As they drove off, Floyd asked MacMillen to stay off the main highways and go on the side roads. He said, "I suppose you know who I am."

"Don't believe I do," MacMillen responded.

"I am Floyd, 'Pretty Boy.' The radios are flashing it all over the country, the papers are full of it. I'm a dangerous man. Your life is as much at stake as mine." He also said he was desperate and a killer, and had to get away.

"I don't know of it," the young man answered. "I am just back from Canons Mill and haven't been reading the papers except funnies or looking through the paper for a job. My name is MacMillen."

He also vehemently denied that he was a constable, detective, or policeman as Floyd pulled his coat up and showed off his gun.

"Isn't that kind of large?" MacMillen said.

Floyd didn't respond.

MacMillen was now afraid and wanted desperately to escape. They passed a car, the only one they had encountered so far.

He pretended they were low on gas by pulling the choke. The car stopped and Floyd got out to push it.

The driver let it drift back into a ditch, where it had to be pulled out. The car was overheated, and Floyd went to a nearby house, where he got a bucket of water for the radiator. He put it in and tried unsuccessfully to start the engine.

MacMillen told Floyd, "I am out of gas. Let's go up and get some gas."

"Well, come on, don't make any movement with your eyes or blow anything," Floyd responded.

"Okay."[5]

They went up to a greenhouse and Floyd asked its owner, sixty-year-old James Baum, "How about getting some gas? I will pay you for it."

Baum did not like his looks, but he did not recognize Public Enemy No. 1.

"I haven't any gas," he responded.

"How about draining some out of your car?" Floyd asked him. Baum said he could not get it out, and MacMillen told Floyd it was very hard to get gas out of that kind of car.

"Let's get him to take us to a gas station," the gangster said to MacMillen. Thinking that it was a good idea because they might be able to get help there, the young man agreed.

Calm, unhurried, and polite, Floyd did not seem like a bad character, so Baum agreed to drive them in his 1929 Nash sedan. As they moved along, Floyd said, "Old man, I have a surprise for you. I want you to keep on driving—don't stop!" He laid his gun on the seat and told them he did not mean to harm them.

Noticing that Floyd had two guns, MacMillen tried to get one of them. "How about giving me the gun, so if we get in trouble I can do some shooting?"

"Nuts to you," Floyd replied.

The gangster proceeded to tell them about the gunfight at Wellsville in which he had been slightly wounded, and showed them a hole in his coat close to the small of the back. The two men did not see any blood.

Floyd said that they were "shooting at me with shotguns," that he had discarded his machine gun about three houses over the bank from the brickyard, and that the young man could have it as a reward for his help. But MacMillen said he didn't want it, nor did he want the ten dollars Floyd had given him.

"Keep it. You will need it when you are leaving," Floyd replied.

They continued to travel in circles, about sixty miles over obscure country roads, then found themselves just a few miles from where they had started.[6]

Around one in the afternoon, Fultz stopped at the sheriff's office at Lisbon, reported the gunfight, and said that Floyd was headed that way in a black Ford sedan with an East Liverpool license, number unknown. He asked that they blockade the road.

Since the sheriff was away, deputy sheriffs George Hayes, armed with a revolver, and Charley Patterson, who carried a shotgun, formed the roadblock near a bridge on the highway that led from Wellsville and East Liverpool at 2:45 in the afternoon. Vehicles were stopped from both directions; only one was allowed through at a time.

Forty-five minutes later, they saw a big tan Nash come down the hill and turn left onto a road leading to a closed copper mill. From a vantage point on the bridge, Patterson saw that boxcars along a siding blocked the Nash so that it was forced back onto the highway. It then headed away from the roadblock.

With Hayes driving, the lawmen went after the Nash.

Because of the traffic, they could not catch up to the car and remained about five cars behind.

The Nash turned left on Roller Coaster Road, aptly named because of its steep hills and frequent dips and turns.

Hayes followed it and started to blow his horn; about half a mile down the road, the cars stopped about fifty yards apart, with the sheriff's car on one end of a dip and the Nash on the other. Thinking they might be killed if they got too close or that the car would be disabled, Hayes stayed back.

Just as Baum and MacMillen jumped out, Floyd fired one shot out the back window; it went through the windshield and back window of the sheriff's car. Patterson was cut slightly by flying glass as the bullet flew only a few inches from their heads. Hayes later said, "He would have hit me right between the eyes if I had been sitting up straight." He had bent over to reach for the door handle.

The officers got out, and Hayes yelled to the men to come to them with their hands up.

They opened fire when Floyd jumped out and ran in a crouching position to the front of the Nash. Baum took Patterson's buckshot in the left thigh.

Nearby, William MacMillen was working in his garden with his wife and daughter. Suddenly bullets from the officers' guns whistled over their heads. They ducked and ran to the house.

Using the front end of the car and Baum and MacMillen for a shield, Floyd ran into the Spence Woods. He reached an open area about two hundred yards long, crossed it, and disappeared into the woods on the opposite side. Once more he had escaped.

Baum and MacMillen also ran into the woods, but soon came out warily. Hayes yelled for them to raise their hands, and they were taken into custody.

Hayes told Patterson to watch the woods while he went for help.[7]

Hayes recruited a posse of at least a hundred men armed with rifles, old Mausers, and other similar weapons. He warned the local farmers to put their cars away and lock them up. The area was surrounded and searched on Saturday, October 20, but Floyd was gone.[8]

Chief Fultz told anyone who would listen that Floyd was wounded and disarmed, and could not last long. The wound in the chief's foot was not serious, and he wanted to direct the search as soon as it had been treated.[9]

Richetti claimed he was Richard Zamboni. Ninety-eight dollars was found on him, which he said he had won several days before in a card game at Medina, Ohio, near Akron. He had been with a James Warren, whom he had recently met in Toledo and had known several years ago in Oklahoma. Richetti could not explain why they had engaged in a gunfight.[10]

Hayes remembered him as a well-behaved, cooperative prisoner and "a wonderful . . . artist." He later said, "Richetti wasn't difficult to handle. We just slapped him around a few times."[11] While a few men guarded Richetti in the decrepit Wellsville jail, Fultz organized the hunt for Floyd late on Saturday.

The area was in an uproar. Many citizens grabbed rifles and shotguns and joined the hunt. Local possemen plunged through the brush and hills. But it was impossible to completely seal off the large woods, which were guarded against escape until the search got under way on Sunday afternoon, October 21. Four men in a big green sedan swept through Wellsville twice, displaying machine guns and firing into the air.

Floyd probably stayed in the woods, away from any people or developed areas, eating apples and pears from the numerous fruit trees.[12]

Sheriff Ray B. Long of Steubenville, Ohio, happened to be in Chief Fultz's office around noon on Sunday while Fultz continued to interview Richetti. Long, who recognized the gangster from a photo he had been given by the Cincinnati office of the FBI, told Fultz, "That's Adam Richetti. He's wanted by the government for his participation in the Kansas City Massacre."

After looking at the booklet of wanted men published by the William J. Burns National Detective Agency, Fultz identified pictures of Richetti and Floyd. (Richetti would also be identified later by his fingerprints.) Fultz said that if he had known it was Floyd and Richetti, he would not have gone after them. Although he then admitted his identity, Richetti still denied that Floyd was the man with him.

Then Richetti told Fultz and the county prosecutor that he was wanted for jumping bail of fifteen thousand dollars for the Mill Creek job, but denied he and Floyd had been involved in the Kansas City Massacre. He also insisted he had not seen Floyd for nearly a year, had last seen him at Texarkana, Arkansas, and had last heard from him from El Paso. But Richetti did admit he was with Floyd on June 16, 1933, when they had kidnapped Sheriff Killingsworth, and boasted of robberies in Kansas and Oklahoma that he and Floyd had pulled off.[13]

He told Hayes that two women had accompanied them, that their car was damaged, and that the women had gone for help. He also talked about their hideouts in Cleveland, Detroit, and Buffalo.[14]

Later that day two employees of the Tiltonsville bank looked at the gangster. Neither could make a positive identification, but both said the prisoner "resembled" one of the robbers and picked out the picture of Floyd as one of the others.[15] Fultz objected to Long calling the FBI at Cincinnati and insisted the call be paid for by the sheriff.[16]

At this time Melvin Purvis and three other FBI agents, including Herman E. Hollis, who had been involved in the Dillinger and Floyd cases, were at a special headquarters in Cincinnati, working on a kidnapping case. Notified of Richetti's capture early on Sunday afternoon, Purvis immediately called J. Edgar Hoover to ask for permission to drop the kidnapping case and join the hunt for Floyd. Hoover agreed.[17] Where Richetti was, Floyd might also be.

Soon afterward, Hoover received a call from Walter Winchell, who needed a big opening announcement for his Sunday evening radio show. He asked Hoover if there had been any new capture of a notorious criminal, and Hoover said, "We caught Pretty Boy Floyd." Winchell was the first member of the press to be told the big news. That night Winchell reported that Floyd had been killed by the FBI.[18]

At two P.M. the FBI squad left by plane for Wellsville. It would have been a pleasant trip over the beautiful autumn terrain if it had not been on such a grim assignment. The pilot told them that the Wellsville airport was closed because of its bad condition and that it was too small. Government workers were busy enlarging it, and it had no lights whatsoever. They would have to land at Pittsburgh and drive about fifty miles to Wellsville.

But Purvis made such a fuss that the pilot reluctantly agreed to put down there. It was like "landing on a dime," and they were tremendously relieved when they arrived without mishap. Actually, there was a perfectly good airport only twenty-five miles from Wellsville, at Beaver Falls, Pennsylvania, and all the other planes carrying FBI agents going to Wellsville landed there.

Sheriff Long met Purvis and his squad at the airport and briefed them on the events of the last twenty-four hours. Purvis told the sheriff one of his main missions was to get custody of Richetti so he could be tried for the murders at Kansas City. Long replied that Fultz was a difficult man to deal with.

After Purvis set up his headquarters at the Travelers Hotel in East Liverpool, he visited Fultz and made a formal request for Richetti's custody.[19] He introduced himself as "Mr. Marshall" to avoid the publicity that had followed him since the Dillinger case. Later the chief would say, "The Mayor and I were working as hard as we could to locate Floyd and Mr. Purvis came to the Mayor and me under an assumed name, which we resented very much for we were dealing in an open and above-board manner."

Purvis argued that the FBI could place a more serious charge against Richetti and he could be questioned more properly elsewhere. Fultz agreed that agents S. K. McKee and Hollis could have a private interview with Richetti.

On Sunday evening the police chief said he had no time to hunt Floyd and spent three hours with newspapermen.[20]

Also on that evening Floyd's machine gun was found. Fultz refused to give the gun to the FBI, which desperately wanted it to run ballistics tests to link it to the Kansas City Massacre.[21]

At first the chief would not release Richetti to Kansas City officers and to federal agents because the prisoner "wounded one of my men and I'm going to prosecute him." Futhermore, Purvis did not have the paperwork to take custody of Richetti.[22]

About two dozen FBI agents from Pittsburgh, Cleveland, Detroit, Louisville, Cincinnati, New York, Chicago, and Indianapolis came by plane and car on Sunday and Monday morning, reinforcing the local lawmen. Roadblocks were set up on all bridges across the Ohio River. Police in eastern Ohio abandoned all other work to join in the search. More than two hundred searchers combed Spencer Woods. Two Ohio state policemen were sent to Wellsville to help out. Underworld haunts in Youngstown and Akron were watched closely.

West Virginia and Pennsylvania authorities blocked all roads leading from Wellsville.[23]

At 2 A.M. the posse was called in by Chief Fultz and Purvis, who feared searchers might fire on their own men or be ambushed by Floyd. Although it was raining heavily, the ring around the woods was maintained through the night.[24]

At daybreak on Monday, October 22, the manhunt resumed, with squads moving in wider and wider circles through the woods.

Baum (who said that Floyd was not wounded) and others were questioned by Purvis and his squad. They described Floyd as six feet tall, although he was only five feet eight and a quarter inches. Purvis said, "But a man with a gun in his hand certainly would look a big six feet to anybody."[25]

That morning, FBI Inspector S. P. Cowley and Sheriff Thomas Bash arrived by plane in Wellsville. Cowley had warrants for the National Motor Vehicle Theft Act violation and conspiracy to obstruct justice, and Sheriff Bash had warrants for the murder of two Missouri officers. These two distinguished lawmen were later referred to in Purvis's book, *American Agent,* simply as a sheriff and a special agent.[26]

They were met with defiance from Fultz. Cowley later said, "I tried for 48 hours to persuade Wellsville authorities to the importance of assisting the Government. They refused, evidently because of jealousy of Purvis. They kept us waiting for hour after hour, promising us now that we could have him, then again that we couldn't."[27]

Bash, whose sole opportunity to speak to Richetti for only a few minutes was at his fingerprinting, was angry at the treatment given him and Cowley. But it was open house for townspeople, who could ask him all the questions they wanted. Although Bash even offered a reward of two hundred dollars out of his own pocket, as well as medical treatment for the wounded lawmen, they still would not let him have the prisoner.[28] Also on that day in Kansas City, a federal grand jury was convened to investigate the Kansas City Massacre.[29]

Now Purvis could concentrate on searching for Floyd.

In the morning the manhunt began to cool, and it was feared that Floyd had made another of his spectacular escapes. But Purvis told the press he was sure the gangster was still in the region. The woods, heavy with brush and timber, were fifty miles in radius. Floyd could be within ten feet of the searchers at any time and they would not know it. Fultz thought Floyd was hiding at some house along the highway.

Purvis divided the FBI agents into squads of three or four men each. Three squads were sent to patrol the highways near the general area of Floyd's disappearance. Raids on the homes of Richetti's relatives near Dillonvale, Ohio, forty miles to the south, were without result. Cabdrivers and rental-car agencies were asked to be on the lookout. One squad visited hospitals, clinics, and doctors to see if Floyd had tried to get medical aid. Residents were told to look out for strangers.

Purvis also arranged for a plane to fly low over the woods.

All tips were investigated immediately. There were rumors Floyd had been shot by an agent but had escaped, and that an FBI agent had been shot in the head.

Purvis stayed at the Travelers Hotel, listening to the phone reports of his men on their various assignments. In the early afternoon he received a call from one of his agents who told him he had just interviewed a farmer near the Bell Schoolhouse. When he was shown the gangster's photo, he said that he had just given a meal to a man whom he identified as Floyd. Purvis had a feeling that this was the real thing.

When Hoover called Purvis to see what was going on, Purvis told him that he was leaving the hotel with three men to centralize the search for Floyd near the Bell Schoolhouse, and there would be no one to answer the phone.

Someone also called Agent H. E. Hollis, who in turn called the East Liverpool police.

When Purvis arrived at the schoolhouse, an agent pointed out the direction Floyd had taken earlier.

Since Purvis had heard many reports that Floyd had been trying to get to Youngstown to seek refuge with a friend, he stopped at a farmhouse and called the Youngstown police chief and asked him to watch out for the fugitive.

Several times they saw a lone man on a distant hill, only to rush up and find it was not Floyd.

The men joked about Purvis being chased by a ram in a farmyard while he was trying to question a woman on the farmhouse porch.

About three in the afternoon, Purvis and the three agents accompanying him—D. K. Hall, W. E. Hopton, and S. K. McKee—came upon four East Liverpool policemen—Chief Hugh J. McDermott at the wheel, Herman H. Roth, Chester C. Smith, and Glenn G. Montgomery—driving down the road.

After a conference they decided to join forces. The East Liverpool police knew the area and could guide Purvis's group.

McKee and Hopton carried machine guns, and Hall and Purvis packed revolvers. Purvis had a .38 police detective special, officers Smith and Roth had 32-20 rifles, and Roth also brought along a .45 revolver. Shotguns were the weapons of choice for McDermott and Montgomery.

The two cars proceeded, with the East Liverpool police car in front. They stopped occasionally to ask if Floyd had been seen, showed photos (no one had seen him), and searched some abandoned structures.

On one place Purvis was searching a barn while the other officers were scattered over the farm. When Purvis, who dreaded the confrontation with Floyd, heard a sound of rustling of cornstalks in the barn's basement, he drew his gun and listened intently, "with every nerve in my body tingling." Someone was coming up the ladder. When it proved to be a special agent, Purvis felt immense relief. After leaving the barn and looking at the beautiful wooded countryside, he thought, "Strange that Death should stalk in that beautiful spot."

According to Purvis, "We began to feel that there would be little hope of capturing Floyd, as it seemed that all of our efforts were futile, and we knew that darkness would be coming soon and after that there would be a period of twelve hours during which no effective search could be made."

At one farmhouse the tired and hungry lawmen ate some fruit and filled their overcoats with more for later use.

They continued on to the farmhouse of Mrs. Ellen Conkle, a widow.[30]

13

You Got Me This Time

About 10 o'clock Monday morning, October 22, 1934, Arthur Conkle, whose farm was close by that of his widowed sister-in-law, saw a man dodging behind fodder shocks in his cornfield. Shortly before noon he glimpsed him again in a field belonging to his neighbor, Robert Robinson. Conkle told Robinson and another of his neighbors, Constable Clyde O. Birch, about the mysterious stranger.

Meanwhile, the hungry fugitive, who had not eaten anything for two days except fruit he had picked, came out of hiding about 12:30 P.M. and went to the Robinson farmhouse, near the Bell Schoolhouse. He had traveled eight miles as the crow flies in the last forty-eight hours. Dressed in a navy blue suit with a very dirty white shirt open at the collar, the hatless Floyd was haggard, in need of a shave, and disheveled; his hands were red and scratched.

Robinson was suspicious of his visitor's appearance and manners even when Floyd courteously asked if could have something to eat and offered to pay a dollar.

As Robinson's daughter prepared a sandwich, the stranger was allowed to wash up.

When Robinson refused to drive him to Youngstown, Floyd asked for directions to that city.

After Floyd had started out on foot, walking north along the highway, Robinson realized who the stranger was and told Conkle he had just fed the fugitive. He then flagged down Constable Birch as the latter drove by.

Robinson and Birch drove to a gas station six miles away, where they found some FBI men. After Robinson told about his suspicious-looking lunch guest, he was shown a picture of Floyd and identified him.[1]

At ten minutes to three in the afternoon (about the same time Purvis had met the East Liverpool police officers), Mrs. Conkle, who lived alone on Spruceville Road, about two miles south of Clarkson, Ohio, and seven miles northeast of East Liverpool, was cleaning her smokehouse. Her brother and sister-in-law, Mr. and Mrs. Stewart L. Dyke, were husking corn in a nearby field.

A stranger appeared and told her he was lost and hungry. He asked if he could pay to get something to eat, "just meat and bread." The widow, who didn't read the papers much and had no idea he was Public Enemy No. 1, said she would prepare a meal for him.

He and his brother had been "hunting squirrels or rabbits or anything" on Sunday near Beaver Creek, had become lost, and had separated in the darkness, Floyd claimed.

"You don't hunt squirrels at night, do you?" she replied suspiciously.

"To tell the truth, lady, I got drunk last night and I don't know where I am exactly."

Told to go outside while the food was being prepared, Floyd had a sweeping view of the countryside and could see anyone coming from any direction. He basked in the sunshine that shone through the brilliant foliage.

Mrs. Conkle could tell he had not been drinking, but he appeared to be watchful and nervous. She became more apprehensive when she saw he was carrying a gun.

After he was given permission to wash his hands, Floyd sat at the table and immediately asked for a newspaper. He read about himself as he ate what was to be his last meal: pork chops, potatoes, rice, and coffee, with doughnuts and pumpkin pie for dessert.

He asked directions to Youngstown and wanted matches, which she gave him.

While eating, Floyd asked about the old jalopy next to a wooden corncrib.

"It belongs to my brother," Mrs. Conkle said. "He's out back working."

"Do you think he'd drive me to Youngstown?" Floyd asked.

Mrs. Conkle replied that after work her brother might take him part of the way to Youngstown, thirty-eight miles distant, on his way home.

He proclaimed the dinner was "fit for a king," and over Mrs. Conkle's protests gave her a dollar bill.

The gangster said he would wait for her brother at his car.

"I look like a wild man, don't I?" Floyd yelled as he walked toward the car. Mrs. Conkle just smiled.

"I feel just that way."

Mrs. Conkle, who stayed in the backyard, stopped paying attention to him until her brother and sister-in-law came from the fields about 4 P.M. and approached their car. They saw a strange man sitting in the driver's seat of their model A Ford. Dyke said later he had seen such a man walking through the pasture earlier, a "poor devil" with big shoulders, "the best built man he had ever seen."[2]

Floyd, who had found the car keys, was about to take off when Stewart Dyke walked up beside the car before the gangster had even noticed him.

Grinning, Floyd said, "Hello, there."

"Hello," replied Dyke.

"I'm lost. Your sister said you would take me to the bus line," Floyd said.

Dyke asked him which one, and Floyd said he did not care, as long as it was a bus line.

The nearest stop was in Columbiana. Dyke told him, "I don't think I could take you to any bus line."

"Take me to [highway] Number Seven, then."

Dyke again refused.

After Floyd asked for directions, Dyke finally agreed he could take him as far as Clarkson.

Amazed at how many Spanish needles there were on the man's

clothes, even in his shirt collar, Dyke said, "Well, one thing is for sure, there are no Spanish needles left where you have been."

Saying he would be right back, he left Floyd at the car and walked to his sister, who asked him, "Did you see the man?"

He told her the man wanted to get someplace where he could catch a bus. He said he "didn't know" when Mrs. Conkle asked, "Who is that man?"

Dyke went back to the car when his sister ordered him to "get him out of here. I don't like it."

Although Mrs. Dyke did not want the man to ride with them, Stewart made her get in the back seat and said, "I will take care of him."

Meanwhile, a brisk wind had risen and was scattering the leaves and stirring the branches overhead, as Floyd walked to the road and looked in both directions before rejoining Dyke at the car and starting to get in the back seat.

"Come and get in front," Dyke urged Floyd, putting his hand on Floyd's shoulder. Dyke had spotted two cars coming down the hill on the narrow country road—and he knew something was going to happen. Floyd had not seen them, but as Dyke was backing the car, his wife remarked about the two cars approaching.

Turning pale, Floyd reached for his gun and cursed as he ordered Dyke to "drive behind that building, they are looking for me."

Dyke drove up to the corncrib, reached over, opened the door, and said, "Get out, you son of a bitch." He realized at that very moment that his passenger was Pretty Boy Floyd!

Floyd jumped out, hesitated briefly, and started to crawl under the corncrib (which was a little over twelve inches above the ground and about thirty yards from the road). Then he seemed to consider getting back into the car.

Instead, the gangster, who had made many miraculous escapes and might do it again, decided to make a run for the woods some two hundred yards away.[3]

Two years before, it had been predicted, "At the end of the trail for you, there is probably a little run in the open for the shelter of a thicket, the bark of a posseman's rifle and a lifeless fall. A pitiful end for the father of a fine son."[4]

. . .

It was East Liverpool Officer Glenn Montgomery who first identified the man skulking behind the corncrib as Charles Floyd. In the meantime the Federal agents arrived and the police yelled, "There he is, back of the corncrib." The two cars stopped in the driveway and Chief Hugh McDermott ordered, "Get out of the car, everyone. Quick." As they spread out in a long half-circle to avoid being good targets and gradually approached, they saw a pair of blue-trousered legs underneath the corncrib. Later all the law officers would claim they called out the orders, "Halt, or we'll shoot" and "Floyd, come to the road. If you don't, we will shoot."

"Look out, he's going to run," McDermott yelled.

Floyd ran behind a small garage at the rear of the corncrib and came out into the open, moving in a zigzag pattern across the rolling open cornfield toward the woods. With a .45 automatic pistol in his right hand, he frequently looked over his right shoulder, but he did not shoot at his pursuers scarcely two hundred feet away.[5]

Officer Chester Smith said later that night that Floyd "made a great mistake by not staying behind that corncrib and fighting it out. He had a better chance there than in the open even if he is a fast runner. Floyd ran with a sort of twisting motion, but I'm telling you he sure could run."[6]

Thinking a machine gun would be the most effective weapon, Melvin Purvis ordered Agent D. K. Hall, who had only a pistol, to drop to the ground.[7]

Then McDermott and Purvis gave the order, "Let him have it," and at least fifty shots echoed—from rifles, shotguns, machine guns, and revolvers.[8] Purvis himself fired six shots from his .38 revolver.[9] They could hardly miss.[10]

Mrs. Dyke later said she heard "bullets whistling through the apple tree, cutting off twigs and leaves that fluttered to the ground. It was so loud we couldn't hear anything right for an hour afterward." Afterward Purvis told the Dykes they were lucky they were not killed.[11]

Floyd's right arm jerked as he was hit in the forearm by a smaller caliber bullet, probably from a rifle.[12] A .45 slug entered below his left shoulder blade and lodged in the rib cage in the upper left chest, shattering the eighth rib and taking part of the lung. Another .45 entered on the right side and came to rest below the heart. The two bullets had crisscrossed, both nicking his heart.[13]

He ran over a meadowed incline and fell on his face, having gone only about twenty yards. He rose to his knees, then fell again and rolled over on his back.

Floyd desperately tried to fire his automatic—but could not, because of his wounded arm—as the lawmen approached cautiously.

Purvis, the first to reach him, kicked the gun out of his hand and picked it up. It was "quite an ingenious device" that could be made fully automatic by one press of the trigger.

When Floyd reached with his left hand for his other gun, in his belt on his left side, Montgomery grabbed that hand and held it down as Roth's arm came over Montgomery's right shoulder and yanked the weapon out.

Floyd tried several times to rise to his feet, but he was kept flat on the ground.

Montgomery asked him what his name was, and he said he was Murphy. Again he was asked, and again he said "Murphy."

"Are you Pretty Boy Floyd?" Purvis said as he put handcuffs on him.

"I'm Charles Arthur Floyd," he said with indignation.

Montgomery also asked if he was Charles "Pretty Boy" Floyd.

"Yes, that's my name, I am Floyd."

One of the agents again said, "Your name's Floyd?" Floyd did not reply. He was asked the question again. Floyd half smiled and said, "I am Floyd."[14]

Since Mrs. Conkle did not have a phone, Purvis set out to telephone Hoover from a store in Clarkson. He made Stewart Dyke come with him to show him the way. He told him to "hold onto something. I don't want you to break your neck," as Agent Hall drove eighty miles an hour on the back road. Purvis made his call to Hoover and obtained a five-gallon can of gasoline.[15]

Meanwhile, patrolmen Chester Smith, Herman Roth, and Montgomery carried the wounded Floyd to the shade of an apple tree next to the main highway. There they asked him about the Kansas City Massacre and other crimes. He answered with profanity each time. One time when he was again asked about the Massacre, Floyd asked them to stand back while he answered, but did not tell them anything.

When Agent S. K. McKee asked him about the Massacre, he raised himself, shouted several obscenities, and then lay back. He was losing his strength.

"I won't tell you nothing. To hell with the Union Station!" snarled Floyd.

Chief McDermott asked, "How bad are you hurt?"

As if making an accusation, the gangster replied, "I am done. You got me twice."

The defiant Floyd asked Montgomery where "Ad" was, referring to Richetti. After he had Floyd repeat the question, Montgomery responded, "Ad who?" Floyd said again, "Where's Ad?" When Montgomery told him, "I don't know," Floyd yelled, "Oh, hell." Again he asked, "Where's Eddie?," also referring to Richetti.

"Who in hell tipped you off?" the gangster said, as he raised himself on one elbow. "I'm Floyd, all right. You got me this time."

Told he was dying, he replied, "I know I'm through."

He swore at the police officers and special agents W. E. Hopton and McKee, then said, "Fuck you. Fuck you. Fuck you." Shortly afterward his last words were "I'm going." He died about 4:25, fifteen minutes after he had been shot.[16]

His body was searched hurriedly; the only wounds found had been inflicted minutes before his death. In his pockets were $122 (twelve $10 bills and two $1 bills), coins, a key, matches, a loaded clip for a .45 caliber automatic pistol, and apples. He also had a Gruen pocket watch and a silver half dollar (with ten notches on it!) attached to a chain, and a cameo ring on the fourth finger of his right hand.

About five minutes after Floyd died, Purvis returned, without an ambulance. They put the body in the back seat of the federal car to take him to the Sturgis Funeral Home in East Liverpool, where it was examined by a Dr. Schoolnic.[17]

At 10 P.M. Coroner E. R. Sturgis of East Liverpool and the county prosecutor called on Purvis at the Travelers Hotel to tell him there would be an inquest into the death of Floyd. A stenographer was procured, and Special Agent McKee made a sworn statement. Sturgis said he was going to get sworn testimony from several persons and hand down the verdict based upon that testimony. On October 25, Sturgis ruled it was justifiable homicide: "I find he was justly shot to death by a combined force of agents of the Department of Justice and officers of the East Liverpool police while making an armed attempt to escape."[18]

About 4:20 P.M. Purvis called Hoover with the big news: Floyd had been shot down and was dying. He reassured the director that none of his agents had been hurt in the melee.[19] Hoover immediately went to the attorney general and told him, "General, I am happy to report that our men have just mortally wounded 'Pretty Boy' Floyd." The very pleased Attorney General Homer Cummings replied, "Congratulations!"[20]

That day the FBI director had numerous calls from the press. He told a Scripps Howard reporter, "We had been very anxious to get Floyd because he had killed one of our men in the Kansas City Massacre." The reporter asked if Hoover thought Floyd was as bad as Dillinger. Hoover replied, "It was pretty hard to evaluate the badness of such men; that none of them would have the courage to fight unless they had a gun in their hands . . . frankly, a lot of their alleged viciousness and badness was a build-up that the press gave them, that however, they were a bunch of vicious individuals who had to be exterminated."[21] To another reporter he said, "A Federal agent was killed, and my boys today were paying back Floyd in his own coin."[22]

When Francis Connor of the *Chicago Daily News* called and asked who fired the fatal shot, Hoover said he would not say anything about that.[23] He told Rex Collier of the *Washington Evening Star* that Floyd had tried to make a deal for his life in return for a life sentence. Hoover had rejected the offer because, he said, "He killed one of our men and he must take the consequences. Moreover, we don't deal with gangsters." The next day Hoover said that on four separate occasions Floyd had offered to surrender if there were no death sentence. A little more than two weeks before, a surrender offer had been made. But there were no deals with the FBI.[24]

At a press conference Hoover boasted, "There've been so many of them [public enemies], I can't even keep track of them." Floyd "was as yellow as Dillinger. There never was a rat really brave, nor even dangerous in the sense that normal persons think about such things." In his words, Floyd was "just a yellow rat who needed extermination."

Of course any rat will fight when cornered, but with an even break they will run first. That was the way with Floyd. He would fight if he was armed and you were not. But in a fair fight he lacked courage.

. . . Of course we do admit some sentiment in the matter. When one of these yellow curs kills one of our men we are going to get him and will never stop until we do.

That was one of the things we had against Floyd, which caused him to be referred to as Public Enemy No. 1.[25]

Hoover, whose relations with Purvis were good at the moment, but soon would turn sour, sent a congratulatory telegram to the agent:

The successful termination of the hunt for Floyd was, I know, in large part due to the splendid work performed by you in directing the activities of the Division in Ohio. The courage and efficiency of the representatives of the Division will I know prove to be of great value in the work which we are all attempting to do in connection with the current warfare against the criminal element.[26]

In reality the press treated Purvis, not Hoover, as the main hero. Papers featured pictures of Purvis with Hoover and assistant to the attorney general William Stanley under the headline "And Again Melvin Purvis Triumphs."[27] Numerous newspaper and radio editorials praised Purvis personally, such as one in the *El Reno Daily Tribune*, entitled "Oklahoma Indebted to Purvis," which stated that "Purvis is rapidly winning for himself the title of No. 1 federal operative in the drive against major criminals."[28] Many letters to the FBI praised Purvis and the FBI in general without referring to Hoover, who resented this greatly.[29]

Hoover asked Purvis if he had fired any shots at Floyd and Dillinger. Purvis answered that he had not shot at Dillinger, but had fired six shots from his .38 revolver at Floyd.[30]

The FBI director did not want his men to stay over in the Wellsville area, and wanted no motion pictures or newspaper pictures of his agents there (especially Purvis, who left the day of Floyd's killing, after Hoover ordered him to leave immediately), in order to avoid publicity. It was convenient for Hoover that Purvis was ill for a few days after the killing, for he wanted him to avoid contact with the press.[31]

Purvis's safety was threatened by Juanita, who said he would be placed on the "spot" by the underworld.[32]

Purvis himself later wrote, "The world was almost as electrified as it had been at the death of Dillinger."[33] The *New York Times* called Floyd "the most dangerous man alive." Some papers and lawmen, such as McDermott, believed that he "died yellow," because he had turned tail and run. One author wrote, "But whereas 20,000 thus paid homage to a hero [at his funeral], it would be fair to say that 20,000,000 other Americans felt that Floyd had been nothing but a cheap crook who had gotten what was coming to him."[34]

Charles K. Campbell of Sunbury, Pennsylvania, wrote a blood-thirsty letter to the FBI about Floyd: "He and his ilk are vultures and do not deserve any consideration from decent people." He hoped "you will *never arrest* any of these birds, but instruct your men to kill outright. Your curse [sic] is approved by practically *all law-abiding citizens.* Why bother with a trial." Hoover sent a letter to Campbell thanking "the public spirited citizen."[35]

"A Good Citizen" wrote to the *Tulsa Tribune:*

> It is appalling the extreme tolerance taken by so many suppos-edly intelligent human beings in regard to the killing of "Pretty-boy" Floyd.
>
> Has our sense of fairness become so unbalanced by the com-mon occurrence of lawlessness that we can lament the "injus-tice" done a proved murderer. How much of injustice did he in-flict upon his many victims? . . .
>
> Probably all that most of us know of the bandit is through the publication on the front pages of our newspapers of his "handsome" face accompanied by enlarged details of his "brav-ery" as told by drama-loving folks with large imaginations, who like to compare a man who should be a disgrace to their state, to Robin Hood. We forget the real details of his life. . . .

Any person living a life of hidden debaucheries and robbing and killing to make friends along his rotten path by strewing stolen favors is not a hero to me.[36]

A typical editorial on Floyd's death appeared in the *Tulsa Daily World*:

INFAMOUS CAREER ENDED

Floyd . . . probably inherited no vicious traits; his family was an industrious and respected one. He was lusty and venturesome, and the sordid school of the small-town poolroom soon claimed him. . . . How many men he killed or how many banks he robbed is not definitely known, but he had a long score in each instance. There was a disposition to heroize him, and he was a favorite of many women, but his desperate deeds were so frequent and so shocking that he never was dramatized as some other and lesser outlaws were. . . .

The large part of his career as a killer was outside Oklahoma, but his infamy will always be associated with Oklahoma. Part of his prosperity was due to the ineptness of Oklahoma officers and the bad habit many of our hill people have of harboring outlaws. It is probable, however, Floyd did not, in late years, regard his immunity as reliable. There has not, for ten years, been any question of how he would finish his malign career. . . .

The law is gaining, steadily and remorselessly. . . . Terror must abide in the haunts of the gangsters, for it is known now that if the "federals" get rightly on a man's track, his capture or death is only a matter of time.[37]

A few wrote letters favorable to Floyd to the papers and FBI. "H. H. M." sent a Western Union message to the FBI on October 23, 1934: "Like to invite entire Dept. to last rites of one loved in the Ole South. His loot was given to poor and needy. Congratulations. It was inevitable."[38]

The underworld also reacted. When Baby Face Nelson and his associate Joseph Raymond "Fatso" Negri heard the news of Floyd's death on the radio, it greatly irritated Nelson, who said, "It saved me the trouble." Apparently he had a grudge against Floyd and was jealous that he was labeled "Public Enemy No. 1," just as he had been jealous of Dillinger.[39]

Chief John Fultz received a threatening letter, signed "the gang," saying, "You got Floyd and Richetti. But we will get the ones who turned them up." Fultz shrugged and said, "If they're no tougher than Floyd and Richetti, I wouldn't be afraid of a carload of them."[40]

There were precautions against an attempt to free Richetti and to protect those who helped capture the gangsters. When three men asked for directions to the home of Constable Clyde Birch (who had tipped off police to Floyd), four of his brothers were assigned to guard his house.[41]

Chief Fultz investigated the theory that one or more accomplices had left Floyd and Richetti along the Ohio River bank while they drove the gang's car away on some mission.[42]

Hundreds went to the Conkle farm in the next few days, trampling the fields, visiting the spot where Floyd fell and the apple tree under which he died. Mrs. Conkle was offered as much as a hundred dollars for Floyd's dinner plate, but she would not part with it.[43]

Richetti refused to believe the officers who finally told him about Floyd's death on the night of the killing, until he was shown accounts in a newspaper. He said, "I don't see why he stuck around so long."[44]

Fultz told reporters that local authorities would take care of Richetti:

Richetti tried to take my life. He shot one of my citizens and he nicked me, therefore I feel that we have a right to take care of our case. I think I should keep him here where I can keep an eye on him until he comes to trial. We'll see that he doesn't get away.[45]

Richetti had been visited by relatives that night. He refused to give his cameo ring to a weeping sister as a keepsake.[46]

It was like a circus sideshow when thousands came to see Richetti the next day. Hundreds were permitted to go down the narrow staircase to the basement of the Wellsville city hall and view the bad man in his cell. Outside, hundreds more waited their turn. A woman who thought Richetti or Floyd might be her son, missing for years, visited Richetti in his cell.[47]

On October 23, Richetti was arraigned, pleaded guilty to the charge of carrying a concealed weapon, and was fined seventy-five dollars; he pleaded not guilty to shooting Fultz with the intent to kill. Bond was set at fifty thousand dollars.[48]

On Wednesday, October 24, the heavily shackled Richetti was taken from Wellsville to the Columbiana County jail at Lisbon in a six-car procession led by Chief Fultz. Hundreds of farmers stood outside their homes to see Richetti pass. Officers paused at the Lisbon schoolhouse, next to the county jail, to let the students have a good look at a living example that crime does not pay. Richetti was brought out of his cell twice that day for the curious.

When one of the officers told him Floyd's body had left East Liverpool, Richetti wept.

Extra guards were placed at the ninety-five-year-old jail, and it was lit up with floodlights. The jail, built for eighteen prisoners, held sixty-six, with four or five in each cell. Twice it had been condemned as unfit, most recently in 1932, when the federal government had condemned it for federal prisoners. From 1930 to 1932 four prisoners had escaped. Richetti was in a cell with three small-time criminals. The sheriff said, "We're ready for anything and anybody that wants to come."

Richetti told officers he would resist attempts to extradite him to Kansas City. "I want a lawyer," he said. Missouri and Ohio authorities fought over his custody.[49]

Fultz resented the FBI's lack of cooperation with him. Purvis had come to him under an assumed name and obtained valuable information on the whereabouts of Floyd. Then Purvis left without offering any cooperation. He was also "sore" at the fifteen-man East Liverpool police for not cooperating with his two-man force, although he was the best of friends with Chief "Hughie" McDermott.[50] Fultz issued a statement the day after Floyd's death:

Mr. Purvis and his men walked out and would not cooperate with us, and instead went to another city after we had given full details of the case, full descriptions of Floyd and the vicinity where we felt he was. He was captured only a short distance away from where we had mentioned.[51]

As one newspaperman later put it, "Some hold that, like every other triumph of G-Men, the credit belongs to local police who listened to Hoover's plea to call in his crime fighters, only to be robbed of glory."[52]

On the night of Floyd's death, Hoover had ordered that renewed efforts be made to gain custody of Richetti.[53]

Referring to a telephone call from newspaperman Rex Collier, Hoover wrote on October 24:

Mr. Collier remarked that the Chief is complaining because Mr. Purvis came to him under an assumed name. I stated this was in order to avoid publicity, and the truth of the matter is that the Chief is upset because he did not participate in the capture of Floyd; that he had given out a story Sunday night to the effect that Floyd had been shot in the stomach, which later was found not to be true.[54]

The previous day Hoover had told Sam Bledsoe of the Associated Press, "these authorities are evidently publicity seekers." Finally Hoover ordered that no assistance be given Wellsville authorities by the FBI, such as sending them fugitive and crime bulletins.[55]

The press supported Hoover's views of Chief Fultz. The *Washington Herald* of October 24, 1934, stated that although Chief Fultz took his position supposedly out of pique over "Federal interference," it was really because Wellsville officers were not in at the "kill."[56]

According to an editorial, "Floyd Let Chief Fultz Down," in the *Kansas City Star*:

There seems to be little doubt that an unkind fate is dogging the footsteps of Police Chief John H. Fultz. . . . The unfortunate extermination of Floyd . . . by Melvin Purvis and party, seems to have been a detail not altogether expected by the Wellsville chief, and . . . he is being hounded by the same malicious fate that kept the late Sir John Falstaff from appearing the hero he doubtless really was.

Let us consider first the details of Chief Fultz's exploit, as re-

lated in his own simple, unassuming way, under his own by-
line: "I shot Pretty Boy Floyd in the stomach. He is badly
wounded. . . . Besides being wounded, he is disarmed." Those
who were present, however, at the death of Floyd, after Purvis
and party had finished with him, found that Floyd was not shot
in the stomach; that he was struck by four bullets, three in the
back and one in an arm. And he carried two automatic pistols,
fully loaded.

This would seem to leave Chief Fultz's version of Saturday's
affair 100 per cent wrong, which is altogether too wrong for
credibility, even for a police chief. . . . Clearly the blame is all
Floyd's. He let the chief down.[57]

A few weeks later Missouri authorities finally got custody of Richetti for the killing of a Missouri sheriff and patrolman in June 1933.[58]

The Oklahoma hill country was full of sorrow. But there were few
tears. Floyd's mother was at first dubious when she heard of her son's
death from Mrs. D. A. Gean, wife of the editor of a weekly newspaper
at Sallisaw. Mrs. Floyd said, "It can't be true," when told by the *Tulsa
Daily World* at 5 P.M. But when she was sure he was dead, she
"gripped the front door . . . tightly and stared, dry-eyed, out the door,
into space."

The front yard filled quickly with relatives, friends, and the curious. Except for his weeping sister Mary, Floyd's relatives were angry.

They were especially angry at the press for what they felt was un-
fair treatment of Floyd. Mrs. Floyd told Mrs. Gean, "I don't want any
newspaper reporters around my home. If I catch any, I'll have them
arrested for trespassing. There will be no cameras around here either.
I don't mean maybe. I mean no."[59]

She told a *Tulsa Daily World* reporter:

Regardless of what the newspapers have to say, Charles has
not done one thousandth of the crimes he has been accused of.
His sense of loyalty to his family and friends was his chief
characteristic. As a little boy he would tell the truth regardless
of the consequences.

I am positive he was not in the Kansas City shooting. Between my anxiety for Charles and the nagging of newspapermen, my life has been made miserable during all the time he has been hunted. Charles was always courteous and truthful and that is something that you cannot say about newspaper reporters.

Charles was not a bad boy at heart and he has always warned all boys to steer clear of violations of the law. My one and only thought now is to get my boy for he is with his enemies and not a loved one there.[60]

Ruby and Jackie, whose home had been at Bixby since September, were appearing on stage at Fort Smith. Showing no outward sign of emotion, Ruby said, "As I expected. I wonder how many poor farmers are indebted to him for paying off mortgages on their farms or renting them places to live." She added, "He had gone too far to surrender."

The last time she had seen him, she claimed, was at Wewoka, Oklahoma, the day after the Kansas City Massacre. She doubted he took part in that crime, because "he was not that type. He fired his gun only to stop people chasing him. If he ever killed, I did not know it."

Ruby said that when Floyd had been released from prison, he came to her at her father's farm at Bixby and "we resolved to start life over and he got a job in the oil field at Earlsboro. We were happy until one day they arrested Charles for a robbery. He was released, but the idea that he would be arrested because he was a former convict discouraged him."

She admitted Floyd had not sent her any money for the last two years. "I guess he just didn't have any money. And, of course, he was afraid to communicate with me."[61]

Floyd's brother Bradley said, "I guess it's better as it is. I haven't seen Charley in six months."[62]

Juanita and Rose had fled from East Liverpool when they heard the news of the gunfight at Wellsville, and made no attempt to find Floyd and Richetti. They attended Floyd's funeral.[63]

The widow of Sheriff Erv Kelley, whom Floyd had killed, said, "I'm glad it happened." She had been apprehensive because their son had been hunting Floyd ever since his father's death in 1932. Kelley's brother, though gratified, said, "I would much rather have done it myself."[64]

. . .

Floyd's body was taken to the Sturgis Funeral Home in East Liverpool in the FBI car. On the way there, McDermott had wanted to take the handcuffs off the dead man, but Purvis objected. The $122 they had taken from Floyd was given to the Sturgis Funeral Home for Floyd's relatives when they came for his body.[65]

A pottery worker made a plaster death mask of Floyd's face for Deputy Sheriff George Hayes. An undertaker, Frank A. Dawson, later said, "The nickname 'Pretty Boy' was no misnomer; you could see where he plucked his eyebrows." And the nails of his fingers, officers were startled to observe, were trimmed to a point. Souvenir hunters stole the clothes from the body of a transient laborer who had died that day at the Swaney Airfield. "Somebody, somewhere has a pair of shoes he thinks were Floyd's," said Dawson.[66]

Fingerprint impressions were taken and sent to FBI headquarters. Fingers 7 to 10 had a frayed appearance, as if sandpapered; the results were merely blotches. But the remaining six prints were clear enough to identify Floyd.[67]

Photographers had a flip attitude about Floyd's body. One said, "That'll make a dandy picture, undertaker."[68]

Chief McDermott received a wire from Floyd's mother that night, but it was too late to comply with it: "I am the mother of Charles Floyd. If he has been killed, turn the body over to a reliable undertaker and prevent any pictures being taken of him and bar the public. Pass this request to the U.S. Department of Justice. Hold body until I arrive."[69]

She had said, "The law has reaped its reward and I would appreciate seeing my wishes carried out." McDermott did not allow the public in the next day.[70]

One newspaper wrote, "all of eastern Ohio has made his death the occasion for a holiday."[71]

A crowd of at least five hundred gathered outside of the undertaking parlor, struggling to get a glimpse of the dead man. They pushed their way into the building after the body was carried in on a stretcher.

The crowd had increased to five thousand when Floyd's body was placed on public view at 8:30 P.M. A line of people, two abreast, who thought Floyd deserved his nickname and were impressed by his excellent physique, passed the body until 11:15 P.M.

Before the night was over, up to twenty thousand people had

milled through the streets of East Liverpool. The porch railing of the funeral home was torn off, hedges and shrubbery were badly trampled, and the lawn was completely ruined.

Police Chief McDermott, meeting each of the thousands of persons as they filed through, stood at the head of a small, low cot. Floyd looked as though he were sleeping, his form solid under a rose-colored coverlet.

When news photographers came on the front porch, the crowd cheered and surged forward, hoping to get into the pictures. Police had to hold them back. People raised their hands, some were boosted to others' shoulders, and hats were waved toward the cameramen.

The excited mob, shouting and talking incessantly, pressed against the porch. Police forced the crowd back to the sidewalk and set up ropes. But many dodged under and got in by the rear or side doors.

The crush of bodies extended far out into the street and for a hundred feet on both sides. As newsboys added to the noise, trying to sell extra editions of newspapers, the story of Floyd's death and how he had boasted that he would "never be taken alive" was told again and again. People went back and forth, seemingly with no goal in mind. Crowds formed around anyone, such as policemen, who might know something. Cars jammed the streets. Many stores stayed open until midnight and did a thriving business. Several thousand people were still waiting when the viewing was closed.[72]

Immediately afterward an autopsy was performed by doctors Roy Costello and Edward W. Miskall, who found Floyd had been shot just three times. There was an old wound in the left ankle, which was consistent with reports he had been wounded there at the time he had killed Sheriff Erv Kelley in 1932.[73]

There was no wound in the left shoulder, although it had been reported he had been wounded there during the Kansas City Massacre. This was believed by many to jeopardize the FBI's case, because it was contrary to the FBI's main witness, James LaCapra. But the FBI argued that the wound might have faded away.[74]

Death was due to internal hemorrhage.

A steel-jacketed .44 or .45 caliber bullet, believed fired from the gun of East Liverpool policeman Herman Roth, had proven fatal. Entering the body on the right side, it had passed through the liver and was removed from below the heart, where it had come to rest.

Another .45 caliber bullet had pierced the left side and lodged in the rib cage in the upper left chest, taking part of the lung. Visible as a red protrusion that nearly broke the skin of the chest, it was removed and given to Chief McDermott.

A smaller caliber bullet, probably from a rifle, had passed through his right forearm.

There was no injury to the spleen, but there was a jagged wound on the right kidney, several perforations of the small intestines and the ascending colon, and an extensive penetrating wound of the pancreas.[75]

The body was enclosed in a cloth-lined shipping case and a pine "rough box" as it left East Liverpool for Sallisaw about 11:30 the morning after Floyd's killing, unaccompanied by any family members because the Floyd family could not raise enough money to travel to East Liverpool. A fund of $127.50 had been raised by friends of the family to transport Floyd's body home.[76]

Two men tried to get to the body on the railroad car, but were chased away. Only thirty people, mostly newspapermen and photographers, saw it leave.[77] Some two hundred citizens met the train when it got to Sallisaw on October 26, in chilly darkness at two in the morning. Several became hysterical and one woman fainted. They escorted the body to the funeral home and then to E. W. Floyd's home. One hundred people volunteered to sit up with the body the rest of the night.[78]

Floyd's mother invited everybody but newspaper reporters to the funeral at Akins on the following Sunday. Over twenty thousand came. It was a circus, with the mob eating peanuts, drinking corn liquor, spreading picnic lunches, carrying pistols, upsetting gravestones, trampling graves, and ripping down fences as they tried to hear the sermon and catch a glimpse of the notorious outlaw. Funeral wreaths were reduced to fragments by souvenir hunters.[79]

 # Epilogue

On the day of Floyd's death, October 22, 1934, the federal grand jury in Kansas City began its investigation into the Kansas City Massacre. Two days later it handed down indictments against Richard and Elizabeth Galatas, Herbert and Esther Farmer, Frances Nash, Louis (Doc) Stacci, Fritz Mulloy, and Vivian Mathias on the charge of conspiracy to obstruct justice by causing the escape of a federal prisoner from the custody of the United States.

All of them were tried and found guilty on January 4, 1935. The next day, Herbert Farmer, Galatas, and Mulloy were each sentenced to two years in Alcatraz and fined ten thousand dollars. Doc Stacci got two years in Leavenworth and a ten thousand-dollar fine.

Frances Nash received immunity and testified for the government. Vivian Mathias, who had already served a year and a day in prison, pleaded guilty at the start of the trial and was granted probation, as were Elizabeth Galatas and Esther Farmer.[1]

Jimmy LaCapra, the government's star witness, still feared for his life when he was released from the Sumner County jail in Wellington, Kansas, on January 2, 1935. FBI Agent Harold Andersen urged him to flee to South America, where he had relatives. But LaCapra refused, and went to New York. On August 21, 1935, his luck failed; his bullet-riddled body was found on a highway near New Paltz, New York.[2]

Attorney General Cummings asked Hoover about the press reports that Purvis had been told by Floyd that he had not participated in the Kansas City Massacre.[3]

During November 1934, Richetti and Floyd were cleared of the charge they had killed two police officers near Mexico, Missouri, when two others admitted to the crime.[4] Richetti was turned over to the Kansas City authorities to be tried for murder in the Kansas City Massacre; on June 10, 1935, his trial began. Mrs. Lottie West was one of the few to testify. A week later, exactly two years after the Massacre, Richetti was found guilty and sentenced to hang.[5]

Richetti convincingly acted insane, but some FBI officials believed he feigned insanity to avoid his fate.[6] His talented legal help was able to delay his execution for years. He was executed on October 7, 1938, at the Missouri State Penitentiary at Jefferson City, not by hanging but in the newly decreed "humane" gas chamber. It was an ugly scene, with Richetti being dragged to the execution site imploring, "What did I do to deserve this?" A few minutes after midnight he was strapped to the chair. He blubbered and declared he was innocent. As the doors closed, he screamed and was seen through the observation window cringing in the chair. Soon he was silent.[7]

Juanita and Rose, who had attended Floyd's funeral, were arrested by the FBI on November 15, 1934, at the home of Floyd's mother. They told the FBI about their life with Floyd and Richetti, and also that they had been in Buffalo most of the time since the Massacre. Their story checked out. For example, the key found on Floyd's body opened the door of their Buffalo apartment. Juanita had said that Purvis had been put on the "spot" by the underworld, but there was nothing to this. For some unexplained reason the women were not prosecuted for harboring Floyd. Later they became involved with Texas drug peddlers.[8]

Although an official FBI memorandum the day after Floyd's death stated that agents were "rendered excellent cooperation and assistance by Chief of Police Hugh J. McDermott of East Liverpool, Ohio, and Sheriff Ray Long," Hoover was not impressed. Purvis, who thought "McDermott was very cooperative during the chase," did not know whether McDermott became involved in the case at his request or through another lead. Actually, Special Agent Herman Hollis had asked McDermott for his aid. Still, Purvis was undecided about a letter of commendation, but thought a reward of $250 to each policeman involved should be given, to increase police support for the bureau.[9]

S. P. Cowley concurred on the reward, although he definitely believed there should not be any letter of commendation. He thought McDermott did not furnish information to the FBI and did not do anything particular to merit commendation—only what any officer would do under the circumstances. He also believed Sheriff Long was not cooperative.

Assistant FBI Director Clyde Tolson did not want to pay a reward or send a letter of commendation to either Sheriff Long or Chief McDermott. Hoover wrote to Tolson, "I agree. I can't quite understand Cowley or Purvis wanting us to pay something but write nothing."[10]

One local resident wrote to Hoover, asking him to write a letter of commendation to deputy sheriffs George Hayes and Charley Patterson. He did not.[11]

Many claims were made about whose gun brought Floyd down. Did the credit belong to East Liverpool Officer Smith or Roth, or to Special Agent McKee? Huge rewards had been reported in the press, but almost none were paid. Robert Robinson, Clyde O. Birch, Mrs. Conkle, and Chief McDermott (for his police pension fund) asked for the rewards for providing information. As far as is known, only Robinson received a hundred-dollar reward from *True Detective Mysteries.* The widows of lawmen killed in the Kansas City Massacre did receive five thousand dollars from Congress. Fultz tried to get Floyd's machine gun from the FBI as his reward, but he failed.[12]

Purvis's career with the FBI and his public reputation peaked with the Floyd case. At the time he was considered by many to be the number one law enforcement officer in the nation. Even Hoover congratulated him. But Hoover forced him to resign in 1935 and tried to make Purvis an "unperson" by writing him out of histories of the FBI.

Purvis cashed in on his fame in several different ways. He wrote a book, *American Agent,* in 1936 and formed the Junior G-Men for a breakfast cereal, Post Toasties. Gradually the public forgot about him as he tried several different jobs. Hoover refused to see him again and gave him bad evaluations that hampered his search for work. The FBI director even refused to send the Purvis family a letter of condolence after Purvis committed suicide in 1960. But after his death the public remembered Purvis again.[13]

C. C. Patterson, a member of the Pretty Boy Floyd gang who had been captured and shot up so badly that he was crippled when the gang robbed the Boley, Oklahoma, bank, spent many years in the Oklahoma State Penitentiary at McAlester. After his release he worked at a filling station in Arizona, where he was occasionally visited by Major H. C. McCormick, who had been at the Boley robbery.[14]

After Floyd's death his family led quiet lives. Ruby wed again shortly afterward. She died of cancer on July 29, 1970. One of his brothers, E. W. Floyd, served with distinction as sheriff of Sequoyah County for twenty-two years until his death in 1970. Floyd's mother, who lived to be almost a hundred years old, was an active churchgoer and lived in Sallisaw until her death on June 16, 1978. In 1974 she and her family had served as consultants for a TV movie about Pretty Boy Floyd.

Soon after Floyd's death his son Jack moved in with his maternal grandfather on an Oklahoma farm. During World War II he served in the navy, and after the war settled in Richmond, California, where he married and had two children.

He had several jobs, including working in poker casinos in the San Francisco area for seventeen years and serving as a consultant on another movie about his father. In 1981 he decided to open his own poker casino in Martinez, California, that also memorialized his father as a museum of sorts.[15]

Jack, who had once had an assumed name at school, said, "People were very good to me and my mother. I guess they felt sorry for us. But my father's reputation was never held against us by the people we know."

Jack felt his father was a "warm, wonderful person" to his only son.

He was very good to everyone he knew. But I've never really felt bitter about losing my father.

If he did kill people, like they say, he did it as a basic law of nature, survival of the fittest. But I don't think he ever went looking to kill people. . . . It's surprising but people here don't say much bad about him. They consider him part of the folklore. . . . Actually I think he was considered more or less one of their [the Midwest's] own people.

His family and friends thought Floyd could have been successful in an honest job. But he met the wrong people in Kansas City and "he just got started wrong."[16]

But Jack was "not trying to whitewash him. If any young people think it was a glamorous life, they should look at the outcome. He died when he was thirty years old, he was always on the run and he ended up with hardly any money, and he was denied the opportunity to be with his family."[17]

After Floyd's death, the FBI was riding high. In quick succession all of the remaining major public enemies of the period were killed or captured. Barely a month after Floyd's demise, Baby Face Nelson met his end in Illinois on November 27, 1934, after a gunfight with the FBI. But the FBI paid a heavy price with the deaths of two agents, Samuel Cowley and Herman Hollis, who had played a major role in the Dillinger and Floyd cases. A few weeks later, on January 16, 1935, Ma Barker and Freddy Barker died in Florida in another sensational gunfight with the FBI. Now there was only one major public enemy left, Alvin Karpis. After two robberies and several escapes, he was finally arrested in New Orleans in May 1936 by FBI agents led by Hoover himself. This marked the end of the gangster era.[18]

Hoover said at the Attorney General's Conference on Crime in December 1934:

John Dillinger, the flagbearer of lawlessness, is dead, killed by Federal bullets. "Pretty Boy" Floyd, who for years laughed at the law—lies in his grave, dead of gunshot wounds inflicted in open battle by our special agents. The career of "Baby Face" Nelson is over: he died of seventeen bullet wounds while two of the finest men I ever knew gave their own clean lives that they might serve society by ending his filthy one. Wilbur Underhill no longer carries the name of the Tri-State Terror. He too is gone, as well as such men as Homer Van Meter, Tommy Carroll, and others. That is progress.[19]

In the museum at FBI headquarters in Washington, the Floyd exhibit was "one of the most popular and widely known of the exhibits."

It included his guns (which showed a lot of wear) and a picture of a short chain from which dangled his watch and his "lucky piece," a silver half-dollar. On the watch, ten notches were on the inside works and ten notches on the crystal, and another ten notches were on the "lucky piece," apparently carved by Floyd as an indication of the number of men he had killed.[20] On February 4, 1935, Hoover had told a congressional committee about the notches and called them a form of "self-flattery." The FBI had returned the watch and a cameo ring to Floyd's mother.[21]

Actually the FBI held Floyd responsible for eleven deaths: Jim Mills, the two Ash brothers, patrolman Ralph Castner, Prohibition Agent Curtis C. Burks, Oklahoma Sheriff Erv A. Kelley, and the five men killed in the Kansas City Massacre, including an FBI agent.

Hoover often gave special tours for VIPs and showed them trophies of the public enemy era. Shirley Temple was given such a tour in the summer of 1938 and later wrote about it:

J. Edgar Hoover's car picked us up, all seven and a half tons of it sheathed in armor and one-inch-thick bulletproof glass. His office was heaven. In a corner stood a tall American flag; plaques and garishly beribboned certificates plastered his walls, and an entrancing assortment of mysterious mementos was scattered on his desk and ranged along the bookcase. He pointed out two life-sized white plaster casts, identifying them as death masks of Pretty Boy Floyd and Baby Face Nelson. Never having seen a dead hoodlum, I examined each carefully, two pale old men, eyes closed and faces reposed in sleep.[22]

But the FBI was not popular everywhere. Floyd's neighbors in Sequoyah County threatened to shoot its agents.[23]

There are many conflicting accounts of the details of Floyd's last two days, although the major points are agreed on. But some of the details are of more than trivial importance, because they involve the reputation of one of America's most idealized institutions—the FBI.

Even at the time there were some who believed Floyd's killing was unjustified. For example, there was Oswald Garrison Villard, one of the founders of the NAACP and the liberal editor of *Nation* magazine. Hoover referred to him as "Our old subject . . . of the war days & then later of the radical movement."[24] Villard wrote a column in the *Chattanooga News* entitled "Cold-Blooded Murder; Department of Justice Hurts Law Enforcement by 'Lynching' of Floyd and Other Criminals—Crime Never Stopped by Sensational Methods":

Is it not time to call a halt upon the Department of Justice's cold-blooded murder of gangsters? The other night I ran across two distinguished judges of the State of New Jersey. They asked me what I thought of the killing of "Pretty Boy" Floyd. I said that it seemed to me lynching, pure and simple. They replied that it was far worse than lynching because it was done by officers of the law, sworn to uphold the law and the orderly processes of the courts . . . and declared that so far from helping enforcement of justice in the United States it was hurting it. . . . They agreed with me that such a thing could happen in no other country in the world, expect among the Nazis and others, who deliberately murder men and declare that they were "shot while escaping." They dwelt with particular horror on the pumping of thirteen bullets into "Pretty Boy" Floyd when he was surrounded and escape was impossible. They were convinced that the majesty of the law would have been much better served had Floyd been taken into court and sent to the electric chair by the regular procedure. . . .

A member of the younger generation asked me very seriously whether it was not better to exterminate outlaws as Floyd was killed than to have them running around the country killing and robbing. This was obviously beside the mark. That these men should be run down and imprisoned, or, if the law requires it, executed, is obvious. But when Government resorts to the methods of Messrs. Purvis and Hoover, it admits that it has sunk to the level of the gangsters, that the regular procedure has broken down, and that the Government's law-enforcement machinery is so weak that it has itself to resort to extralegal methods to rid the country of these public enemies. . . .

When one sees the publicity given to Purvis and Hoover . . . one begins to wonder whether there isn't some other motive behind the spectacular character of these exterminations. Certainly, familiarizing the whole underworld with their personalities cannot add to their efficiency as detectives.[25]

On November 30, 1934, at the annual convention of the Illinois Bar Association, several lawyers criticized the "trigger-happy" FBI.[26]

FBI officials insisted that the killing of Floyd was justified even as they lied about it. For example, reporter Rex Collier, who named Inspector Samuel P. Cowley as the leader of the special agents who killed Floyd instead of Purvis, wrote:

Federal Bureau of Investigation agents have been accused of shooting him [Floyd] in the back "in cold blood."

> There were rumors among critics of the bureau that Floyd fell on his knee and begged for mercy as ruthless agents poured lead into his body. . . .

> There is no doubt there was considerable sympathy in scattered places for this notorious outlaw and killer from the Cookson hills of Oklahoma.

> Yet this was the man . . . who killed, kidnaped and plundered his way to the top of the list of public enemies. . . .

> Hoover ordered his men to intensify their hunt for Floyd and Richetti, but it can be said definitely that at no time were "shoot on sight" or "shoot to kill" orders issued to the G-men by Hoover or anyone else.[27]

The most serious charge was by one of the patrolmen in the posse that killed Floyd, Chester C. Smith. *Time* magazine of September 24, 1979, in an article entitled "Blasting a G-Man Myth," reported that Smith claimed he was the first to see Floyd trying to get away. Smith said, "I knew Purvis couldn't hit him, so I dropped him with two shots from my .32 Winchester rifle."

Floyd was not seriously wounded, and Smith disarmed him. Purvis, according to Smith, then came up and ordered: "Back away from that man. I want to talk to him." Floyd was defiant and shouted several curses. Purvis then told Herman Hollis, "Fire into him," and Hollis killed Floyd with a tommy-gun burst.

Smith insisted there had been an FBI coverup and said, "Sure was, because they didn't want it to get out that he'd been killed that way."

He claimed he was now telling the truth because he was the only living person connected with the killing. No one would be hurt any longer.

Smith also said that while Floyd was dying, he had asked him why he did not stop when the lawmen first yelled at him to halt.

"He said, 'My object was to get into the woods, and if I did, I would have killed you all.'"

According to Smith, Purvis told him, "My orders from Mr. Hoover was to bring him in dead."

But there are many inconsistencies in Smith's accounts. The autopsy report does not support him. And Special Agent Hollis was not in the party that killed Floyd.

Smith was also known to have made up tales about having known Floyd when he was supposedly operating in East Liverpool in the mid-1920s.[28]

He was also wrong about being the only person involved in the Floyd killing still alive. W. E. (Bud) Hopton, one of the agents involved, branded the *Time* article "totally false." He wrote, "As is too often the case in recent years with the news media and publications such as yours, you are being taken in by publicity seekers without making any effort to determine whether the allegations are true."[29]

Time implied that it was making sensational new charges about Floyd's death. But in reality Smith had been saying those things for years. For example, the *Los Angeles Times* of October 19, 1974, reported that Floyd had been "murdered" by one shot from Hollis's revolver, after Smith had wounded Floyd with one shot.

Robert Bruce Nathan, the head of the FBI's Kansas City office during the early 1930s, wrote to the *Los Angeles Times* on November 9, 1974: "At no time was there any hint that Floyd was killed deliberately while in custody. We wanted him alive for questioning, hoping that this would assist in solving other cases. . . . It seems a shame that after 40 years there is this effort to besmirch the character of these men [Hollis and Purvis]."[30]

The *Times* even had an editorial, entitled "Questions for the FBI":

From the long past, a curious and bizarre story. A retired policeman, 79, of East Liverpool, Ohio, says Charles Arthur (Pretty Boy) Floyd, a notorious gangster of the 1930s, was deliberately shot to death by order of an FBI agent as Floyd lay wounded in an Ohio cornfield.

The policeman is the only survivor of the seven law enforcement men present at Floyd's death in 1934, and his story, according to reports, was corroborated by another retired law officer, who says the same account was told to him in confidence 40 years ago by other participants. The FBI version at the time in 1934 said Floyd died in a burst of gunfire.

Does the FBI have evidence in its files to dispute the claim of the retired officer? Has the FBI questioned him or the other officer said to have verified the story? After four decades, these questions in connection with the death of a gangster may appear to be quixotic. They are not.[31]

The FBI director at the time, Clarence M. Kelley, in a letter to the *Times*, wrote: "Forty years have elapsed since Floyd's death, and the FBI remains convinced of the accuracy of the essential facts as they exist in our files and in Coroner Sturgis' report. You may be certain that we would have instituted an exhaustive inquiry into this matter were this not the case."[32]

The retired law officer who had corroborated Smith's account was Deputy Sheriff George E. Hayes, who had engaged Floyd in a gunfight at Lisbon, Ohio.[33]

Other factors supporting Smith are the statements of Hoover and other FBI officials, already mentioned, that sanctioned the summary killing of Floyd.

According to Chief McDermott, he had sent Purvis to call an ambulance. By the time he returned, Floyd was dead. McDermott asked Purvis if he had called the ambulance, and he said "no," that instead he had called the "big boss" in Washington.[34]

When Floyd's mother saw her son's body, she wondered how he could speak with such terrible wounds.[35]

Another contrary fact is that Mrs. Conkle, Stewart Dyke, and his wife all denied at the coroner's inquest that they had heard the lawmen give any commands to halt.[36]

Hundreds of thousands of words have appeared written about Charles "Pretty Boy" Floyd. Accounts of his life have appeared in books, detective magazines, newspapers, movies, radio, television, and pulp magazines, as well as in histories of the FBI. Today we come upon such oddities as a racehorse, an Australian boxer, and a heavy metal band named after him.[37]

These were typical of the doggerel at the time:

Of how Pretty Boy Floyd was a doggone fool. When he went to buy a dinner near East Liverpool.[38]

And

> Poor Charles Floyd was the bandits' pride—
> They knew him in the hills where he did hide—
> But Columbiana County ain't no Ozark Hill
> And down in Ohio they shoot to kill.[39]

In John Steinbeck's *The Grapes of Wrath,* Ma Joad says:

I knowed Purty Boy Floyd. I knowed his Ma. They was good folks. He was full of hell, sure, like a good boy oughta be. . . . He done a little bad thing an' they hurt 'im, caught 'im an' hurt him so he was mad, an' the next bad thing he done was mad, an' they hurt 'im again. An' purty soon he was mean-mad. They shot at him like a varmint, an' he shot back, an' then they run him like a coyote, an' him a-snappin' an' a-snarlin', mean as a lobo. An' he was mad. He wasn't no boy or no man no more, he was jus' a walkin' chunk a mean-mad. But the folks that knowed him didn't hurt 'im. He wasn't mad at them. Finally they run him down an' killed 'im. No matter how they say it in the paper how he was bad—that's how it was.[40]

Woody Guthrie promoted Pretty Boy Floyd's image as a Robin Hood. According to his famous song, Floyd took to a crime career only after a deputy insulted his wife and he killed him. But he robbed to help the poor, such as paying the mortgages of poor farmers:

> Well, as through this world I've rambled,
> I've seen lots of funny men,
> Some rob you with a six-gun,

Others with a fountain pen.
As through this world you travel,
As through this world you roam,
You'll never see an outlaw
Drive a family from their home.

A revue, *Outside the Law*, performed in New York City in 1989 by the Irondale Ensemble and derived from Shakespeare's *As You Like It*, is a contemporary morality tale with such real-life figures as Floyd, J. Edgar Hoover, and Oliver North.[41]

With Floyd's death the days of the so-called Robin Hood bandits were coming to an end. Although he deserves the condemnation any killer and robber must receive, he had many virtues, such as courage, loyalty to his family and friends, and compassion for those who struggled to survive during the bleak years of the Depression.

 # Notes

FBI documentation of the 1930s was not consistent. For example, the four-digit-maximum number added to the FBI file number (for example, 62-28915-2655) was often omitted. At other times the number was illegible. Memorandums usually listed the names of the persons who prepared them as well as to whom they were sent, but there are instances where the documents contain no personal names.

Introduction

1. Bob L. Blackburn, "Law Enforcement in Transition: From Decentralized County Sheriffs to the Highway Patrol," *The Chronicles of Oklahoma* 56 (Summer 1978): 200. To simplify matters, the term *FBI* is used for the entire history of the organization even though it was not officially named "Federal Bureau of Investigation" until July 1935.

2. J. Edgar Hoover, Address to Hi-Y Clubs of America, June 22, 1936 (FBI Office of Congressional and Public Affairs).

3. Lew Louderback, *The Bad Ones: Gangsters of the '30s and Their Molls* (Greenwich, Conn.: Fawcett, 1968), 7–11; *Oklahoma City Daily Oklahoman*, June 2, 1932.

4. Louderback, *Bad Ones*, 8–9; *Oklahoma City Oklahoma News*, Oct. 26, 1934.

5. Blackburn, "Law Enforcement," 195.

6. *Tulsa Daily World*, Sept. 18, 1932.

7. Blackburn, "Law Enforcement," 200.

8. *Tulsa Daily World*, Mar. 17, 1929; May 29, June 9, 1931.

9. Courtney Ryley Cooper, "Bandit Land," *Saturday Evening Post* 207 (Aug. 4, 1934): 30.

10. Louderback, *Bad Ones*, 131; Michael Wallis, *Pretty Boy: The Life and Times of Charles Arthur Floyd* (New York: St. Martin's Press, 1992), passim.

11. Louderback, *Bad Ones*, 130.

12. *Oklahoma News*, Oct. 26, 1934.

13. Louderback, *Bad Ones*, 132.

14. *Tulsa Daily World*, Oct. 14, Aug. 21, 1933; *New York Times*, Oct. 23, 1934; *Oklahoma News*, Oct. 25, 1934.

15. Louderback, *Bad Ones*, 133.

16. David Einstein, "Son's Poker Palace Revives Legend of 'Pretty Boy' Floyd," Associated Press, Oct. 20, 1981; Louderback, *Bad Ones*, 132; *Oklahoma News*, Oct. 26, 1934.

17. Louderback, *Bad Ones*, 132.

18. *Tulsa Daily World*, Jan. 4, Apr. 10, 1932; *Oklahoma News*, Oct. 26, 1934; Louderback, *Bad Ones*, 132.

19. Louderback, *Bad Ones*, 131; Einstein, "Son's Poker Palace."

20. *Oklahoma News*, Oct. 26, 1934; *St. Louis Globe-Democrat*, May 6, 1934.

21. *Tulsa Daily World*, Mar. 13, 1934.

22. Ibid., Apr. 9, 1934.

23. Ibid., Mar. 5, 1934.

1. A Cornbread Living

1. *Muskogee Daily Phoenix*, Oct. 29, 1934.

2. Ibid., Oct. 28, 1934; Louderback, *Bad Ones*, 169–70.

3. *Muskogee Daily Phoenix*, Oct. 29, 1934.

4. *Tulsa Daily World*, Oct. 29, 1934; *Muskogee Daily Phoenix*, Oct. 29, 1934.

5. *Muskogee Daily Phoenix*, Oct. 29, 1934.

6. Ibid.

7. Ibid.; *Tulsa Daily World*, Oct. 29 1934; *Daily Oklahoman*, Oct. 31, 1934.

8. *Muskogee Daily Phoenix*, Oct. 29, 1934.

9. Ruth Floyd Wofford, "Floyd, Walter," in *The History of Sequoyah County, 1828–1975* (Sallisaw, Okla.: Sequoyah County Historical Society, 1976), 250–51; *Tulsa Daily World*, Oct. 23, 1934.

10. Wofford, "Floyd, Walter," 250–51.

11. Ibid.; Wallis, *Pretty Boy*, 24, 35, 87, 134.

12. Wofford, "Floyd, Walter," 250–51.

13. *Oklahoma News*, Oct. 26, 1934.

14. Wallis, *Pretty Boy*, 116.

15. Ibid., 176.

16. Paul I. Wellman, *A Dynasty of Western Outlaws* (Lincoln: University of Nebraska Press, 1986), 313–24.

17. *Oklahoma News*, Oct. 26, 1934.

18. Wofford, "Floyd, Walter," 250–51.

19. *Tulsa Daily World*, Apr. 17, 1932; Kent L. Steckmesser, "The Oklahoma Robin Hood," *The American West* 7 (Jan. 1970): 39.

20. "Homage to an Outlaw," *People Weekly* 38 (July 6, 1992): 83–86.

21. Steckmesser, "Oklahoma Robin Hood," 39; Louderback, *Bad Ones*, 132.

22. *Oklahoma News*, Oct. 25, 1934; *Muskogee Daily Phoenix*, Oct. 24, 23, 1934.

23. J. H. Harkrider interview by Grace Kelly, May 20, 1937, in Indian Pioneer Papers 39:49 (available at the University of Oklahoma Library, Western History Collections).

24. *Tulsa Daily World*, Apr. 17, 1932.

25. Dick O'Connor, *G-Men at Work: The Story of America's Fight Against Crime and Corruption* (London: John Lang, 1939), 8.

26. *Tulsa Daily World*, Apr. 17, 1932.

27. *Sallisaw (Okla.) Sequoyah County Democrat*, May 19, 1922; various court records of the District Court of the United States for the Eastern District of Oklahoma concerning "Charley" Floyd and J. Harold Franks, Fort Worth branch of the National Archives, file 7660.

28. Wallis, *Pretty Boy*, 118.

29. *Tulsa Daily World*, Oct. 23, 1934.

30. Ibid.; FBI Identification Order no. 1194, June 22, 1933 (Charles Floyd) (available at FBI Research Unit).

31. Louderback, *Bad Ones*, 132–33.

32. *Toledo News-Bee*, Nov. 2, 1934; *Muskogee Daily Phoenix*, Oct. 24, 1934; *Kansas City Times*, Oct. 24, 1934.

33. *Toledo News-Bee*, Nov. 2, 1934; *Tulsa Daily World*, June 21, 1934.

34. Wellman, *Dynasty*, 325–27.

35. *Tulsa Daily World*, Aug. 21, 1933.

36. James Evetts Haley, *Robbing Banks Was My Business: The Story of J. Harvey Bailey* (Canyon, Tex.: Palo Duro Press, 1973), 74–75.

37. Ibid., 75–76.

38. Louderback, *Bad Ones*, 135; *Toledo News-Bee*, Nov. 2, 1934; Wallis, *Pretty Boy*, 141.

39. *St. Louis Globe-Democrat*, Sept. 18, 1925.

40. Ibid.

41. *St. Louis Post-Dispatch*, Aug. 23, 1925.

42. *St. Louis Globe-Democrat*, Sept. 18, 1925.

43. Ibid., Sept. 16, 17, 1925; *St. Louis Post-Dispatch*, Oct. 23, 1934.

44. *St. Louis Globe-Democrat*, Sept. 18, 17, 12, 1925; *St. Louis Post-Dispatch*, Sept. 11, 12, 1925, May 6, 1992.

45. *St. Louis Globe-Democrat*, Sept. 12, 16, 18, 1925.

46. Ibid., Sept. 15, 16, 1925; *Muskogee Daily Phoenix*, Oct. 24, 1934.

47. *St. Louis Globe-Democrat*, Sept. 16, 1925.

48. *Muskogee Daily Phoenix*, Oct. 24, 1934.

49. *St. Louis Globe-Democrat*, Sept. 17, 1925.

50. Ibid., Sept. 18, 1925.

51. Ibid.; Missouri State Prison record of Charles Floyd (available from State Archivist, Missouri Office of Secretary of State); Wallis, *Pretty Boy*, 151.

52. Donald Schroeger, "The Course of Corrections in Missouri, 1833–1983," in *Official Manual, Missouri, 1983–1984* (Jefferson City: Office of Missouri Secretary of State, 1983), 1–23; "MSP Historical Information," *The Jefftown Journal*, historical ed. (Summer 1972).

53. Missouri State Prison record of Charles Floyd.

54. *Jefferson City (Mo.) Post Tribune*, Oct. 23, 1934.

55. Ibid.; Missouri State Prison record of Charles Floyd.

56. *Jefferson City (Mo.) Post Tribune*, Oct. 23, 1934.

57. *Tulsa Daily World*, Feb. 28, 1934.

58. Ibid., Oct. 23, 1934.

59. Missouri State Prison record of Alfred Lovett (available from State Archivist, Missouri Office of Secretary of State).

60. *Tulsa Daily World*, Oct. 23, 1934.

2. *They Just Wouldn't Let Me Alone After I Got Out*

1. Merle Clayton, *Union Station Massacre: The Shootout That Started the FBI's War on Crime* (New York: Leisure Books, 1975), 35–40.

2. Louderback, *Bad Ones*, 136.

3. FBI Identification Order for Charles Floyd.

4. *Tulsa Daily World*, Oct. 23, 1934.

5. Louderback, *Bad Ones*, 136.

6. Ibid., 138–39; *Oklahoma News*, Oct. 25, 1934; Report, John B. Little, Oklahoma City, Nov. 23, 1934, FBI File 62-28915-3237.

7. Report, John B. Little, Oklahoma City, Nov. 23, 1934, FBI File 62-28915-3237; *Oklahoma News*, Oct. 25, 1934.

8. Louderback, *Bad Ones*, 136.

9. Wallis, *Pretty Boy*, 176–80.

10. Report, John B. Little, Oklahoma City, Nov. 23, 1934, FBI File 62-28915-3237.

11. Ibid.

12. FBI Identification Order for Charles Floyd; *Pueblo* (Colo.) *Star-Journal*, Oct. 23, 1934.

13. FBI Identification Order for Charles Floyd; *Tulsa Daily World*, Dec. 6, 1932.

14. *Sallisaw Democrat-American*, Nov. 22, 1929; Report, John B. Little, Oklahoma City, Nov. 23, 1934, FBI File 62-28915-3237; Louderback, *Bad Ones*, 135; *Tulsa Daily World*, Apr. 17, 1932; Wallis, *Pretty Boy*, 182.

15. *Tulsa Daily World*, Dec. 6, 1932; *Kansas City Star*, Dec. 3, 1929.

16. *Kansas City Star*, Dec. 3, 1929.

17. Ibid., Dec. 4, 1929.

18. Report, John B. Little, Oklahoma City, Nov. 23, 1934, FBI File 62-28915-3237.

19. *Akron Beacon Journal*, March 13, 1930.

20. Ibid.

21. Ibid., Oct. 23, 1934.

22. *Toledo News-Bee*, Feb. 6, 1930.

23. *Akron Beacon Journal*, Mar. 10, 1930.

24. Ibid., Mar. 8, 1930.

25. Wallis, *Pretty Boy*, 201.

26. *Akron Beacon Journal*, Mar. 10, 1930.

27. Ibid, Oct. 23, 1934.

28. *Cleveland Plain Dealer*, Oct. 23, 1934.

29. *Akron Beacon Journal*, Mar. 10, 13, 1930; Wallis, *Pretty Boy*, 202.

30. Wallis, *Pretty Boy*, 195.

31. *Toledo News-Bee*, Mar. 12, 1930.

32. *Akron Beacon Journal*, Mar. 13, 1930.

33. *Toledo News-Bee*, March 15, 1930; *Akron Beacon Journal*, May 22, 1930.

34. *Akron Beacon Journal*, May 22, 1930.

35. *Toledo News-Bee*, May 22, 1930.

36. Report, John B. Little, Oklahoma City, Nov. 23, 1934, FBI File 62-28915-3237.

37. *Toledo News-Bee*, Nov. 11, 1930; *Akron Beacon Journal*, Oct. 23, 1930.

38. *Toledo News-Bee*, Nov. 25, 1930, Oct. 23, 1934.

39. Wallis, *Pretty Boy*, 196–97.

40. *Toledo News-Bee*, Nov. 25, 1930, Oct. 23, 1934.

41. Ibid., Apr. 17, 1931, Oct. 23, 1934.

42. Wellman, *Western Outlaws*, 314–15, 328.

43. *Toledo News-Bee,* Apr. 17, 1931, Oct. 23, 1934.
44. Ibid., Oct. 23, 1934.
45. Ibid.

3. Billy "the Killer" Miller

1. Report, John B. Little, Oklahoma City, Nov. 23, 1934, FBI File 62-28915-3237.
2. FBI Identification Order for Charles Floyd.
3. *Toledo News-Bee,* Apr. 17, 1931.
4. Ibid., Apr. 17, 18, 1931; *Kansas City Star,* Mar. 28, 1931.
5. Report, John B. Little, Oklahoma City, Nov. 23, 1934, FBI File 62-28915-3237.
6. Ibid.; *Tulsa Daily World,* Mar. 10, 1931.
7. Louderback, *Bad Ones,* 138–39.
8. *Kansas City Star,* Mar. 26, 1931; Letter, Special Agent in Charge (SAC), Kansas City, to Hoover, Aug. 22, 1934, FBI File 62-28915-2280 (includes official Kansas City, Kansas, police report on the Ash killings).
9. *Kansas City Star,* Mar. 26, 1931.
10. Report, John B. Little, Oklahoma City, Nov. 23, 1934, FBI File 62-28915-3237; *Tulsa Daily World,* May 17, 1932.
11. *Louisville* (Ky.) *Courier-Journal,* Apr. 7, 1931; Report, John B. Little, Oklahoma City, Nov. 23, 1934, FBI File 62-28915-3237; *Toledo News-Bee,* Apr. 18, 1931.
12. *Toledo News-Bee,* Apr. 14, 1931.
13. Ibid., Apr. 17, 1931.
14. Ibid.
15. Ibid., Apr. 17, 18, 20, 1931.
16. Ibid., Apr. 17, 1931.
17. Ibid., April 18, 1931.
18. Ibid., Apr. 20, 1931; Report, John B. Little, Oklahoma City, Nov. 23, 1934, FBI File 62-28915-3237.
19. *Toledo News-Bee,* Apr. 23, 1931.
20. Ibid., Apr. 17, 18, 20, 1931.
21. Louderback, *Bad Ones,* 140–41; *Oklahoma News,* Oct. 25, 1934.
22. *Kansas City Star,* July 21, 1931.
23. Ibid.
24. Ibid.
25. Ibid., July 21, 25, 1931; *Tulsa Daily World,* July 22, 1931.

4. The Phantom of the Ozarks

1. Leon E. Smith, *High Noon at the Boley Corral* (Detroit: Leeann Publications, Plus, n.d.), 9.
2. Myron J. Quimby, *The Devil's Emissaries* (New York: A. S. Barnes, 1969), 66–67; Louderback, *Bad Ones,* 141–42; Wallis, *Pretty Boy,* 221–24.
3. Quimby, *Devil's Emissaries,* 67.
4. Ibid., 67–68.
5. Smith, *High Noon,* 9, 26–27.
6. *Tulsa Daily World,* Oct. 23, 1934.
7. Smith, *High Noon,* 35, 40–44, 54.

8. Louderback, *Bad Ones*, 131–32; Henry Lysing (pseud. of John Leonard Nanovic), *Men Against Crime* (New York: David Kemp, 1938), 191.

9. *Muskogee Daily Phoenix*, Jan. 15, 1932.

10. *Tulsa Daily World*, Jan. 4, 1932.

11. Ibid., Apr. 10, 1932.

12. *Muskogee Daily Phoenix*, Aug. 5, 1931.

13. Ibid., Sept. 9, 1931.

14. Ibid., Sept. 30, 1931.

15. Ibid., Oct. 1, 1931; *Sallisaw Democrat-American*, Oct. 1, 1931.

16. *Muskogee Daily Phoenix*, Oct. 15, 1931.

17. Ibid., Nov. 6, 1931.

18. Ibid., Dec. 24, 27, 1931.

19. Ibid., Jan. 6, 1932; Report, Dwight Brantley, SAC, Oklahoma City, Nov. 20, 1934, FBI File 62-28915-3272.

20. *Tulsa Daily World*, Jan. 3, 4, 5, 6, 1932.

21. *Daily Oklahoman*, Jan. 4, 1932.

22. *Muskogee Daily Phoenix*, Jan. 4, 1932.

23. Ibid.; Jan. 15, 1932.

24. *Tulsa Daily World*, Jan. 15, 1932.

25. Ibid.; *Daily Oklahoman*, Jan. 15, 1932.

26. *Daily Oklahoman*, Jan. 15, 1932.

27. *Tulsa Daily World*, Jan. 15, 1932.

28. *Daily Oklahoman*, Jan. 16, 1932.

29. Ibid.

30. Ibid.

31. Ibid., Jan. 17, 1932.

32. Ibid.

33. Louderback, *Bad Ones*, 142; *Tulsa Daily World*, Jan. 17, 1932.

34. *Muskogee Daily Phoenix*, Jan. 18, 1932.

35. *Daily Oklahoman*, Jan. 17, 1932.

36. Ibid., Jan. 26, 1932.

37. *Tulsa Daily World*, Jan. 21, 1932.

38. *Muskogee Daily Phoenix*, Jan. 25, 1932.

39. *Daily Oklahoman*, Jan. 25, 1932.

40. *Tulsa Daily World*, Feb. 5, 1932.

41. *Daily Oklahoman*, Jan. 26, 1932.

42. *Tulsa Daily World*, Jan. 28, 1932.

43. Wallis, *Pretty Boy*, 217–18.

44. *Tulsa Daily World*, Oct. 23, 1934.

45. David Einstein, "Son's Poker Palace."

46. Wallis, *Pretty Boy*, 219–21, 226.

47. *Fort Smith* (Ark.) *Southwest American*, Oct. 23, 1934; *Akron Beacon Journal*, Oct. 23, 1934.

48. *Fort Smith Southwest American*, Oct. 23, 1934.

49. *Tulsa Daily World*, Oct. 23, 1934.

50. Ibid., Nov. 2, 1932.

51. Ibid., Feb. 12, 1932; *Tulsa Tribune*, Oct. 23, 1934.

52. *Muskogee Daily Phoenix*, Feb. 2, 1932.

53. *Tulsa Daily World*, Feb. 12, 1932; *Tulsa Tribune*, Oct. 23, 1934.

54. *Muskogee Daily Phoenix*, Feb. 9, 1932.

55. *Tulsa Daily World*, Feb. 9, 1932.

56. Louderback, *Bad Ones*, 143.

57. *Tulsa Daily World*, Feb. 9, 1932.

58. Ibid., Feb. 10, 1932.

59. Ibid., Feb. 11, 1932; Louderback, *Bad Ones*, 143.

60. *Tulsa Daily World*, Feb. 12, 1932.

61. *Muskogee Daily Phoenix*, Feb. 14, 1932.

62. *Tulsa Daily World*, Feb. 12, 13, 1932.

63. Ibid., Feb. 14, 15, 1932.

64. Ibid., Feb. 12, 13, 14, 1932.

65. *Oklahoma City Times*, Feb. 13, 1932.

66. *Tulsa Daily World*, Feb. 15, 1932.

67. Ibid., Feb. 24, 1932.

68. Ibid., Oct. 23, 1934; Cooper, "Bandit Land," 32.

5. All I Know Is You'll Never Catch Him

1. Louderback, *Bad Ones*, 143–44.

2. *Tulsa Daily World*, Apr. 10, 1932.

3. *Oklahoma News*, Oct. 30, 1934.

4. *Tulsa Daily World*, Apr. 17, 1932.

5. Ibid., Apr. 10, 1932.

6. *Muskogee Daily Phoenix*, Apr. 12, 1932.

7. Wallis, *Pretty Boy*, 257–58.

8. *Tulsa Daily World*, Apr. 10, 1932.

9. Ibid., Apr. 11, 1932.

10. Ibid., Apr. 10, 1932.

11. Ibid., Apr. 13, 1932.

12. Ibid., Apr. 14, 1932.

13. Ibid.

14. Ibid.

15. Ibid., May 8, 1932.

16. Ibid., May 7, 1932.

17. Ibid., Apr. 17, 1932.

18. Ibid., May 26, 1932; Wallis, *Pretty Boy*, 257–58.

19. *Muskogee Daily Phoenix*, Apr. 23, Nov. 25, 1932.

20. *Tulsa Daily World*, Apr. 22, 1932.

21. Ibid., Apr. 23, 1932.

22. Ibid., June 8, 1932.

23. *Daily Oklahoman*, June 8, 1932.

24. Ibid.

25. *Muskogee Daily Phoenix*, June 9, 1932.

26. *Tulsa Daily World*, June 10, 1932.

27. Ibid., June 12, 1932.

28. Ibid., June 10, 1932.

29. Louderback, *Bad Ones*, 145.

30. Ibid.

6. The Luckiest Bandit That Ever Lived

1. Report, John B. Little, Oklahoma City, Nov. 23, 1934, FBI File 62-28915-3237.
2. *Tulsa Daily World*, Dec. 6, 1932; Report, John B. Little, Oklahoma City, Nov. 23, 1934, FBI File 62-28915-3237.
3. *Oklahoma News*, Oct. 25, 1934.
4. *Muskogee Daily Phoenix*, July 28, 1932.
5. *Tulsa Daily World*, Dec. 6, 1932.
6. Wallis, *Pretty Boy*, 267, 295.
7. *Tulsa Daily World*, June 18, 1932; *Muskogee Daily Phoenix*, July 2, 1932; *Daily Oklahoman*, July 8, 1932.
8. *Tulsa Daily World*, Aug. 4, 5, 6, 7, 1932.
9. Ibid., Sept. 4, 1932.
10. *Muskogee Daily Phoenix*, July 27, 1932.
11. Ibid., July 30, 1932.
12. Ibid.
13. *Tulsa Daily World*, Sept. 28, 1932.
14. Louderback, *Bad Ones*, 145–46; *Muskogee Daily Phoenix*, Aug. 30, 1932.
15. *Muskogee Daily Phoenix*, Aug. 4, Sept. 4, 1932; *Tulsa Daily World*, Nov. 2, 1932.
16. *Tulsa Daily World*, Nov. 2, 1932.
17. Ibid.; *Muskogee Daily Phoenix*, Nov. 2, 1932; *Oklahoma News*, Nov. 2, 1932; "Oklahoma's 'Bandit King,'" *The Literary Digest* 114 (Dec. 10, 1932): 26–27; Louderback, *Bad Ones*, 146.
18. *Toledo News-Bee*, Nov. 3, 1934.
19. *Oklahoma News*, Oct. 28, 1934.
20. *Toledo News-Bee*, Nov. 3, 1934.
21. Cooper, "Bandit Land," 9.
22. *Tulsa Daily World*, Nov. 8, 1932.
23. Louderback, *Bad Ones*, 147.
24. Smith, *High Noon*, 55; *Tulsa Daily World*, Nov. 24, 1932.
25. *Daily Oklahoman*, Nov. 24, 1932.
26. *Muskogee Daily Phoenix*, Nov. 25, 1932.
27. *Daily Oklahoman*, Nov. 25, 1932.
28. *Muskogee Daily Phoenix*, Nov. 25, 1932.
29. Louderback, *Bad Ones*, 148.
30. Quimby, *Devil's Emissaries*, 75.
31. Ibid.
32. *Tulsa Daily World*, Oct. 29, 1932.
33. Ibid., Oct. 24, 1934.
34. "Oklahoma's 'Bandit King,'" 26–27.

7. The Pretty Boy Floyd Gang

1. Louderback, *Bad Ones*, 149.
2. Letter, SAC, Kansas City, to Director of Probation and Parole, Jefferson City, Missouri, Sept. 22, 1938, FBI File 62-28915; Report, Bliss Morton, Indianapolis, Oct. 10, 1934, FBI File 62-28915-2729.
3. Wallis, *Pretty Boy*, 290; *Kansas City Journal-Post*, Oct. 23, 1934.

4. Report, R. C. Suran, Chicago, Oct. 11, 1934, FBI File 62-28915.

5. Report, Bliss Morton, Indianapolis, Oct. 10, 1934, FBI File 62-28915-2729.

6. *Muskogee Daily Phoenix*, Oct. 22, 1934; *Tulsa Daily World*, Oct. 23, 1934; Report, W. E. Miller, Kansas City, June 6, 1934, FBI File 62-28915-1717.

7. Quimby, *Devil's Emissaries*, 76–77.

8. Ibid., 77.

9. *Oklahoma News*, Oct. 30, 1934.

10. Letter, Chipman to SAC, Oklahoma City, Sept. 16, 1933, FBI File 62-28915-587; *Muskogee Daily Phoenix*, Dec. 22, 1932.

11. Letter, Chipman to SAC, Oklahoma City, Sept. 16, 1933, FBI File 62-28915-587.

12. *Muskogee Daily Phoenix*, Apr. 27, 1933; *Daily Oklahoman*, Oct. 31, 1934.

13. *Daily Oklahoman*, Apr. 30, 1933.

14. Ibid., May 14, 1933.

15. Ibid., May 30, 1933.

16. Ibid., May 31, 1933.

17. Ibid., May 30, 1933; Lysing, *Men Against Crime*, 191.

18. *Muskogee Daily Phoenix*, Dec. 2, 1933; *Memphis Commercial Appeal*, Dec. 3, 1933.

19. *Memphis Commercial Appeal*, Dec. 3, 1933.

20. Louderback, *Bad Ones*, 149.

21. *Tulsa Daily World*, May 31, 1933.

22. *Muskogee Daily Phoenix*, May 30, 1933.

23. Report, Dwight Brantley, Oklahoma City, July 9, 1934, FBI File 62-28915-1952.

24. Louderback, *Bad Ones*, 149.

25. *Tulsa Daily World*, Oct. 23, 1934; Letter, SAC, Dallas, to Director, July 11, 1934, FBI File 62-28915.

26. *Tulsa Daily World*, Oct. 23, 1934.

27. Ibid., June 4, 1933.

28. Ibid.

29. *Muskogee Daily Phoenix*, June 5, 1933; *Oklahoma News*, June 6, 1933.

30. *Muskogee Daily Phoenix*, June 6, 1933.

31. Report, Dwight Brantley, Oklahoma City, July 31, 1934, FBI File 62-28915-2116.

32. *Tulsa Daily World*, June 16, 17, 18, 1933.

33. Ibid., June 15, 1933.

34. Ibid., June 17, 18, 21, 22, 1933; Report, H. A. Dietz, Kansas City, Jan. 7, 1936, FBI File 62-28915-3799.

35. Report, H. A. Dietz, Kansas City, Jan. 7, 1936, FBI File 62-28915-3799; Letter, SAC, Kansas City, to SAC, Buffalo, Dec. 13, 1934, FBI File 62-28915.

8. Machine Gun Challenge to the Nation

1. John Toland, *The Dillinger Days* (New York: Random House, 1963), 52.

2. Clayton, *Union Station Massacre*, 7–22.

3. *Kansas City Star*, July 8, 1932.

4. Toland, *Dillinger Days*, 52; Report, R. E. Vetterli, Kansas City, June 26, 1933, FBI File 62-28915-92.

5. Report, R. E. Vetterli, Kansas City, June 26, 1933, FBI File 62-28915-92; Toland, *Dillinger Days*, 52–53.

6. Report, R. C. Suran, Chicago, Oct. 6, 1934, FBI File 62-28915-2655.

7. Report, R. E. Vetterli, Kansas City, June 26, 1933, FBI File 62-28915-92.

8. Report, R. C. Suran, Chicago, Oct. 6, 1934, FBI File 62-28915-2655.

9. Ibid.; Report, W. F. Trainor, Kansas City, July 29, 1933, FBI File 62-28915-406.

10. Report, R. C. Suran, Chicago, Oct. 6, 1934, FBI File 62-28915-2655.

11. Report, R. E. Vetterli, Kansas City, June 26, 1933, FBI File 62-28915-92.

12. Clayton, *Union Station Massacre*, 111–12.

13. Report, R. C. Suran, Chicago, Oct. 6, 1934, FBI File 62-28915-2655; Toland, *Dillinger Days*, 53–54.

14. Clayton, *Union Station Massacre*, 23; Quimby, *Devil's Emissaries*, 88–90.

15. Report, W. F. Trainor, Kansas City, Sept. 5, 1934, FBI File 62-28915-2370.

16. Ibid.; Hayten Preston, *They Shoot to Kill (Secrets of the G-Men)* (London: Readers Library, 1938), 92–93.

17. Report, W. F. Trainor, Kansas City, Sept, 5, 1934, FBI File 62-28915-2370.

18. Report, R. C. Suran, Chicago, Oct. 6, 1934, FBI File 62-28915-2655; Toland, *Dillinger Days*, 55.

19. Statement from Vivian Mathias, Sept. 30, 1934; Cowley to Hoover, Chicago, Oct. 1, 1934, FBI File 62-28915-2602.

20. Toland, *Dillinger Days*, 55.

21. Ibid., 56.

22. Report, R. E. Vetterli, Kansas City, June 26, 1933, FBI File 62-28915-92.

23. Toland, *Dillinger Days*, 56.

24. Report, R. E. Vetterli, Kansas City, June 26, 1933, FBI File 62-28915-92.

25. Ibid.

26. Report, W. F. Trainor, Kansas City, Mo., Oct. 19, 1934, FBI File 62-28915-2850.

27. Ibid.

28. Letter, Gill to Vetterli, SAC, Kansas City, July 12, 1933, FBI File 62-28915.

29. Report, R. E. Vetterli, Kansas City, June 26, 1933, FBI File 62-28915-92.

30. Letter, Gill to Vetterli, SAC, Kansas City, July 12, 1933, FBI File 62-28915.

31. Report, R. E. Vetterli, Kansas City, June 26, 1933, FBI File 62-28915-92.

32. Ibid.

33. Ibid.

34. Letter, Gill to Vetterli, SAC, Kansas City, July 12, 1933, FBI File 62-28915.

35. Report, R. E. Vetterli, Kansas City, June 26, 1933, FBI File 62-28915-92.

36. Louderback, *Bad Ones*, 156–57; Toland, *Dillinger Days*, 58.

37. Report, R. E. Vetterli, Kansas City, June 26, 1933, FBI File 62-28915-92; Clayton, *Union Station Massacre*, 130.

38. Clayton, *Union Station Massacre*, 130.

39. Report, W. F. Trainor, Kansas City, Oct. 19, 1934, FBI File 62-28915-2850.

40. Report, R. E. Vetterli, Kansas City, June 26, 1933, FBI File 62-28915-92.

41. Report, W. F. Trainor, Kansas City, Oct. 19, 1934, FBI File 62-28915-2850.

42. Statement from Vivian Mathias, Sept. 30, 1934; Cowley to Hoover, Chicago, Oct. 1, 1934, FBI File 62-28915-2602.

43. Cowley to Hoover, Chicago, Oct. 1, 1934, FBI File 62-28915-2602.

44. Report, W. F. Trainor, Kansas City, Sept. 5, 1934, FBI File 62-28915-2370.

45. Statement from Vivian Mathias, Sept. 30, 1934; Cowley to Hoover, Chicago, Oct. 1, 1934, FBI File 62-28915-2602.

46. Cowley to Hoover, Chicago, Oct. 1, 1934, FBI File 62-28915-2606; Memorandum for the Director from Tamm, June 14, 1935, FBI File 62-28915-3723.

47. Report, W. F. Trainor, Kansas City, Sept. 5, 1934, FBI File 62-28915-2370; Clayton, *Union Station Massacre*, 152–53.

48. Clayton, *Union Station Massacre*, 144.

9. *The War Against Crime*

1. Clayton, *Union Station Massacre*, 141–42, 151–52.

2. Letter, SAC, Oklahoma City, to Director, July 11, 1933, FBI File 62-28915-316.

3. Clayton, *Union Station Massacre*, 169–70.

4. Letter, SAC, Kansas City, to Director, Oct. 28, 1933, FBI File 62-28915-812.

5. Memorandum for the Director from R. E. Newby, Mar. 14, 1934, FBI File 62-28915-1541.

6. Letter, Gill to SAC, Kansas City, July 12, 1933, FBI File 62-28915.

7. L. L. Edge, *Run the Cat Roads* (New York: Dembner Books, 1981), 9.

8. Quimby, *Devil's Emissaries*, 94.

9. Letter, Gill to SAC, Kansas City, July 12, 1933, FBI File 62-28915; Letter, SAC, Kansas City, to Director, Nov. 6, 1934, FBI File 62-28915-3122.

10. Letter, Director to SAC, Kansas City, Aug. 7, 1934, FBI File 62-28915-2121.

11. Letter, SAC, Kansas City, to Director, May 9, 1935, FBI File 62-28915-3667.

12. Memorandum for the Director from E. A. Tamm, Nov. 7, 1934, FBI File 62-28915-3128; Memorandum for the Director from E. A. Tamm, Feb. 26, 1935, FBI File 62-28915; Letter, SAC, Kansas City, to Director, Nov. 6, 1934, FBI File 62-28915-3122.

13. Louderback, *Bad Ones*, 161–62; Edge, *Cat Roads*, 1–10.

14. Clayton, *Union Station Massacre*, 146.

15. Letter, SAC, Kansas City, to SAC, Portland, May 8, 1936, FBI File 62-28915-3829.

16. Louderback, *Bad Ones*, 158–59.

17. Letter, SAC, Kansas City, to Director, Feb. 27, 1935, FBI File 62-28915-3586.

18. Louderback, *Bad Ones*, 161.

19. Ibid.

20. Letter, SAC, Portland, to SAC, Kansas City, Jan. 26, 1934, FBI File 62-28915; Henry "Blackie" Audett, *Rap Sheet* (New York: William Sloane, 1954), 148–52.

21. Clayton, *Union Station Massacre*, 143; *Kansas City Times*, July 5, 1933.

22. *Tulsa Daily World*, July 7, 1933.

23. Clayton, *Union Station Massacre*, 148, 159.

24. Edge, *Cat Roads*, 156; Louderback, *Bad Ones*, 159.

25. Letter, SAC, Kansas City, to Director, Jan. 29, 1934, FBI File 62-28915.

26. Quimby, *Devil's Emissaries*, 100.

27. Clayton, *Union Station Massacre*, 177–79.

28. Letter, SAC, Kansas City, to Director, Nov. 10, 1933, FBI File 62-28915-819; Letter, SAC, Kansas City, to Director, July 24, 1935, FBI File 62-28915-3741.

29. Letter, Director to SAC, Kansas City, Jan. 18, 1934, FBI File 62-28915-1055; "Watch for These Mad Dogs!" *Liberty*, Sept. 15, 1934, 45; Richard G. Harris, "A Mad Dog Is Caught," *Liberty*, Nov. 17, 1934, 33.

30. Clayton, *Union Station Massacre*, 162–63.

31. Ibid., 163–64.

32. Ibid., 180–81.

33. Report, T. H. Tracy, New York, Dec. 5, 1933, FBI File 62-28915-924.

34. Clayton, *Union Station Massacre,* 180–82; Memorandum for the Director from R. E. Newby, Dec. 1, 1933, FBI File 62–18915-899.

35. Clayton, *Union Station Massacre,* 172–77, 185–87.

36. Letter, Director to SAC, Kansas City, Aug. 7, 1934, FBI File 162-28915-2121.

37. Clayton, *Union Station Massacre,* 189–90.

38. Ibid., 190–92.

39. Ibid.; Letter, SAC, Kansas City, to SAC, St. Paul, April 21, 1934, FBI File 62-28915; Statement from Vivian Mathias, Sept. 30, 1934; Cowley to Hoover, Chicago, Oct. 1, 1934, FBI File 62-28915-2602.

40. *Tulsa Daily World,* Oct. 11, 1934.

41. Toland, *Dillinger Days,* passim.

42. Carl Sifakis, *The Encyclopedia of American Crime* (New York: Facts on File, 1982), 596–97; Toland, *Dillinger Days,* 269.

43. Louderback, *Bad Ones,* 163.

44. Ibid.

45. Ibid.

46. Ibid., 163–64.

47. Ibid., 164.

48. Ibid.

49. Ibid.; *Tulsa Daily World,* Mar. 4, 1934.

50. *Muskogee Daily Phoenix,* May 12, 1934.

51. *Tulsa Daily World,* July 29, 1934.

52. Ibid., Aug. 12, 1934.

10. *We Are Going to Kill Him, If We Catch Him*

1. Louderback, Bad Ones, 164–65; Report, Dwight Brantley, SAC, Oklahoma City, Oct. 25, 1934, FBI File 62-28915-2967.

2. *Tulsa Daily World,* July 31, 1933.

3. Michael Wallis, *Oil Man: The Story of Frank Phillips and the Birth of Phillips Petroleum* (New York: Doubleday, 1988), 355–58.

4. *Muskogee Daily Phoenix,* July 15, 1934.

5. *Tulsa Daily World,* Aug. 8, 1933.

6. Ibid., June 25, July 2, 1934.

7. Ibid., Aug. 14, 1934.

8. Louderback, *Bad Ones,* 162–63.

9. Ibid., 164; Letter, SAC, Oklahoma City, to Director, Apr. 2, 1934, FBI File 62-28915-1556; *Daily Oklahoman,* Feb. 20, 1934.

10. Louderback, *Bad Ones,* 164–65.

11. Report, H. T. Arterberry, Dallas, Sept. 12, 1934, FBI File 62-28915-2430.

12. *Muskogee Daily Phoenix,* Nov. 4, 1933.

13. *Tulsa Daily World,* Oct. 7, 1934.

14. *St. Louis Globe-Democrat,* May 6, 1934.

15. *Muskogee Daily Phoenix,* June 25, 1934.

16. Teletype, Purvis to Director, July 30, 1934, FBI File 62-28915-2103.

17. "Watch for These Mad Dogs!," *Liberty,* Sept. 15, 1934, 45; "Watch for These Mad Dogs!," *Liberty,* Nov. 3, 1934, 55.

18. "Watch for These Mad Dogs!," *Liberty,* Nov. 3, 1934, 55.

19. Letter, SAC, Oklahoma City, to SAC, Kansas City, Nov. 23, 1933, FBI File 62-28915-2430.

20. Memorandum for Mr. Cowley from Director, May 16, 1934, FBI File 62-28915-1653; Memorandum for Mr. Cowley from Director, May 17, 1934, FBI File 62-28915-1667; Letter, SAC, Oklahoma City, to Director, June 8, 1934, FBI File 62-28915.

21. *Muskogee Daily Phoenix*, Dec. 5, 1933; *Fort Smith Southwest American*, Oct. 23, 1934.

22. *Tulsa Daily World*, Dec. 17, 1933.

23. *Muskogee Daily Phoenix*, Mar. 2, 1934.

24. *Tulsa Daily World*, May 7, 1934.

25. Ibid., June 3, 1934.

26. *Muskogee Daily Phoenix*, June 18, 1934.

27. Letter, SAC, Dallas, to Director, June 26, 1934, FBI File 62-28915.

28. *Muskogee Daily Phoenix*, June 18, 1934.

29. Ibid., July 1, 1934.

30. Memorandum to Mr. Nathan, Mr. Tamm from Director, June 28, 1934, FBI File 62-28915; *Kansas City Journal-Post*, Sept. 4, 1934.

31. *Kansas City Journal-Post*, July 2, 1934; Report, Dwight Brantley, Oklahoma City, Aug. 23, 1934, FBI File 62-28915-2301.

32. *Kansas City Journal-Post*, Sept. 4, 1934.

33. Ibid., Sept. 5, 1934.

34. *Tulsa Daily World*, Sept. 4, 1934.

35. Ibid., June 10, 1934.

36. Memorandum for the Director from R. E. Newby, Mar. 14, 1934, FBI File 62-28915-1541.

37. Letter, SAC, Kansas City, to SAC, Los Angeles, Feb. 15, 1934, FBI File 62-28915.

38. Memorandum for Mr. Cowley from Director, July 10, 1934, FBI File 62-28915; Memorandum for Mr. Nathan from Director, June 23, 1934, FBI File 62-28915-1863.

39. Letter, SAC, Kansas City, to SAC, Los Angeles, Feb. 15, 1934, FBI File 62-28915.

40. Memorandum, Oct. 21, 1934, FBI File 62-28915-2862; Memorandum from the Director for Mr. Tamm, Mr. Nathan, June 23, 1934, FBI File 62-28915-1838.

41. Letter, SAC, Kansas City, to SAC, Little Rock, Aug. 16, 1934, FBI File 62-28915.

42. Memorandum for Mr. Tamm from Director, June 6, 1934, FBI File 62-28915-1729.

43. Memorandum for the Director from E. A. Tamm, Oct. 9, 1934, FBI File 62-28915-2991.

44. Letter, R. B. Nathan to Director, Kansas City, June 29, 1934, FBI File 62-28915-1915.

45. Memorandum for Mr. Smith from Director, June 2, 1934, FBI File 62-28915-1710; Memorandum for the Director from H. H. Clegg, Mar. 25, 1934, FBI File 62-28915-1474.

46. Letter, Director to SAC, Oklahoma City, July 31, 1934, FBI File 62-28915-2099.

47. Memorandum for Mr. Smith from Director, June 2, 1934, FBI File 62-28915-1710; Memorandum for the Director from E. A. Tamm, July 6, 1934, FBI File 62-28915.

48. Letter, SAC, Oklahoma City, to Director, Aug. 3, 1934, FBI File 62-28915.

49. Letter, SAC, St. Louis, to Director, May 6, 1934, FBI File 62-28915-1621.

50. Report, Dwight Brantley, Oklahoma City, Sept. 13, 1934, FBI File 62-28915-2439.

51. *Daily Oklahoman*, Oct. 18, 1933.

52. Letter, SAC, Dallas, to Director, June 26, 1934, FBI File 62-28915; Letter, Acting SAC, Oklahoma City, to Director, Apr. 26, 1934, FBI File 62-28915; Memorandum for Mr. Cowley from Director, May 16, 1934, FBI File 62-28915-1653; Memorandum for Mr. Cowley from Director, May 17, 1934, FBI File 62-28915-1667; Letter, SAC, Dallas, to Director, July 3, 1934, FBI File 62-28915; Letter, SAC, Dallas, to Director, July 12, 1934, FBI File 62-28915.

53. Letter, SAC, Dallas, to Director, June 26, 1934, FBI File 62-28915.

54. Letter, SAC, Dallas, to Director, July 3, 1934, FBI File 62-28915.

55. Letter, Isaac D. Dalton, Collinsville, Ill., to Attorney General, May 7, 1934, FBI File 62-28915.

56. Memorandum to Mr. Nathan, Mr. Tamm from Director, June 28, 1934, FBI File 62-28915; *Muskogee Daily Phoenix*, July 1, 1934.

57. Memorandum to Mr. Tamm, Mr. Nathan from Director, June 23, 1934, FBI File 62-28915-1838; Memorandum for Mr. Nathan, Mr. Tolson, Mr. Tamm from Director, June 27, 1934, FBI File 62-28915-1890.

58. Memorandum for Mr. Nathan, Mr. Tolson, Mr. Tamm from the Director, June 27, 1934, FBI File 62-28915-1890; Memorandum for Mr. Nathan, Mr. Tamm from the Director, June 28, 1934, FBI File 62-28915.

59. Letter, SAC, Oklahoma City, to Director, May 18, 1934, FBI File 62-28915; Letter, SAC, Oklahoma City, to Director, June 23, 1934, FBI File 62-28915.

60. Letter, SAC, Oklahoma City, to Director, June 29, 1934, FBI File 62-28915; Memorandum to Mr. Nathan, Mr. Tamm from Director, June 28, 1934, FBI File 62-28915; Memorandum to Mr. Tamm, Mr. Nathan from Director, June 23, 1934, FBI File 62-28915-1838.

61. Memorandum to Mr. Tamm, Mr. Nathan from Director, June 23, 1934, FBI File 62-28915-1838.

62. Memorandum for the Director from E. A. Tamm, July 28, 1934, FBI File 62-28915-2157.

63. Memorandum for Mr. Tamm from Director, June 6, 1934, FBI File 62-28915-1729.

64. Memorandum for Mr. Nathan from Director, June 23, 1934, FBI File 62-28915; Letter, Nathan to SAC, Little Rock, Aug. 31, 1934, FBI File 62-28915.

65. *Kansas City Times*, Aug. 25, 1934.

66. Memorandum for Mr. Nathan, Mr. Tamm from Director, June 28, 1934, FBI File 62-28915.

67. *Tulsa Daily World*, July 24, 1934.

68. Ibid.

69. *Toledo News-Bee*, July 24, 1934.

70. Ibid.

71. Letter, Harold Nathan to Director, Aug. 18, 1934, FBI File 62-28915-2250.

72. Letter, Director to Nathan, Oklahoma City, Aug. 20, 1934, FBI File 62-28915.

73. Memorandum for the Director from E. A. Tamm, Aug. 25, 1934, FBI File 62-28915; Report, Dwight Brantley, Oklahoma City, Oct. 10, 1934, FBI File 62-28915-2743.

74. Letter, Director to S. P. Cowley, Chicago, Sept. 6, 1934, FBI File 62-28915-2347.

75. Memorandum for Mr. Tamm from Director, Oct. 1, 1934, FBI File 62-28915-2654.

76. Memorandum for the Director from E. A. Tamm, Oct. 11, 1934, FBI File 62-28915.

77. Letter, Director to S. P. Cowley, Chicago, Oct. 5, 1934, FBI File 62-28915; Letter, Director to SAC, Kansas City, Aug. 17, 1934, FBI File 62-28915.

78. Memorandum, Oct. 6, 1934, FBI File 62-28915-2661; *Tulsa Daily World*, Oct. 13, 1934.

79. *Tulsa Daily World*, Oct. 11, 1934.

80. Ibid., Oct. 12, 1934.

81. *Muskogee Daily Phoenix*, Oct. 14, 17, 19, 21, 1934; *Time*, Oct. 22, 1934, 17.

82. *Time*, Oct. 22, 1934, 17.

83. *Tulsa Daily World*, Oct. 13, 1934.

84. Report, Dwight Brantley, Oklahoma City, Oct. 25, 1934, FBI File 62-28915-2967.

85. *Muskogee Daily Phoenix*, Oct. 19, 1934.

86. *El Paso Morning Times*, Oct. 13, 1934.

87. Report, R. C. Coulter, St. Paul, Oct. 19, 1934, FBI File 62-28915-2848.

11. On the Lam

1. Letter, SAC, Cincinnati, to SAC, Detroit, Oct. 12, 1934, FBI File 62-28915; Report, D. E. Hall, Detroit, Nov. 21, 1934, FBI File 62-28915-3223.

2. Report, W. F. Trainor, Kansas City, Sept. 5, 1934, FBI File 62-28915-2370.

3. Letter, SAC, Cincinnati, to SAC, Detroit, Oct. 12, 1934, FBI File 62-28915; Report, D. E. Hall, Detroit, Nov. 21, 1934, FBI File 62-28915-3223.

4. Report, J. P. MacFarland, Buffalo, Nov. 19, 1934, FBI File 62-28915-3202.

5. Wallis, *Pretty Boy*, 325–26.

6. Report, J. P. MacFarland, Buffalo, Nov. 19, 1934, FBI File 62-28915-3202.

7. Report, S. K. McKee, New York City, Oct. 21, 1933, FBI File 62-28915-726.

8. Report, John B. Little, Oklahoma City, Nov. 23, 1934, FBI File 62-28915-3237.

9. Letter, SAC, Buffalo, to Director, Nov. 23, 1934, FBI File 62-28915.

10. "Kansas City Massacre," *The Investigator* (Jan. 1945): 1–6. (FBI publication)

11. Report, John B. Little, Oklahoma City, Nov. 23, 1934, FBI File 62-28915-3237.

12. Report, J. P. MacFarland, Buffalo, Nov. 19, 1934, FBI File 62-28915-3202.

13. Ibid.

14. Ibid.

15. Ibid.; Report, J. P. MacFarland, Buffalo, N.Y., Nov. 20, 1934, FBI File 62-28915-3211.

16. Letter, SAC, Oklahoma City, to SAC, Kansas City, Nov. 13, 1934, FBI File 62-28915; Report, John B. Little, Oklahoma City, Jan. 18, 1935, FBI File 62-28915-3479.

17. Report, G. V. Doherty, Buffalo, Dec. 19, 1934, FBI File 62-28915-3355.

18. Report, J. P. MacFarland, Buffalo, Nov. 19, 1934, FBI File 62-28915-3202; Report, J. D. Cunningham, Buffalo, Dec. 11, 1934, FBI File 62-28915; Letter, SAC, Kansas City, to SAC, Buffalo, Dec. 13, 1934, FBI File 62-28915.

19. Report, J. D. Cunningham, Buffalo, Dec. 11, 1934, FBI File 62-28915; Report, C. F. Graham, Buffalo, Mar. 14, 1935, FBI File 62-28915.

20. Report, John B. Little, Oklahoma City, Nov. 23, 1934, FBI File 62-28915-3237.

21. *Tulsa Daily World*, May 15, 1934; Letter, SAC, Kansas City, to SAC, Oklahoma City, Aug. 11, 1934, FBI File 62-28915-2184; Letter, SAC, Dallas, to Director, July 11, 1934, FBI File 62-28915; *Tulsa Daily World*, Oct. 23, 1934.

22. Letter, SAC, Dallas, to Director, July 11, 1934, FBI File 62-28915; Letter, SAC, Kansas City, to SAC, New Orleans, Aug. 11, 1934, FBI File 62-28915; Report, Dwight Brantley, Oklahoma City, Sept. 13, 1934, FBI File 62-28915-2439.

23. Letter, SAC, New Orleans, to Director, July 23, 1934, FBI File 62-28915-2050; Letter, Harold Nathan, Assistant Director, to SAC, New Orleans, Aug. 7, 1934, FBI File 62-28915; Report, L. A. Kindell, New Orleans, Sept. 18, 1934, FBI File 62-28915-2469.

24. Alvin Karpis with Bill Trent, *The Alvin Karpis Story* (New York: Coward, McCann & Geoghegan, 1971), 180–81.

25. Toland, *Dillinger Days*, 307–13.

26. Jay Robert Nash and Ron Offen, *Dillinger: Dead or Alive?* (Chicago: Henry Regnery, 1970), 57–58.

27. Letter, Director to SAC, Chicago, Jan. 9, 1935, FBI File 62-28915-3478; Report, C. C. Spears, Portland, Dec. 31, 1934, John Paul Chase, FBI File 62-29777.

28. Toland, *Dillinger Days*, 307–13.

29. Wallis, *Pretty Boy*, 327–28.

30. Report, F. S. Smith, Kansas City, Mar. 11, 1935, FBI File 62-28915-3613.

31. Letter, Frank D. Butler, manager, South Side office, Toledo Trust Co., to Dept. of Justice, Nov. 5, 1934, FBI File 62-28915-3077; Letter, Director to Butler, Toledo, Nov. 13, 1934, FBI File 62-28915-3077.

32. Report, F. S. Smith, Kansas City, March 11, 1935, FBI File 62-28915-3613.

33. Report, John B. Little, Oklahoma City, Nov. 23, 1934, FBI File 62-28915-3237; Letter, SAC, Oklahoma City, to SAC, Kansas City, Nov. 13, 1934, FBI File 62-28915; Report, J. P. MacFarland, Buffalo, Nov. 19, 1934, FBI File 62-28915-3202; Report, F. S. Smith, Kansas City, Mar. 11, 1935, FBI File 62-28915-3613.

12. Death Hunt

1. Report, John B. Little, Oklahoma City, Nov. 23, 1934, FBI File 62-28915-3237.

2. Melvin Purvis, *American Agent* (Garden City, N.Y.: Doubleday, 1936), 234.

3. Letter, SAC, Detroit, to Director, Jan. 30, 1935, FBI File 62-28915-3547 (includes Coroner's Investigation in re: Death of Charles "Pretty Boy" Floyd).

4. Ibid.

5. Ibid.

6. Ibid.

7. Ibid.; *East Liverpool* (Ohio) *Evening Review,* Oct. 9, 1984.

8. *East Liverpool Evening Review,* Oct. 9, 1984.

9. Ibid.

10. Ibid.

11. Ibid.

12. Ibid.

13. Report, S. K. McKee, Chicago, Oct. 26, 1934, FBI File 62-28915-2965; Purvis, *American Agent,* 235.

14. *East Liverpool Evening Review,* Oct. 9, 1934.

15. *Muskogee Daily Phoenix,* Oct. 22, 1934.

16. Report, S. K. McKee, Chicago, Oct. 26, 1934, FBI File 62-28915-2965.

17. Purvis, *American Agent,* 232–37.

18. Neal Gabler, *Winchell: Gossip, Power and the Culture of Celebrity* (New York: Alfred A. Knopf, 1994), 201.

19. Purvis, *American Agent,* 232–37.

20. Memorandum for Mr. Tamm from Director, Oct. 21, 1934, FBI File 62-28915-2854; *Cincinnati Enquirer,* Oct. 24, 1934.

21. *Cincinnati Enquirer,* Oct. 24, 1934.

22. *Toledo News-Bee,* Oct. 23, 1934; Purvis, *American Agent,* 236.

23. Purvis, *American Agent,* 237.

24. Report, S. K. McKee, Chicago, Oct. 26, 1934, FBI File 62-28915-2965.

25. Ibid.

26. Purvis, *American Agent,* 236–37.

27. *Cincinnati Times-Star,* Oct. 24, 1934.

28. *Kansas City Journal-Post,* Oct. 24, 1934.

29. *Toledo News-Bee,* Oct. 22, 1934.

30. Purvis, *American Agent,* 237–40; Report, S. K. McKee, Chicago, Oct. 26, 1934, FBI File 62-28915-2965; *East Liverpool Evening Review,* Oct. 9, 1984; *Wellsville* (Ohio) *News,* Oct. 23, 1934; Memorandum for Mr. Tamm from the Director, Oct. 22, 1934, FBI File 62-28915-2903.

13. You Got Me This Time

1. Letter, Director to Robinson, East Liverpool, Ohio, Nov. 7, 1934, FBI File 62-28915; Letter, Robinson, East Liverpool, Ohio, to Dept. of Justice, Oct. 29, 1934, FBI File 62-28915; Letter, M. C. Reagle to Hoover, Dec. 19, 1934, FBI File 62-28915-3410; Letter, Robinson to Attorney General Cummings, Feb. 4, 1935, FBI File 62-28915-3462; Letter, Hoover to Robinson, Feb. 13, 1935, FBI File 62-28915-3462; Report, S. K. McKee, Chicago, Oct. 26, 1934, FBI File 62-28915-2965; *Youngstown Vindicator,* Oct. 23, 1934. Hoover rejected Robert Robinson's claim of a reward for providing information about Floyd.

2. *Tulsa Daily World,* Oct. 23, 1934; Letter, SAC, Detroit, to Director, Jan. 30, 1935, FBI File 62-28915-3547 (includes Coroner's Investigation in re: Death of Charles "Pretty Boy" Floyd).

3. Letter, SAC, Detroit, to Director, Jan. 30, 1935, FBI File 62-28915-3547 (includes Coroner's Investigation in re: Death of Charles "Pretty Boy" Floyd).

4. *Oklahoma City Times,* Feb. 13, 1932.

5. Letter, SAC, Detroit, to Director, Jan. 30, 1935, FBI File 62-28915-3547 (includes Coroner's Investigation in re: Death of Charles "Pretty Boy" Floyd); *Tulsa Daily World,* Oct. 23, 1934; *East Liverpool Evening Review,* Oct. 9, 1984, Oct. 18, 1969.

6. *East Liverpool Evening Review,* Oct. 18, 1969; *Tulsa Daily World,* Oct. 23, 1934.

7. Purvis, *American Agent,* 241.

8. Letter, SAC, Detroit, to Director, Jan. 30, 1935, FBI File 62-28915-3547 (includes Coroner's Investigation in re: Death of Charles "Pretty Boy" Floyd).

9. Memorandum for the Director from Clyde Tolson, Nov. 6, 1934, FBI File 62-28915-3088.

10. Letter, SAC, Detroit, to Director, Jan. 30, 1935, FBI File 62-28915-3547 (includes Coroner's Investigation in re: Charles "Pretty Boy" Floyd).

11. *East Liverpool Review,* Oct. 18, 1969.

12. Letter, SAC, Detroit, to Director, Jan. 30, 1935, FBI File 62-28915-3547 (includes Coroner's Investigation in re: Charles "Pretty Boy" Floyd).

13. Ibid.; Letter, Director to SAC, Kansas City, Dec. 14, 1934, FBI File 62-28915; *East Liverpool Evening Review,* Oct. 9, 1984; *Wellsville News,* Oct. 23, 1934.

14. *Tulsa Daily World,* Oct. 23, 1934; Report, S. K. McKee, Oct. 26, 1934, FBI File 62-28915-2965; Letter, SAC, Detroit to Director, Jan. 30, 1935, FBI File 62-28915-3547; Purvis, *American Agent,* 240–42.

15. *East Liverpool Evening Review,* Oct. 9, 1984.

16. Report, S. K. McKee, Chicago, Oct. 26, 1934, FBI File 62-28915-2965; Letter, SAC, Detroit, to Director, Jan. 30, 1935, FBI File 62-28915-3547 (includes Coroner's Investigation in re: Death of Charles "Pretty Boy" Floyd).

17. Report, S. K. McKee, Chicago, Oct. 26, 1934, FBI File 62-28915-2965.

18. Letter, SAC, Detroit, to Director, Jan. 30, 1935, FBI File 62-28915-3547 (includes Coroner's Investigation in re: Death of Charles "Pretty Boy" Floyd).

19. Purvis, *American Agent*, 242; Memorandum for Mr. Tamm from Director, Oct. 22, 1934, FBI File 62-28915-2894.

20. Memorandum for Mr. Tamm from Director, Oct. 22, 1934, FBI File 62-28915-2576; Drew Pearson, "Merry-Go-Round," *Philadelphia Record*, Oct. 31, 1934.

21. Memorandum for Mr. Tamm from Director, Oct. 22, 1934, FBI File 62-28915-2902.

22. *Pittsburgh Press*, Oct. 23, 1934.

23. Memorandum for Mr. Tamm from Director, Oct. 22, 1934, FBI File 62-28915-2893.

24. *New York Evening Post*, Oct. 23, 1934; *Daily Oklahoman*, Oct. 24, 1934.

25. *Toledo News-Bee*, Oct. 23, 1934; *Oklahoma News*, Oct. 23, 1934.

26. Letter, Hoover to Purvis, Oct. 23, 1934, FBI File 62-28915; Richard Gid Powers, *Secrecy and Power: The Life of J. Edgar Hoover* (New York: Free Press, 1987), 535–36.

27. *New York Evening Post*, Oct. 23, 1934.

28. As reprinted in *Daily Oklahoman*, Oct. 28, 1934.

29. Letter, Clyde D. Sargent, Special Investigator, Sabine County, Missouri, to SAC, Kansas City, no date, FBI File 62-28915; Letter, C. O. Garshwiler to Dept. of Justice, Los Angeles, no date, FBI File 62-28915; Letter, Hoover to C. O. Garshwiler, Nov. 13, 1934, FBI File 62-28915.

30. Memorandum for the Director from Clyde Tolson, Nov. 6, 1934, FBI File 62-28915-3088.

31. Memorandum for Mr. Tamm from Director, Oct. 22, 1934, FBI File 62-28915-2885; Memorandum, Oct. 24, 1934, FBI File 62-28915-2946.

32. Memorandum from E. A. Tamm to the Director, Nov. 1, 1934, FBI File 62-28915.

33. Purvis, *American Agent*, 242.

34. *New York Times*, Oct. 23, 1934; *Akron Beacon Journal*, Oct. 23, 1934; Jo Chamberlin, "Putting Gangdom on the Spot," *Review of Reviews* 90 (Dec. 1934): 47–50.

35. Letter, Charles K. Campbell to Director, Oct. 24, 1934, FBI File 62-28915-2997; Letter, Director to Campbell, Oct. 30, 1934, FBI File 62-28915-2997.

36. *Tulsa Tribune*, Oct. 27, 1934.

37. *Tulsa Daily World*, Oct. 24, 1934.

38. Telegram, H. H. H. to Director, Oct. 23, 1934, FBI File 62-28915-3150.

39. Letter, Director to SAC, Chicago, Jan. 9, 1935, FBI File 62-28915-3478; Report, C. C. Spears, Portland, Dec. 31, 1934, John Paul Chase, FBI File 62-29777.

40. *Muskogee Daily Phoenix*, Oct. 25, 1934.

41. *Tulsa Daily World*, Oct. 26, 1934.

42. Ibid.

43. *East Liverpool Review*, Oct. 18, 1969.

44. *Muskogee Daily Phoenix*, Oct. 24, 1934.

45. *New York Times*, Oct. 23, 1934.

46. *Youngstown Vindicator*, Oct. 23, 1934.

47. *Pittsburgh Press*, Oct. 23, 1934; *Tulsa Daily World*, Oct. 26, 1934.

48. *Kansas City Journal Post*, Oct. 24, 1934.

49. *Tulsa Daily World*, Oct. 25, 1934.

50. *Cincinnati Post*, Oct. 26, 1934.

51. *Cincinnati Times-Star*, Oct. 24, 1934.

52. Walter Trohan, "J. Edgar Hoover, the One Man Scotland Yard," *Chicago Tribune*, June 21, 1936.

53. *Daily Oklahoman*, Oct. 23, 1934.

54. Memorandum for Mr. Tamm from Director, Oct. 24, 1934, FBI File 62-28915.

55. Memorandum for Mr. Tamm from Director, Oct. 23, 1934, FBI File 62-28915-2945.

56. Telegram, W. W. Griffith, editor of the *Youngstown Vindicator*, Youngstown, Ohio, Oct. 24, 1934, FBI File 62-28915-3084; *Washington Herald*, Oct. 24, 1934.

57. *Kansas City Star*, Oct. 24, 1934.

58. *Muskogee Daily Phoenix*, Nov. 28, 1934.

59. Ibid., Oct. 23, 1934; *Tulsa Daily World*, Oct. 23, 1934.

60. *Tulsa Daily World*, Oct. 23, 1934.

61. *Muskogee Daily Phoenix*, Oct. 23, 1934.

62. Ibid.

63. Memorandum for Mr. Tamm from Director, Oct. 28, 1934, FBI File 62-28915.

64. *Muskogee Daily Phoenix*, Oct. 23, 1934.

65. Purvis, *American Agent*, 242; Letter, McDermott to Hoover, Nov. 28, 1936, FBI File 62-28915-3871; Report, S. K. McKee, Chicago, Oct. 26, 1934, FBI File 62-28915-2965.

66. *Youngstown Vindicator*, Oct. 23, 1934; *East Liverpool Review*, Oct. 18, 1969.

67. Report, S. K. McKee, Chicago, Oct. 26, 1934, FBI File 62-28915-2965.

68. *Akron Beacon Journal*, Oct. 23, 1934.

69. *Muskogee Daily Phoenix*, Oct. 23, 1934.

70. *Tulsa Daily World*, Oct. 23, 1934.

71. *Akron Beacon Journal*, Oct. 23, 1934.

72. Ibid.

73. Ibid.; Letter, SAC, Detroit, to Director, Jan. 30, 1935, FBI File 62-28915-3547; *East Liverpool Evening Review*, Oct. 9, 1984; *Tulsa Daily World*, Oct. 25, 1934.

74. *Tulsa Daily World*, Oct. 25, 1934.

75. *Wellsville News*, Oct. 23, 1934; Letter, Director to SAC, Detroit, Feb. 9, 1935, FBI File 62-28915-3547 (includes autopsy of Floyd, Oct. 22, 1934).

76. *Muskogee Daily Phoenix*, Oct. 25, 1934.

77. *Pittsburgh Sun-Telegraph*, Oct. 25, 1934.

78. *Pittsburgh Press*, Oct. 26, 1934.

79. *Tulsa Daily World*, Oct. 29, 1934.

Epilogue

1. Clayton, *Union Station Massacre*, 199–200.

2. Ibid.; Memorandum for Mr. Tamm from Director, Aug. 21, 1935, FBI File 62-28915-3753.

3. Memorandum from Director, Oct. 24, 1934, FBI File 62-28915-2946.

4. *Muskogee Daily Phoenix*, Nov. 28, 1934.

5. Clayton, *Union Station Massacre*, 201.

6. Report, F. S. Smith, Kansas City, Mar. 11, 1935, FBI File 62-28915-3613.

7. *New York Post*, Oct. 7, 1938.

8. Report, John B. Little, Oklahoma City, Nov. 23, 1934, FBI File 62-28915-3237; Letter, SAC, Buffalo, to Director, Nov. 31, 1936, FBI File 62-28915; Memorandum for the

Director from E. A. Tamm, Nov. 20, 1934, FBI File 62-28915-3213; Letter, SAC, San Antonio, to SAC, Oklahoma City, May 25, 1938, FBI File 62-28915-3941.

9. Memorandum, Oct. 23, 1934, FBI File 62-28915-3152; Memorandum for the Director from Clyde Tolson, Nov. 2, 1934, FBI File 62-28915-2926.

10. Memorandum for the Director from Clyde Tolson, Nov. 2, 1934, FBI File 62-28915-2926.

11. Letter, Ernest H. Van Fasseu to Director, Oct. 26, 1934, FBI File 62-28915-3144; Letter, Director to Van Fasseu, Nov. 3, 1934, FBI File 62-28915-3144.

12. *East Liverpool Evening Review*, Oct. 9, 1984; Letter, John Shuttleworth, editor, *True Detective Mysteries*, Dec. 11, 1934, FBI File 62-28915; Memorandum for Mr. Tolson, Apr. 25, 1936, FBI File 62-28915-3826; Letter, Nathan to Fultz, Dec. 15, 1938, FBI File 62-28915-3980.

13. Powers, *Secrecy and Power*, 223–26.

14. Quimby, *Devil's Emissaries*, 74.

15. Einstein, "Son's Poker Palace."

16. *Daily Oklahoman*, July 14, 1970.

17. Einstein, "Son's Poker Palace."

18. Louderback, *Bad Ones*, passim.

19. Nathan Douthit, "Police Professionalism and the War Against Crime in the United States, 1920s–30s," in George L. Mosse, ed., *Police Forces in History* (Beverly Hills, Calif.: Sage, 1974), 330.

20. Memorandum for Mr. Naughten from Dennis A. Flinn, July 30, 1938, FBI File 62-28915-3952; Letter, Purvis to Director, Oct. 26, 1934, FBI File 62-28915-3238.

21. *Oklahoma City Times*, Feb. 4, 1935.

22. Shirley Temple Black, *Child Star: An Autobiography* (New York: McGraw-Hill, 1988), 231.

23. Letter, SAC, Oklahoma City, to Director, Nov. 20, 1934, FBI File 62-28915-3274; Letter, Alvin E. Evans, University of Kentucky, Lexington, to Director, Sept. 21, 1936, FBI File 62-28915.

24. Memorandum, Nov. 3, 1934, FBI File 62-28915-A.

25. *Chattanooga* (Tenn.) *News*, Nov. 3, 1934.

26. *Chicago Tribune*, Dec. 1, 1934.

27. *Daily Oklahoman*, Aug. 6, 1936.

28. *Time*, Sept. 24, 1979, 25; *Lisbon* (Ohio) *Morning Journal*, Oct. 21, 1984.

29. "Horton Brands Article in *Time* on Floyd Killing Totally False!" *Grapevine* 43 (Dec. 1979): 34–35.

30. *Los Angeles Times*, Oct. 19, Nov. 9, 1974.

31. Ibid., Oct. 28, 1974.

32. Ibid., Nov. 23, 1974.

33. *Lisbon Morning Journal*, Oct. 21, 1984.

34. Letter, McDermott to Hoover, Nov. 28, 1936, FBI File 62-28915-3871.

35. Edge, *Cat Roads*, 216.

36. Letter, SAC, Detroit, to Director, Jan. 30, 1935, FBI File 62-28915-3547 (includes Coroner's Investigation in re: Death of Charles "Pretty Boy" Floyd).

37. *East Liverpool Review*, Oct. 18, 1969.

38. Timothy R. Brookes, "Pretty Boy Floyd," *Timeline* 7, no. 4 (Aug.–Sept. 1990): 2.

39. Ibid., 15.

40. Louderback, *Bad Ones*, 133.

41. *New York Times*, Apr. 7, 1989.

 # Select Bibliography

Books

Audett, Henry "Blackie." *Rap Sheet*. New York: William Sloane, 1954.

Breuer, William B. *J. Edgar Hoover and His G-Men*. Westport, Conn.: Praeger, 1995.

Bruns, Roger. *The Bandit Kings: From Jesse James to Pretty Boy Floyd*. New York: Crown, 1995.

Clayton, Merle. *Union Station Massacre: The Shootout That Started the FBI's War on Crime*. New York: Leisure Books, 1975.

Cooper, Courtney Ryley. *Here's to Crime*. Boston: Little, Brown, 1937.

Corey, Herbert. *Farewell, Mr. Gangster!: America's War on Crime*. Foreword by J. Edgar Hoover. New York: D. Appleton-Century, 1936.

Crump, Irving, and John W. Newton. *Our G-Men*. New York: Dodd, Mead, 1937.

Cunningham, William. *Pretty Boy*. New York: Vanguard Press, 1936. (Fiction)

Douthit, Nathan. "Police Professionalism and the War Against Crime in the U.S., 1920s–1930s." In *Police Forces in History*, 317–33. Ed. G. L. Mosse. Beverly Hills, Calif.: Sage, 1974.

Draper, W. R. *On the Trail of "Pretty Boy" Floyd: A Reporter's Thrilling Pursuit of an Outlaw's Story*. Girard, Kan.: Haldeman-Julius, 1946.

Edge, L. L. *Run the Cat Roads: A True Story of Bank Robbers in the 30's*. New York: Dembner Books, 1981.

Girardin, George Russell, with William J. Helmer. *Dillinger: The Untold Story*. Bloomington: Indiana University Press, 1994.

Gish, Anthony. *American Bandits*. Girard, Kan.: Haldeman-Julius, 1938.

Hamilton, Sue. *Pretty Boy Floyd*. Minneapolis: Abdo & Daughters, 1989. (children's book)

Hoover, John Edgar. *Persons in Hiding*. Boston, Little: Brown, 1938.

Kooistra, Paul Gregory. "American Robin Hoods: The Criminal as Social Hero." Ph.D. diss., University of Virginia, 1982.

Louderback, Lew. *The Bad Ones: Gangsters of the '30s and Their Molls*. Greenwich, Conn.: Fawcett, 1968.

Lysing, Henry (pseud. of John Leonard Nanovic). *Men Against Crime*. New York: David Kemp, 1938.

Nash, Jay Robert. *Bloodletters and Badmen: A Narrative Encyclopedia of American Criminals from the Pilgrims to the Present*. New York: M. Evans, 1973.

O'Connor, Dick. *G-Men at Work: The Story of America's Fight Against Crime and Corruption*. London: John Lang, 1939.

Potter, Claire Bond. "Guarding the Crossroads: The FBI's War on Crime in the 1930's." Ph.D. diss., New York University, 1990.

Poveda, Tony. *Lawlessness and Reform: The FBI in Transition*. Pacific Grove, Calif.: Brooks/Cole, 1990.

Powers, Richard Gid. *G-Men: Hoover's FBI in American Popular Culture*. Carbondale: Southern Illinois University Press, 1983.

———. *Secrecy and Power: The Life of J. Edgar Hoover*. New York: Free Press, 1987.

Preston, Hayten. *They Shoot to Kill (Secrets of the G-Men)*. London: Readers Library, 1938.

Purvis, Melvin. *American Agent*. Garden City, N.Y.: Doubleday, 1936.

Quimby, Myron J. *The Devil's Emissaries*. New York: A. S. Barnes, 1969.

Sifakis, Carl. *The Encyclopedia of American Crime*. New York: Facts on File, 1982.

Smith, Leon E. *Hidden Heroes on the Checkerboard Plains*. Detroit: Diversified Publishers, 1992.

———. *High Noon at the Boley Corral*. Detroit: Leeann Publications, Plus, n.d.

Toland, John. *The Dillinger Days*. New York: Random House, 1963.

Ungar, Robert. *The Union Station Massacre: The Original Sin of J. Edgar Hoover's FBI*. Kansas City: Andrews McMeel Publishing, 1997.

Wallis, Michael. *Pretty Boy: The Life and Times of Charles Arthur Floyd*. New York: St. Martin's Press, 1992.

Wellman, Paul Iselin. *A Dynasty of Western Outlaws*. Lincoln: University of Nebraska Press, 1986.

Whitehead, Donald F. *The FBI Story: A Report to the People*. Foreword by J. Edgar Hoover. New York: Random House, 1956.

Wofford, Ruth Floyd. "Floyd, Walter." In *The History of Sequoyah County, 1828–1975*, 250–51. Sallisaw, Okla.: Sequoyah County Historical Society, 1976.

Magazine Articles

Blackburn, Bob L. "Law Enforcement in Transition: From Decentralized County Sheriffs to the Highway Patrol." *The Chronicles of Oklahoma* 56 (Summer 1978): 194–207.

"Blasting a G-Man Myth." *Time,* Sept. 24, 1979, 25.

Brookes, Timothy. "Pretty Boy Floyd." *Timeline* 7, no. 4 (Aug.–Sept. 1990): 2–15.

Chamberlin, Jo. "Putting Gangdom on the Spot." *Review of Reviews* 90 (Dec. 1934): 47–50.

Cooper, Courtney Ryley. "Bandit Land." *Saturday Evening Post* 207 (Aug. 4, 1934): 8, 9, 30, 32.

Helmer, Bill. "Deadly Combination: Did Pretty Boy Floyd Join the Dillinger Gang." *Oklahombres* 7, no. 4 (Summer 1996): 9–10.

Helmer, William J. "The Depression Desperados: A Study in Modern Myth-Making." *Mankind* 5, no. 2 (1975): 40–46.

King, Jeffery S. "Pretty Boy Floyd and the Akins Post Office Burglary." *Oklahombres* 7, no. 4 (Summer 1996): 8.

Maxwell, Gloria. "The Kansas City Union Station Massacre. Part 1." *Oklahombres* 2, no. 3 (Spring 1991): 3–9.

———. "The Kansas City Union Station Massacre. Part 2." *Oklahombres* 2, no. 4 (Summer 1991): 6–15.

———. "The Kansas City Union Station Massacre. Part 3." *Oklahombres* 3, no. 1 (Fall 1991): 1–8.

Meyer, Richard E. "The Outlaw: A Distinctive American Folktype." *Journal of the Folklore Institute* 17, no. 2–3 (1980): 94–124.

"Oklahoma's 'Bandit King.'" *The Literary Digest* 114 (Dec. 10, 1932): 26–27.

O'Reilly, Kenneth. "A New Deal for the FBI." *Journal of American History* 69 (Dec. 1982): 638–58.

Seagle, William. "The American National Police." *Harpers* 169 (Nov. 1934): 752–61.

Steckmesser, Kent L. "The Oklahoma Robin Hood." *The American West* 7 (Jan. 1970): 38–41.

Webb, Michael. "Pretty Boy's Visit to the Gateway City." *Oklahombres* 4, no. 3 (Spring 1993): 17–20.

Newspapers

Akron Beacon Journal
East Liverpool (Ohio) *Evening Review*
Kansas City Journal-Post
Kansas City Star
Muskogee (Okla.) *Daily Phoenix*

New York Times
Daily Oklahoman
Toledo News-Bee
Tulsa Daily World

Original Sources

FBI Identification Order no. 1194, June 22, 1933 (Charles Floyd).
FBI File 62-28915 (Charles "Pretty Boy" Floyd).
Missouri State Prison record of Charles Floyd.
Various court records concerning "Charley" Floyd and J. Harold Franks of the
    District Court of the United States for the Eastern District of Oklahoma re-
    lating to a 1922 burglary of the Akins, Oklahoma, post office. Located at
    the Fort Worth, Texas, branch of the National Archives under File no. 7660.

Index

The Life and Death of Pretty Boy Floyd
was designed by Will Underwood;
composed in 9^1/$_2$/13 Trump Medieval on
a Power Macintosh in Quark XPress
by Generic Compositors;
printed by sheet-fed offset lithography
on 50-pound Lions Falls Turin Book Natural stock
(an acid-free, totally chlorine-free paper)
with halftones printed on 70-pound
Westvaco enamel gloss stock, and notch bound
in signatures over binder's boards in
Arrestox B cloth with Rainbow endpapers
and wrapped with dust jackets printed in
three colors finished with film lamination
by Thomson-Shore, Inc.;
and published by
The Kent State University Press
Kent, Ohio 44242